Caroline Krantz and

Series Adviser

Navigate

Coursebook

with video and Oxford Online Skills

Upper-intermediate → **B2**

Contents

Oxford 3000™ *Navigate* has been based on the Oxford 3000 to ensure that learners are only covering the most relevant vocabulary.

Communication

1.1 The rules of conversation

GOALS ■ Talk about conversation in different cultures ■ Use different question types

Vocabulary & Speaking conversation

1a Look at situations a–c, which show conversations between people from different cultures. In each there has been a cross-cultural misunderstanding. With a partner, discuss what has caused the misunderstanding.

How much do you earn?

b Check the answers on page 126.

2 Look at the list of things that can happen in a conversation. Check you understand the words in bold in the phrases. Put a tick next to the things you would aim to do and a cross next to the ones you would try to avoid.

- have a **row**
- put someone **at ease**
- listen **enthusiastically**
- **establish** shared interests
- ask **appropriate** questions
- have a **misunderstanding**
- have some **awkward** silences
- **put your foot in it**
- make **small talk**
- make a good **impression**
- tell an **entertaining** story
- **offend** someone
- **dominate** the conversation
- **hit it off** with someone

Cross-cultural communication quiz

1 Think about the distance at which two people who are not close friends stand when they are having a casual conversation. This distance varies between cultures. In North America the distance is 45 cm. Do you think this distance is greater or smaller in the following places? Write *G* (greater) or *S* (smaller).

   a Western Europe ___   **c** the Middle East ___
   b Japan ___

2 Which of these nationalities finds silences awkward in conversation?

   a East Asian ___   **b** Spanish ___   **c** American ___

3   Work in groups and do the following. Tell the others in the group about ...

   1   a person you know who is good at putting people at ease and how they do it.

   2   a person you know who tends to dominate the conversation.

   3   a time when you or someone you know put his/her foot in it.

   4   a person you hit it off with as soon as you met them.

   5   how easy or difficult you find it to make small talk.

Grammar & Speaking   using different question types

4   How much do you know about cross-cultural communication? With a partner, read and discuss the answers to the quiz.

5   **1.1**))) Listen to a talk by a trainer in cross-cultural communication. Check your answers to the questions in the quiz.

6   **1.1**))) Listen again and answer the questions.

   1   In the Middle East, how far apart do two people, who are not friends, stand during a conversation?

   2   Why are silences in conversation a positive thing in some parts of East Asia?

   3   In which country is it acceptable to ask somebody about their salary?

   4   In the Philippines, what can you be arrested for?

---

7   Discuss in small groups. What advice would you give a visitor to your country about the following?

   • personal space   • making eye contact
   • common gestures   • conversation topics
   • interrupting   to avoid

8   Read the Grammar focus box and choose the correct options to complete the rules.

> ### GRAMMAR FOCUS different question types
>
> • **Subject questions**
>   When *who, which, what* or *whose* is the subject/part of the subject, we **¹ use / don't use** auxiliaries *do* or *did* in a question.
>   *Who said that?* (NOT ~~Who did say that?~~)
>   *Which of these nationalities speaks the loudest?*
>
> • **Indirect questions**
>   If we begin a question with an expression like *Do you think* or *Do you know*, what follows keeps normal word order – the subject goes **² before / after** the verb.
>   *Do you think you'll come to the party?*
>
> • **Questions with prepositions**
>   When a *Wh-* word is the object of a preposition, the preposition usually comes at the **³ beginning / end** of the question.
>   *What are you talking about?*
>
> → Grammar Reference page 136

9   Look again at the highlighted questions in the quiz in exercise **4**. Find examples of ...

   1   subject questions where there is no auxiliary verb.

   2   indirect questions.

   3   questions with a preposition at the end.

10a Put the words in the right order to make questions.

   1   laugh / what / makes / you ?

   2   favourite / about / what's / your / book ?

   3   awake / what / night / keeps / you / at ?

   4   out / do / you / think / go / will / you / tonight ?

   5   most / who / in / your / family / similar / to / are / you ?

   6   your / do / you / why / parents / know / name / chose / your ?

   b   Now discuss the questions with your partner.

11 Work with a partner. You are going to write some questions about languages for your partner. Student A, turn to page 126. Student B, turn to page 132.

12a **TASK** Work with a partner. Choose three topics from the list. For each topic write two questions.

   • family • a holiday • last weekend • job • home

   b   Work with a different partner and ask the questions.

▶ VOX POPS VIDEO 1

> 3   **Who speaks the loudest? Put the nationalities in order from 1–3 (1 = quiet → 3 = loud).**
>
>   a Northern European ___   c East Asian ___
>   b South American ___
>
> 4   **In the UK, which of these questions might you ask when making small talk?**
>
>   a Who do you think will win the World Cup?
>   b How much do you earn?
>   c Whereabouts are you from?
>   d Who will you vote for in the election?
>
> 5   **Where do these gestures cause offence? Match each illustration to two countries or regions.**
>
>   1  2
>
>   a Slovakia   c the Middle East
>   b Greece   d South East Asia

1.2 The letter is dead, long live the letter!

Vocabulary & Speaking written communication

1 With a partner, divide the words in the box into groups 1–3.

> confidential   copy somebody in/cc somebody into
> cross out   delete   emoticon   handwriting   handwritten
> inbox   instant   in tray   texting   postage stamp
> punctuation   stationery

1 electronic communication   3 both
2 paper communication

2a Complete each question with a word or phrase from exercise 1.

1 When did you last send or receive a _handwritten_ _____ letter?
2 Have you ever accidentally sent a _confidential_ email or text to the wrong person?
3 Do you know the cost of a _postage stamp_ _____?
4 Which _emoticon_ (e.g. ☺) do you use most often?
5 How neat is your _____? HANDWRITING
6 Which do you do more, _texting_ messaging or email? Why?

b Ask and answer the questions with a partner.

Grammar & Reading present perfect simple and continuous

3 Read the article and readers' comments and put phrases 1–5 in gaps a–e.

1 send something by post every day
✓2 with the speed and efficiency of digital media
✓3 there is pressure to respond instantly
✓4 life's too short
✓5 written by older generations

4 Read the article again and answer the questions.

1 What are the writer's three main arguments in defence of the handwritten letter?
2 What evidence is given of a renewed interest in letter-writing?
3 What advantages of electronic communication are mentioned in the readers' comments?

5 What are your views about letter-writing? Discuss with a partner.

The death of the handwritten letter?

[1] People have been communicating by letter for at least 2,000 years. Now, however, a _____, the handwritten letter is in serious decline. But have we given enough consideration to what we will lose if we abandon the letter completely?

When we handwrite a letter, we write more thoughtfully. When we receive an email, b _____ and we don't always think carefully about how to express our feelings, often choosing to use emoticons instead.

Writing letters may be hard work, but receiving one can be one of life's greatest pleasures. There is so much to appreciate: the feel of the paper, the style of the handwriting and simply knowing someone has taken the trouble to write to you.

Texts and emails allow instant communication but are quickly deleted, while letters stay around for longer, allowing us to keep a record of our past. Many of us keep special letters c _____. But what correspondence will we leave behind for future generations? Nothing. That for me would be the greatest loss to our culture if letters died out completely.

However, [2] there are signs that people have been writing more letters recently. [3] Newspapers have reported a rise in stationery sales and [4] several internet campaigns have sprung up in an attempt to save the art of letter-writing, such as the annual *Month of Letters*, in which thousands of participants d _____ for a month.

So letter-writing may not be ready to die ... quite yet.

Your comments

CO Cristina Oliveira:
With digital media we write more than ever before. Surely [5] this has had a positive impact on our writing skills?

JB James Brook:
I'm sure [6] I've only written two or three letters in my life. I'd love to write more, but e _____!

LF Luke Francis:
[7] I've always had terrible handwriting. Without email, I'd never write to anybody.

Published: Tuesday, 10.15 a.m.

6 Read the Grammar focus box and match rules a–d to the phrases in blue in the article and *Your comments* column. Some phrases relate to more than one rule.

GRAMMAR FOCUS present perfect simple and continuous

- We use the present perfect to talk about something that started in the past and is continuing now, or is repeated up to now, when <u>how long</u> is mentioned in the sentence, or when how long is clear from the situation.

  a We can often use **either the present perfect simple or the present perfect continuous** when we use *since* or *for* to talk about actions that are still going on.

    He has worked/has been working at the post office since 1987.

  b We usually use **the present perfect continuous** for actions continuing or repeated <u>for a short time up</u> to the present, e.g. with phrases like *all day* and *recently*.

    You've been working on that letter all morning – isn't it good enough now?

  c We usually use **the present perfect simple** to talk about states rather than actions, with verbs like *be*, *have* and *know*.

    Writing has been much easier since spellcheckers were invented.

  d We use **the present perfect simple** to talk about something that happened once, or more than once, at an unspecified time in the past, when there is a <u>link to the present</u>.

    Researchers have found that texting can improve children's spelling.

→ **Grammar Reference** page 137

7a Complete the article with the present perfect simple or continuous form of the verbs in brackets. Sometimes both forms may be possible.

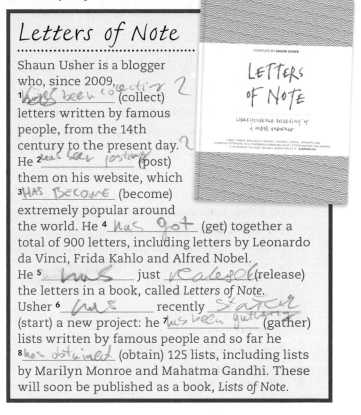

Letters of Note

Shaun Usher is a blogger who, since 2009, **1** *has been collecting* (collect) letters written by famous people, from the 14th century to the present day. He **2** *has been posting* (post) them on his website, which **3** *has become* (become) extremely popular around the world. He **4** *has got* (get) together a total of 900 letters, including letters by Leonardo da Vinci, Frida Kahlo and Alfred Nobel. He **5** *has* just *released* (release) the letters in a book, called *Letters of Note*. Usher **6** *has* recently *started* (start) a new project: he **7** *has been gathering* (gather) lists written by famous people and so far he **8** *has obtained* (obtain) 125 lists, including lists by Marilyn Monroe and Mahatma Gandhi. These will soon be published as a book, *Lists of Note*.

b With a partner, match answers 1–8 in exercise **7a** to rules a–d in the Grammar focus box.

PRONUNCIATION auxiliary verbs *have* and *been*

8a **1.2**))) Listen to the sentences and questions. How do we pronounce *have* and *been*?

I've been working very hard lately.
Have you been waiting long?
How long have you been here?

b **1.3**))) Listen and write the questions you hear.

c Work with a partner. Ask and answer the questions in exercise **8b**.

---

9 **TASK** You are a famous person and you are going to write a letter. Turn to page 126 for more information.

Letter from Elvis Presley to the president

1.3 Vocabulary and skills development

Reading guessing the meaning of new words

1 Work with a partner and discuss the questions.
  1 In which situations do people whistle?
  2 Is whistling acceptable in your culture, for both men and women?

2 **1.4**)) Listen to an extract from a podcast about an ancient whistling language and answer the questions.
  1 Where was the language used? Is it still used?
  2 In the listening, you hear an example conversation between two whistlers. What is it about?
    a a concert   b a party   c a lost sheep

3 Read about Silbo Gomero and put the topics in the order they appear in the article.
  ___ how the language is formed
  ___ its origins
  ___ what it sounds like
  ___ reasons for its disappearance
  ___ attempts to revive it

4a Read the information in the Unlock the code box and use the strategies to help you guess the meaning of the underlined words and phrases in the article.

> 🔓 **UNLOCK THE CODE**
> strategies for understanding new words
>
> When you see a new word in a text, there are several strategies you can use to try to guess its meaning.
>
> • Look at the context (words before and after the new word). This can help you work out the part of speech (adjective, noun, etc.) and give you clues to guess the meaning.
>
>   *ravine* (line 8) 'deep ravines' → it's a noun;
>   it's something which is deep, 'steep hills and deep ravines' → it's probably a kind of valley.
>
> • Look at the different parts of the word. You might already know part of the word.
>
>   *disapprove* (line 31) *dis-* + *approve*
>
> • Use your own language. Sometimes the English word is similar to the word in your language.
>
>   *unique* (line 3) is similar to Italian = *unico*,
>   Slovak = *unikátny*, Indonesian = *unik*.

b Compare your ideas with a partner.

5 Read the article again and answer the questions with a partner.
  1 Why is Silbo Gomero ideal for communicating on La Gomera?
  2 What is known about the origins of the language?
  3 Why is the language in decline?
  4 What efforts have been made to keep the language alive?
  5 What do La Gomera inhabitants think should happen to the language?

Silbo Gomero:
The revival of an ancient whistling language

If you go walking in the hills of La Gomera, you might be lucky enough to hear local people communicating in Silbo Gomero. Silbo is unique in that it is whistled, not spoken. Anybody who hasn't heard of the language could easily
5 confuse it with birdsong.
  La Gomera is a tiny Spanish island, just the tip of a volcano <u>sticking out</u> of the sea, off the coast of north-west Africa. Its steep hills and deep ravines make it difficult to cross. Whistling is perfect for communicating here, as
10 whistles can be heard from up to seven kilometres away.
  Silbo comes from the Spanish *silbar* meaning 'to whistle', and *Gomero* means 'from La Gomera'. When the first European <u>settlers</u> arrived at La Gomera in the 15th century, the islanders – of North African origin – were already
15 communicating with whistles. When the Spanish arrived, the locals adapted the whistling language to Spanish.

Vocabulary & Speaking   verbs + prepositions

6 Read the information about verbs and prepositions in the Vocabulary focus box.

> **VOCABULARY FOCUS** verbs + prepositions
>
> Some verbs are usually followed by a particular preposition. These are followed by a noun, pronoun or verb + -ing.
>
> Verb + preposition + object: *Have you **heard of** Silbo Gomero?*
>
> Verb + object + preposition + object: *It's easy to **confuse** Silbo **with** birdsong.*
>
> *… an attempt to **prevent** the language **from** becoming extinct*

Silbo consists of four vowels and four consonants which can be whistled in different ways to make over 4,000 words. A finger is placed in the mouth to create
20 a stronger whistle and the other hand is cupped next to the mouth to control its direction.

In the 1950s, economic difficulties forced many whistlers to emigrate from La Gomera. This, the growing road network and, later, the development of
25 mobile phones all contributed to the decline of Silbo.

In 1999, in an attempt to prevent the language from becoming completely extinct, Silbo was made a compulsory subject in La Gomera's primary schools. In 2009, the language was awarded the UNESCO Intangible
30 Cultural Heritage of Humanity designation. Some locals disapprove of this, saying it is a peasant language that should be left to die out. Others believe it should be preserved as it is part of the islanders' cultural identity. They also argue that in much of the island you cannot
35 depend on telephone coverage, so it is an essential form of communication.

■ **a peasant** a poor person who works on another person's or their own farm

7 Look at the highlighted verbs and prepositions in the article and complete the table.

Preposition	Verb
of	*hear*
on	DEPEND
to	adapted Century
with	*confuse*
from	PREVENT
in	COMMUNICATING

8a Complete the sentences with the correct form of the verbs in the box.

> ban   bring   disapprove   lead   result

> ### Whistling trivia ...   banned
> 1 Henry Ford, founder of the Ford Motor Company, ~~bring disapproved~~ his workers from whistling.
> 2 In Russia, it is believed that whistling indoors can ~~bring~~ in bad luck. result
> 3 In the USA and Canada, spectators at sports events whistle to express approval. However, in Europe and Brazil they whistle when they disapprove of a referee's decision.
> 4 There is an old tradition amongst sailors that whistling can lead on a storm. bring
> 5 In Sullivan's Island, South Carolina, whistling in public can ~~lead~~ to a fine of $500.
> result, bad

b Add the verbs in the box in exercise **8a** to the table in exercise **7**.

9a Complete the questions with suitable verbs from exercises **7** and **8**.

1 What factors do you think lead c _____ to a person's happiness?
2 What does a healthy diet prevent consist _____ of?
3 Do you think we DEPEND _____ too much on computers?
4 Do you BAN _____ of e-cigarettes? Why/Why not? DISAPPROVE
5 Do you think drivers should be ban _____ from using mobile phones?
ed

b Ask and answer the questions with a partner.

1.4 Speaking and writing

GOALS ☐ Deal with problems on the phone ☐ Write an informal email

Vocabulary & Listening dealing with problems on the phone

1 Work with a partner. Discuss the questions.

   1 On average, how many phone calls do you make in a day?

   2 Do you generally prefer phoning, Skyping or another form of communication? Why?

   3 What things can go wrong when you speak on the phone?

2 **1.5))))** Listen to four phone conversations in which a problem occurred. Match conversations 1–4 to problems a–d.

   a an unclear telephone line
   b one of the speakers is distracted
   c an unwanted sales call
   d a friend wants to talk for too long

3 **1.6))))** Listen and complete the sentences in the Language for speaking box.

LANGUAGE FOR SPEAKING dealing with problems on the phone

Getting rid of unwanted callers
1 I don't a＿＿＿＿ sales calls.
2 Would you remove my b＿＿＿＿ from your database?

Ending a conversation politely
3 It's been great c＿＿＿＿ to you.
4 I'd d＿＿＿＿ get off the phone.
5 I'll let you get on.
6 I've got a e＿＿＿＿ of work to do.
7 I won't take up any more of your time.

Dealing with distractions
8 Just f＿＿＿＿ with me a moment.
9 I'm afraid you've g＿＿＿＿ me at a bad time.
10 Could you just hold the line?

Dealing with a bad phone line
11 The h＿＿＿＿ isn't too good here.
12 You're breaking up …
13 I'm i＿＿＿＿ you again.
14 Could you call me back on my j＿＿＿＿?

Note: We often use the word *Anyway*, … to signal that we want to end a conversation.

4 **1.6))))** Listen again and repeat the sentences.

5 **TASK** Work with a partner. You are going to role-play a phone conversation using the phrases in exercise **3**. If possible, sit back to back to imitate the conditions of a real phone call.

Student A

1 It's 8 p.m. You are a salesperson (decide what you are selling, e.g. a mobile phone). Call Student B and try to sell your product. Try to keep them on the phone for at least two minutes by explaining the benefits of the product. Remember your boss said you need to increase your sales and you're feeling under pressure.

Student B

1 It's 8 p.m. and you are at home watching a film. The phone rings. You are expecting a call from your aunt in Canada. You need to speak to her to give her some important family news. Answer the phone.

You are going to do two more role-plays. Student A, turn to page 126. Student B, turn to page 132.

Writing an informal email giving news

6 Read the email and answer the questions.

1 Are Noemi and Sofia old friends, recent friends or work colleagues?

2 The email is written in an informal style. What features of the email show this?

Sent: TUESDAY 12.29

Hi Noemi,

Seems like ages since we've been in touch! Hope all's well with you. All's well here but life's pretty busy, as ever. I've changed jobs. Still teaching art and design, but at a different college. I've been working there for six months now. I love it, but it's hard work. We're off on a study trip to Amsterdam at the end of the month. Should be fun. I've never been to Amsterdam before.

The other thing that's been keeping me busy is the ukulele. The band that I play in has suddenly become really popular locally and we've been playing loads of gigs. Mainly just small ones, but last weekend we played in front of 300 people at a festival. Fame at last! ;) Is the ukulele as popular in Spain as it is here?

Anyway, the really big news is that my sister is pregnant and she's just found out that she's having twins! She and Tom are over the moon, but quite nervous, too, as you can imagine. And I'm going to be an aunt for the first time. Can't wait!

So, enough about me. How are things with you? What have you been up to? Still living in the same flat? I'd love to come over to Madrid to visit you some time. Maybe during the summer holidays – I'll have plenty of time on my hands then.

It would be really great to catch up properly before that. Shall we try and speak next week? Are you on Skype?

Speak soon, hopefully.

Lots of love,

Sofia

---

7 Read the information about ellipsis in the Language for writing box. Find examples of ellipsis in the email in exercise **6**. Decide if they are examples of type 1 or type 2.

> **LANGUAGE FOR WRITING** ellipsis (leaving out words) for informal writing
>
> In informal writing (and speaking) we often leave out words at the beginning of a sentence. This is known as ellipsis.
>
> Common types of ellipsis include:
>
> 1 leaving out the pronoun:
>   *It sounds amazing. → Sounds amazing.* ✓
>
> 2 leaving out the pronoun and auxiliary verb:
>   *It's great to hear from you. → Great to hear from you.* ✓

8 Make these sentences more informal by leaving out words at the beginning.

1 I'm just writing to say hello.

2 It was great to see you last week.

3 I hope to hear from you soon.

4 Are you going anywhere this summer?

5 I'll see you in a week's time.

6 I miss you!

9 As well as ellipsis, informal writing contains a lot of colloquial vocabulary. Match the highlighted words or phrases in the email to their more formal equivalents, 1–9.

1	a lot of/many	6	exchange news
2	in contact	7	very
3	extremely happy	8	lots of free time
4	a long time	9	What have you been doing?
5	We're going away		

10 **TASK** Write an email to a friend or family member that you haven't seen for a year. Use phrases from the email in exercise **6**. Include information about the following.

• things you have done during the year

• things you have been doing recently

• things you are planning to do

• news about other members of the family

11a Exchange emails with a partner. Has your partner used …?

• fixed informal phrases for opening and closing the email

• a chatty informal style

• correct grammar, vocabulary and spelling

b Find out more about the news in the email and discuss with your partner.

→ HOMEWORK FOR NEXT PiAZ TODAY

1.5 Video

Minority languages in the British Isles

1 Match the sentence halves.

1 An **official** language is a language …

2 An **indigenous** language is a language …

3 A **dominant** language is the language …

4 A **minority** language is an official language that is spoken …

5 A **global** language is spoken …

a that most people in a country speak.

b by just a small number of people in a country or region.

c with special legal status, used by the government, etc.

d all around the world.

e native to a country or region.

2 Look at the photos. In which part of the British Isles do you think they were taken? What aspects of minority language preservation do they show?

3 ▶ Watch the video. Are sentences 1–5 true (T) or false (F)?

1 92% of people in the UK speak English as their first language.

2 In Scotland, Scottish Gaelic is spoken by around 60,000 people.

3 In Ireland, only a few people understand Irish.

4 In Wales, Welsh is spoken by about 50% of the population.

5 In Cornwall, hardly anybody speaks Cornish.

4 ▶ Watch again. Choose the correct options to complete the sentences, according to the video.

1 Welsh, Scottish Gaelic, Irish and Cornish have their roots in *Celtic / Anglo-Saxon* culture.

2 There are Scottish Gaelic communities in northern *Canada / Australia*.

3 The first official language of the Republic of Ireland is *Irish / English*.

4 Welsh is most spoken in the *north / south* of Wales.

5 Cornish is spoken by a few *hundred / thousand* people.

6 Experts predict that *50% / 90%* of the world's languages will die out by the end of the century.

5 **TASK** Work with a partner. Ask and answer the questions.

1 What are your country's official languages? Which are minority languages, and where are they spoken?

2 Do you think governments should spend money on keeping minority languages alive? Why/Why not?

Review

1a Write questions about the underlined pronouns.

1   **A** <u>It</u> arrived this morning.
    B _What arrived this morning?_
    A Your postcard.

2   **A** <u>She</u> collects old typewriters.
    B _Who collects old typewriters_
    A My cousin.

3   **A** I texted <u>him</u> by mistake.
    B _to whom you texted by mistake_
    A Mattias.

4   **A** <u>He</u> often confuses me with my twin brother.
    B _Who confuses me with_
    A My football coach.

5   **A** I had never heard of <u>it</u> before. _had_
    B _About what I never heard_
    A Silbo Gomero.

b Complete each question by adding the missing word.

1   How many friends can you truly rely?
2   Do you think you go abroad this summer?
3   What are you learning English? _FOR_
4   Is there anything you strongly disapprove? _with_

c Ask and answer the questions in exercise **1b** with a partner.

2a Complete the paragraph with the present perfect simple or continuous.

I'm going on a big trip to Argentina soon, so for the last few weeks I've ¹ _tried_ / _been trying_ to brush up my Spanish. I've ² _studied_ / _been studying_ Spanish before, but I've ³ _forgotten_ / _been forgetting_ quite a lot, so I've ⁴ _gone_ / _been going_ to evening classes. They've ⁵ _been_ / _been being_ very helpful. I've ⁶ _downloaded_ / _been downloading_ a Spanish vocabulary app for extra practice and I've also ⁷ _read_ / _been reading_ a book in Spanish. It's a slow process, but I've nearly ⁸ _finished_ / _been finishing_ it.

b Work with a partner. Talk about how long you've been learning English and what you've been doing recently to practise.

3 Complete the article with words from the box.

> appropriate   awkward   ease   impression   offend   row   small

The hidden rules of
weather-speak

It is a well-known fact that the British are fond of talking about the weather, but it is important to realize that British conversations about the weather are not really about the weather at all. _Weather-speak_ is simply a way of helping us feel at ¹ _ease_ in social situations. It is used in three specific contexts:

- as a simple greeting
- as a form of ² _small_ talk leading to conversation about other more important matters
- as a filler when there is an ³ _awkward_ silence during a conversation.

It is seen as a safe, impersonal topic, which is unlikely to ⁴ _row_ anybody or lead to a ⁵ _offend_

Something to bear in mind when speaking to a British person about the weather is that you are expected to agree. If somebody says 'Ooh, isn't it cold?', an ⁶ _appropriate_ reply would be 'Yes, isn't it?' or 'Mmm, very cold'. If you said 'No actually, it's quite mild', you would create a very bad ⁷ _impression_

4 **1.7**)) Listen to eight questions. For each question write _Yes_ or _No_.

5a Complete the sentences from three phone conversations. The first letter is given.

1   The c_____ isn't t_____ good here.
2   I'd b_____ g_____ off the phone.
3   I'm a_____ you've c_____ me at a b_____ time.
4   Could you c_____ me b_____ on my l_____ line?
5   I'll l_____ you get o_____.
6   Just b_____ w_____ me a moment.

b Match the sentences in exercise **5a** to situations a–c.

a   ending a conversation politely
b   dealing with a bad phone line
c   dealing with distraction

c **TASK**   Work with a partner. Choose a sentence from exercise **5b** and role-play a phone conversation.

Escape

2.1 Out of your comfort zone

GOALS ■ Talk about travel and adventure ■ Talk about past events

---

Vocabulary & Speaking talking about travel and adventure

1 Work with a partner. Tell your partner about a place in the world that you would really like to visit one day.

2 **2.1**))) Listen to three people telling their friends about places they would like to go to and why. Match some of the reasons a–g to conversations 1–3.

a wildlife	e weather
b scenery	f physical activity
c personal challenge	g architecture
d atmosphere	

3a Complete the sentences with words or phrases from the box.

> adventurous   appeal   remote   roughing it   season
> soak up   stunning   touristy   wander   zone

1 Apparently, the views are absolutely _STUNNING_.
2 I'm not very good at _TOURISTY_. I like life's little luxuries!
3 You need to be more _ADVENTUROUS_. Step out of your comfort _ZONE_.
4 I'd like to experience being in a completely _____ environment with no one else around.
5 It's just the cold weather that doesn't _____ to me that much.
6 It would be great just to _____ around the old streets and _____ the atmosphere.
7 It gets quite _____ in the summer, so it's probably best to go out of _____.

b **2.1**))) Listen again and check.

4 Work in groups and discuss the questions.
1 Where is the remotest place you've ever been?
2 Is there a monument, a work of art or an animal that you'd like to see with your own eyes?
3 Can you think of a destination that really appeals to you, and one that really doesn't? Why/Why not?

Grammar & Speaking talking about past events

5a Look at the photo and the first paragraph of the article and discuss the questions with a partner.
1 Who is the woman? Where did she go, and when?
2 In what ways do you think she had to step out of her comfort zone?

b Read the rest of the article and make notes of a) Mary Kingsley's achievements, and b) the challenges she faced.

A Fearless Traveller

It's hard to imagine anybody who looks less like an explorer than the Victorian traveller, Mary Kingsley (pictured right), but she was one of the world's toughest and most adventurous explorers. At a time when her friends were doing household chores and going to dances, Mary Kingsley was paddling up rivers in a canoe, eating snakes and poking hippopotamuses with her umbrella in West Africa.

Kingsley was the daughter of a travelling doctor from London. She loved hearing her father's travel stories, but there was no question that she would accompany him on his travels as her mother was frequently unwell and needed to be cared for. Suddenly, though, her life changed when both of her parents died within six weeks of one another. With no family responsibilities, she decided to travel to West Africa, a place she had always dreamt of visiting. She had two missions to complete while she was touring the continent: one was to meet the native people of West Africa, learn about their customs and religions and write a book about the subject. The other was to collect tropical fish and reptiles for the British Museum.

Her father's medical friends had warned her about tropical diseases and other dangers of travelling alone, but she ignored them and in 1893 she sailed to modern-day Sierra Leone on the first of her two long journeys to West Africa.

6 Work with a partner. Match the highlighted words in the article to meanings 1–6.

1 things you must do
2 strongest and bravest
3 moving a boat through water with a single oar
4 a sudden, unexpected meeting
5 something that you are remembered for
6 paid no attention to

7 Without looking at the article, complete these sentences with the correct form of the verbs in brackets. Read the article again and check.

1 She _____ (have) two missions to complete while she _____ (tour) the continent.

2 After she _____ (learn) the necessary skills, she _____ (set) off alone down the river …

3 The crocodile _____ (try) to climb into her canoe, so she _____ (hit) it on the head with a paddle.

She lived for a while with the local people, who taught her how to fish with pineapple leaves. After she had learnt the necessary skills, she set off alone along the river in search of fish and reptiles. During her travels, she became the first woman to climb the active volcano Mount Cameroon, and the first white person to paddle up the Ogowe River and to cross the jungle to the Remboue River.

On her travels, she had to deal with extreme heat, tornadoes and various wild animals. Once, while she was canoeing along the Ogowe River, she had an encounter with a crocodile. The crocodile was trying to climb into her canoe, so she hit it on the head with a paddle. Kingsley describes this and other similar encounters in her two books, *Travels in West Africa* and *West African Studies*, which she wrote when she returned from her travels. The books became bestsellers and are still in print today.

She collected eighteen species of reptile and sixty-five species of fish, two of which were previously unknown and have been named after her. However, that was not her only legacy: she also became well known for her attitude towards the African people. She was the first explorer to show proper respect to the African people and their culture, and helped to change European attitudes towards them.

8 With a partner, name the tenses in exercise 7. Choose from *past simple*, *past continuous* and *past perfect*. Underline two more examples of these tenses in the article.

9 Choose the correct options to complete the rules in the Grammar focus box.

GRAMMAR FOCUS past events – narrative forms

- We use the **¹ past simple / past perfect** to describe the main events of the story.
  In 1893, she sailed to modern-day Sierra Leone.
- We use the **² past continuous / past perfect** to show that a past action or situation took place before another past action.
  She decided to travel to West Africa, a place she had always dreamt of visiting.
- We use the **³ past simple / past continuous** to talk about a) an action or situation that was in progress at the time of the main events or b) two actions in progress at the same time.
  … while she was canoeing along the river, she had an encounter with a crocodile.

→ Grammar Reference page 138

10 Read some more stories about Kingsley. Complete the sentences with the correct form of the verbs in brackets. There may be more than one possibility.

While she ¹_____ (travel) she ²_____ (wear) the same clothing that she ³_____ (wear) at home – a long black dress. She ⁴_____ (claim) that the dress ⁵_____ (save) her life once after she ⁶_____ (fall) into a hole and landed on a spiky branch.
She ⁷_____ (be) one of the first Europeans to see a gorilla, although she later ⁸_____ (comment) that she ⁹_____ (never see) anything so ugly before.
Once, when she ¹⁰_____ (walk) through the jungle, she ¹¹_____ (rescue) a leopard that ¹²_____ (get) caught in a trap. When it ¹³_____ (start) circling her she ¹⁴_____ (stare) back at it and ¹⁵_____ (say) 'Go home, you fool!'.

11 **TASK** Work with a partner. You are going to read about two more famous female travellers. Student A, turn to page 127. Student B, turn to page 132.

▶ VOX POPS VIDEO 2

2.2 An extraordinary escape

GOALS ☐ Use past perfect forms ☐ Talk about feelings

Grammar & Speaking   past perfect forms

1a With a partner, look at the picture and the title of the article. Describe what you can see. Who do you think the man is and why is he in a box? What about the other people?

b Read the article and find out if you were right.

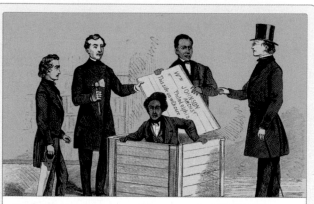

The man who mailed himself to freedom

Early in the morning of March 24, 1849, a box arrived at 107 North Fifth Street in Philadelphia. These were the offices of the Pennsylvania Anti-Slavery Society. Several members of this organization had gathered there that Saturday morning, anxiously waiting for the arrival of this package that had come from Richmond, Virginia.

After receiving the box, the men locked the door so that there would be no interruptions and one of them did something strange. Leaning over the box, he tapped on it and quietly asked, 'Is all right inside?' Even more strangely, a voice replied from inside the box, 'All right.'

Within a few minutes, the men opened the box. Inside was an African-American man in his early thirties by the name of Henry Brown. And he had just succeeded in escaping from slavery by shipping himself as freight to this city in the free state of Pennsylvania. In honour of this very creative but extremely dangerous feat, he became known forever after as Henry 'Box' Brown.

He had an extraordinary story to tell.

■ **freight** goods that are transported by ships, planes, trains or lorries/trucks

■ **feat** an action that needs skill, strength or courage

2 Read the article again and discuss the questions with a partner.
1 Why had the men gathered at the society?
2 Why had Henry Brown chosen Pennsylvania as his destination?
3 What do you think his life had been like in Virginia? What do you think had led him to escape?
4 What dangers do you think he had faced during the journey?

3 2.2))) You are going to hear a talk about what happened before Henry Box Brown arrived. Listen and answer the questions.
1 Where had Brown been working in Virginia?
2 What terrible event had led to his decision to escape?
3 Who had helped him escape?
4 Which forms of transport did he use?
5 How long had he been travelling in the box when it was opened?

4 2.2))) Listen again. Are these sentences true (T) or false (F)? Correct the false sentences.
1 Brown wanted to escape because his owner had been beating him.
2 Nancy's owner sold her even though he had promised not to.
3 Before they were separated, the couple had been living in Brown's owner's house.
4 Brown almost died in the box because he hadn't had anything to drink during the journey.
5 Brown didn't become famous until after he had died.

5 Look at the sentences in exercise **4**. Underline examples of the past perfect simple and the past perfect continuous.

6 Look again at the sentences in exercise **4**. Then complete the rules in the Grammar focus box with *simple* or *continuous*.

GRAMMAR FOCUS past perfect forms

- We use the past perfect when we are already talking about the past and want to talk about an earlier past time.
- We use the past perfect **1**_____ to talk about actions that continued for a period of time up to the moment we are talking about.

    His body hurt because he had been sitting in the same position for hours.
- We use the past perfect **2**_____ to talk about actions that were completed before the moment we are talking about.

    He'd asked for her master's permission before they got married.
- When we are talking about <u>states</u>, rather than actions, for example with verbs like *be, like, have, know*, we use the past perfect **3**_____.

    They hadn't been together long before his wife was sold to another owner.

→ Grammar Reference page 139

---

7 Complete the sentences with the past perfect simple or past perfect continuous form of the verbs in brackets.

1 They _____ (know) each other for a year before they got married.

2 He was exhausted because he _____ (drive) all night.

3 She was in a panic because she _____ (lose) her passport.

4 He _____ (have) the car for just a month when someone crashed into it.

5 The alarm didn't go off because I _____ (forget) to set it.

6 My eyes were hurting because I _____ (stare) at the computer screen all day.

7 I was sorry that the trip was cancelled. I _____ (look) forward it.

8 Continue each sentence with a suitable verb in the past perfect simple or past perfect continuous to explain what had happened/been happening.

1 She felt dizzy because …

2 He was out of breath because …

3 He had oil on his hands because …

4 Her boots were muddy because …

Vocabulary & Speaking adjectives of feeling

9a Complete the mind map with the adjectives in the box.

anxious bitter delighted disorientated down
furious hurt miserable petrified puzzled relieved
satisfied tense terrified

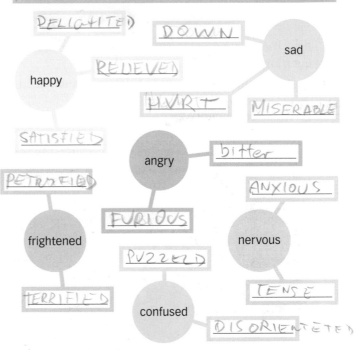

PRONUNCIATION word stress – adjectives (1)

b **2.3** 》 Mark the stress on the adjectives on the mind map. Listen and check. Then listen again and repeat.

---

10 Work with a partner. Think again about the story of Henry Box Brown. Which adjectives from exercise **9a** could you use to describe …?

1 how Brown felt when he heard the news that Nancy was going to be sold

2 how he felt just before his journey in the box

3 how he felt while he was in the box

4 how the luggage handlers would have felt if they had heard a noise coming from inside the box

5 how he felt just after he got out of the box

6 how he felt the next day

11a **TASK** Think of a person who has committed an extraordinary act of bravery. It could be a person you know or a famous historical figure. Make notes about the following.

- Who is it?
- What did he/she do?
- What had happened before the event?

b Work in groups. Tell the story of this person's extraordinary feat. Which story was the most unusual?

2.3 Vocabulary and skills development

Listening understanding North American and British accents

1 Read the article about learning holidays and discuss the questions with a partner.

1 What benefits of a learning holiday are mentioned in the article?

2 Would you be interested in going on any of the learning holidays listed in the article?

3 Does the idea of learning holidays in general appeal to you? If not, why not? If so, what skill would you like to learn?

TRAVEL

Go on holiday, bring back a skill

Have you ever wanted to come home from a holiday with something more lasting than a suntan? Something more useful than a suitcase full of souvenirs? What if you could come back with a new skill instead?

Learning holidays, which combine travel and learning, have become one of the latest new trends in travel. They can give you the opportunity to do something you've always wanted to do, while at the same time truly discovering a country's culture – and they can enrich your life long after the trip is over. These days, travellers can learn how to make chocolates in Italy, how to dance the tango in Argentina or even learn Maasai warrior survival skills in Kenya.

2 2.4))) Listen to the first part of an interview on a travel programme and answer the questions.

1 What does the guest on the programme do for a living?

2 Why has she been invited to speak on the programme?

3 Can you identify the accent of a) the presenter b) the guest?

3a 2.5))) Before you listen to the rest of the interview, read and listen to the information in the Unlock the code box.

> 🔓 **UNLOCK THE CODE**
> understanding different accents
>
> There are many regional accents in both North America and Britain. Below are some of the most important general differences between standard North American English (NAmE) and standard British English (BrE):
>
> • One of the most noticeable differences is the pronunciation of 'o'. In NAmE, 'o' often sounds like /ɑː/ or /ɔː/, for example, *not* /nɑːt/ and *strong* /strɔːŋ/ (in contrast to BrE: *not* /nɒt/ and *strong* /strɒŋ/).
>
> • Some words with /ɑː/ in standard BrE are pronounced with /æ/ in NAmE, for example: *ask* /æsk/ and *aunt* /ænt/ (in contrast to BrE: *ask* /ɑːsk/ and *aunt* /ɑːnt/).
>
> • In NAmE, 't' often sounds like /d/ in the middle of words, for example, *water* /ˈwɔːdər/ and *writer* /ˈraɪdər/.
>
> • In NAmE, 'r' is always pronounced, for example *car* /kɑr/. In standard BrE, it is generally pronounced before a vowel, for example: *career* /kəˈrɪə/.

b 2.6))) Listen to the words. Circle the sound you hear.

1 castle /ɑː/ /æ/

2 arm /ɑː/ /ɑːr/

3 rocket /ɒ/ /æ/

4 learning /ɜː/ /ɜːr/

5 matter /t/ /d/

6 got /ɒ/ /æ/

7 falconry /ɔː/ /æ/

c 2.7))) You will hear the following phrases spoken twice, once with a British accent and once with a North American accent. Write *B* or *NA*.

1 No, not at all. 1 ___ 2 ___

2 You've got a chance to train. 1 A 2 B

3 What an incredible opportunity! 1 ___ 2 A

4 Have you ever wanted to go to space camp? 1 A 2 B

5 I'm more of a water person. 1 B 2 ___

d 2.8))) Listen and complete the sentences you hear. Are the accents British or American? Write *B* or *NA*.

1 You *get a little ... certificate* . B

2 One of *a hottest new trends in travel* . A

3 Where *did you learn to surf* ? A

4 I *read about ... it on the internet* . B

4 Look at the photos of three learning holidays. What skills are the people practising?

3.

1.

2.

5 2.9))) Listen to the rest of the radio interview. Number the photos in the order you hear them and write the country.

6 2.9))) Listen again and complete the sentences with 1–3 of your own words.

las,

1 The castle was built in ~~IRLAND~~ . 1228
2 Walking in the castle grounds with a falcon reminded Ilana of a/an HARRY POTTER film
3 At the Adult Space Academy, you learn how to ~~LAND AND fly~~ a space shuttle. LAUNCH AND LAND
4 Using a flight simulator you can find out what it feels like to walk MOONWALK on the moon
5 Gladiator skills lessons are given by members of 'The HISTORIC Rome'. GROUP
6 At the end of the gladiator course, each participant receives a/an CERTIFICATE

Vocabulary & Speaking North American English

7 The following two extracts from the listening each contain one North American word (underlined). Do you know the British English equivalents?

… there are so many interesting learning <u>vacations</u>.
Last <u>fall</u>, I did a falconry course …

8 Read the information in the Vocabulary focus box about North American English.

> **VOCABULARY FOCUS** North American English
>
> • British English (BrE) and North American English (NAmE) sometimes use different words to describe the same thing:
>
> *car park* (BrE) → *parking lot* (NAmE)
> *motorway* (BrE) → *expressway/freeway/highway* (NAmE)
>
> • In some cases they use the same word to describe different things. For example, *pants* means 'trousers' in North American English and 'underpants' in British English.

9 Replace the North American words in bold in the sentences with British words from the box.

> boot caravan central holiday lorry luggage motorway pavement petrol queue return rubbish single toilet Underground

1 Put the **baggage** in the **trunk**.
2 There was a lot of **garbage** on the **sidewalk**.
3 There was a very long **line** for the **restroom** at the **gas** station.
4 We took the **subway** to **downtown** New York.
5 The **freeway** was closed because a **truck** was on fire.
6 Would you like a **one-way** or a **round-trip** bus ticket?
7 For our last **vacation** we rented a **travel trailer** and drove to the west coast.

10a Write five sentences using a North American word from exercise **9**.

b Work with a partner. Take it in turns to say a sentence to each other. You are in the UK and your partner questions the American word, as in the example.

A *Shall we take the subway?*
B *The subway? Ah … here we call it the Underground.*

2.4 Speaking and writing

GOALS ☐ Tell and react to a story ☐ Write an email of complaint

Speaking telling and reacting to a story

1 Work with a partner and discuss the questions.

1 Which of the forms of transport in photos a–c have you used?

2 When was the last time you travelled in one of these?

3 What things can go wrong when you use these forms of transport?

2 **2.10**)) Listen to two people telling a story about a travel experience and answer the questions.

1 Which conversation is about …?
  a a business trip 2   b a family holiday

2 Which travel experience happened …?
  a not so long ago 2   b a long time ago 1

3 **2.10**)) Listen again and answer the questions.

Conversation 1

1 Why was Jamie annoyed with Liz? MAP

2 Where did Liz and Jamie end up parking for the night?
CHILDREN PLAYGROUND

Conversation 2

3 Why did Sabrina get to the airport late? JAM TRAFIC

4 What went wrong at the airport?

4 Complete the Language for speaking box with the phrases in the box.

> And then, to make matters worse, … We ended up …
> Did you hear about …? This was in the days before …
> You're not going to believe this … That is hilarious!

5a Match 1–6 to a–f to make phrases we use when reacting to someone telling a story.

1 I'm — a were furious!
2 You must have been — b kidding!
3 I bet you — c hilarious!
4 You're — d can't be serious!
5 That is — e so embarrassed!
6 You — f not surprised!

b **2.11**)) Listen and check your answers.

PRONUNCIATION intonation – making exclamations

When you make exclamations, e.g. *You're kidding!*, make sure your voice rises and falls. If you use a flat intonation it can sound like you aren't very interested.

c **2.12**)) Listen to two people making exclamations. Who sounds more interested, A or B?

1 You're kidding!

2 That's hilarious!

3 I bet you were furious!

d Practise the exclamations in exercise **5c**.

6 Think of a memorable travel experience that you have had and make notes.

7 **TASK** Work in groups of three. Take it in turns to tell your story. The other members of the group each choose two of the responses in the Language for speaking box and try to insert them in the story.

LANGUAGE FOR SPEAKING telling and reacting to a story

Introducing the story
Have I ever told you about …?

Giving a time context
This happened … ago.

Adding emphasis
You'll never guess …
But that wasn't the end of the story …

Ending the story/part of the story
In the end, …

Reacting to a story
I'm not surprised.
You can't be serious!
You're kidding!
I bet you were furious/petrified, etc.!

Writing   an email of complaint

8 Have you ever had a bad travel experience and complained about it? What happened? What was the result?

9 Read the email of complaint to an airline and answer the questions.

1 Why is the writer unhappy?
2 What two actions does he want the airline to take?

Customer Complaint

Customer details: Daniel Caudrey
Flight details: HG412   **Booking Reference:** VMHPIT

Describe your complaint

Dear Sir/Madam,

I'm writing to complain about **¹**an incident which occurred during my flight from London to Mexico City, via Miami, on 19 May.

The flight had made a scheduled stop at Miami airport and passengers were asked to **²**remain on board whilst passengers from Miami boarded the plane. **³**We had been informed that cleaning staff would also enter the plane in order to **⁴**prepare the seats for the new passengers. The cabin crew had also **⁵**requested that we leave our seats to make it easier for the **⁶**cleaning staff to do their job.

My partner and I therefore stood up and walked around the aeroplane, as requested, while the seats next to ours were cleaned. Shortly after we **⁷**returned to our seats, I discovered that my MP3 player had disappeared from the pocket of the seat in front. Clearly, it had been stolen by the cleaning staff.

I was extremely upset by this, especially as the MP3 player was brand new and I had loaded it with Mexican music that I was planning to listen to on my holiday.

I feel that the airline should take responsibility for this incident. **⁸**I am therefore requesting compensation for the MP3 player, which had a value of £120. I also suggest that you investigate the matter to **⁹**ensure that this does not happen to other passengers in future.

I look forward to your reply.

Yours faithfully,

Daniel Caudrey

---

10 Look at the tips for writing a successful complaint. Do you think the writer has followed them?
- Be respectful: do not be rude or sarcastic.
- Be brief: avoid including unnecessary details.
- Be clear: explain events in a logical order.
- Be reasonable: if you want compensation, ask for enough, but not too much.

11 Match highlighted phrases 1–9 in the email to more informal phrases a–i.

a got back
b stay on the plane
c asked us to
d get the seats ready
e make sure
f cleaners
g something that happened
h I would like my money back
i somebody had told us

12a **TASK** You are going to write an email of complaint. Either think of your own situation or use the situation below.

> You recently stayed in a hotel. You asked reception to give you a wake-up call at 6 a.m. as you had to catch a plane. You received the wake-up call an hour late and, as a result, you missed your flight and had to pay for another one.

b Write your email of complaint. Use the Language for writing box to help you.

LANGUAGE FOR WRITING
writing an email of complaint

Explaining the reason for writing
I am writing to complain about/express my dissatisfaction with …

Describing the incident
We were told that …
We had been informed that …
I discovered that …
Clearly, …
I am extremely annoyed/dissatisfied/upset about …

Requesting action
I suggest/trust/would ask that you investigate/look into the situation.
I am therefore requesting compensation for …

Closing the email
I look forward to your reply …

13 **TASK** Exchange emails with a partner. Does it explain the incident clearly? Is it written in a formal style?

2.5 Video

Learning holidays

1 Look at the words and phrases in the box. Which can you see in the photos?

> artists' materials   beach resort   fishing boat   harbour
> ocean view   oil paint   paintbrush   still life   studio   tutor

NATURE LIFE (MARTWA NATUR)

2 Work with a partner. Use the words and phrases in exercise **1** to describe the photos. They are of a painting school and of the British seaside town of St Ives, where the school is located. Why do you think this would be a good location for a painting school?

3 ▶ Watch the video. Read the summary and choose the correct options to complete it.

> St Ives is a seaside town in the **1** *south-east / south-west* of Britain. As well as being famous for its **2** *sandy beaches / fish restaurants*, it is well known for its arts scene. By the 1950s, it had become **3** *home / a popular holiday destination* for a large group of influential artists. In the video, the presenter attends a course at the St Ives School of Painting. The school, which opened in **4** *1938 / 1958*, runs courses in **5** *oil painting / a range of art forms*. It is located **6** *in the centre of the town / on the edge of a beach*. The maximum number of students in a class is **7** *six / eight*. The presenter attended a **8** *one-day / two-day* course for beginners, for which the school provided **9** *most / all* of the materials. At the end of her learning holiday, she bought herself a **10** *paintbrush / painting* as a souvenir.

4 ▶ Watch again. What does the presenter say about …?
spectacular
a the features of St Ives *PICTUREST PLACE*
b her previous experience of painting *IN SCHOOL*
c the arts scene in St Ives *COST ST IVES PLACE*
d the school's philosophy *BILLON STUDENT COR*
e her plans to do another painting course *NEW SKILL*

5a **TASK** Work with a partner. Read the task.

> You are going to design a learning holiday to sell to a market of holidaymakers who are looking for a holiday where they can learn a skill in an interesting or beautiful location.

b Choose a skill for the holiday from the list below. Then think of the ideal location for the holiday.

- action/adventure/survival
- cooking/eating/drinking
- art/creative
- designing/building
- culture/language/music

cozy small beach

LOTS OF SCHOOL

Review

1   Choose the correct options to complete the text.

> Kira Salak, born in 1971, is an American writer, adventurer and journalist. She has been described as the toughest – some say the craziest – adventurer of our time.
>
> In 1995, she **1** *went* / *was going* on a solo jungle trek through Papua New Guinea, becoming the first woman to cross the country. She **2** *wrote* / *had written* about this epic adventure in her book *Four Corners*.
>
> In 2002, she **3** *paddled* / *was paddling* alone, in a kayak, 966 km down West Africa's Niger River to Timbuktu. Her goal was to retrace the journey of the Scottish explorer, Mungo Park, who **4** *had died* / *was dying* during the expedition in 1797. While Salak **5** *travelled* / *was travelling*, she experienced many dangers, including tropical storms, diseases and hippos. She **6** *described* / *had described* the trip in her book *The Cruellest Journey*.
>
> Before becoming an adventurer, she **7** *had set* / *was setting* a Wisconsin state record in cross-country running and **8** *had begun* / *was beginning* training for Olympic trials.

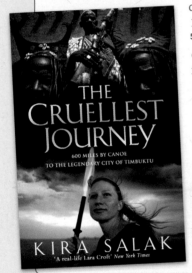

2a   Write answers to the questions. Use the past perfect simple or continuous.

Why was he relieved? Because he'd found his passport.   LEFT

1   Where was his rucksack?   HIS RUCKSACH HAD
2   Why was he so exhausted?   BECAUSE HE HAD blow
3   Why didn't he have any money on him?
4   Why was he feeling anxious?
5   How had he changed since the last time you saw him?

b   Work with a partner. Read out your answers in random order. Your partner guesses the question.

HE HAD SPEND IT

BECAUSE HE HAD BEEN WRITIM ALL DAY
→ HE HAD LOST OF WEIGHT

3   Complete the example sentences with a word from the box. There are two words you don't need.

> comfort   encounter   remote   rough   season   set   step   wander

1   If you ___WANDER___ around a place, you walk around without a particular purpose.
2   If you ___ROUGH___ it, you live in a way that is not comfortable for a short time.
3   If you go somewhere out of ___SEASON___, you go at a time of year when few people go.
4   If you ___STEP___ out of your ___COMFOR___ zone, you do something unfamiliar and challenging.
5   If you go somewhere ___REMOT___, it is far away from places where other people live.

4   Underline the word that is different from the others.

1   relieved   satisfied   happy   tense
2   down   frightened   upset   miserable
3   bitter   disorientated   puzzled   confused
4   anxious   tense   nervous   furious
5   terrified   stressed   scared   petrified

5a   **2.13**))) Listen to eight words in North American English and match them to British English words a–h.

a   rubbish ___7___   e   holiday ___Vac___
b   toilet ___Resin___   f   caravan ___Trace___ 4
c   boot ___6___   g   petrol ___8___
d   lorry ___5___   h   pavement ___

b   Work with a partner. Can you think of more words in North American English? Write them down with their British equivalent.

HIS RUCKSACK AT HOME

6a   Complete the phrases for telling and responding to a story. The first letter is given.

1   And then, to make m___atters___ worse ...
2   You can't be s___ouries___!
3   I b___et___ you were petrified!
4   To cut a long story s___hort___ ...
5   You'll never g___uess___ what happened next ...

b   **TASK**   Work with a partner. Think of a time when you felt disorientated, relieved or terrified. Take it in turns to tell your story. While you are listening, react with interest.

3 Invest

3.1 Invest in your future

GOALS ■ Talk about the future (1) ■ Talk about learning, thinking and knowledge

Grammar talking about the future (1)

1a Work in small groups. How do you think the world of work will change in the next 10–20 years? Think of at least three ways.

b Look at the introduction to a podcast discussion. Do you agree with what it says?

NEWS   BUSINESS   **CAREERS**   TECHNOLOGY   BLOG

// Jobs of the future //

As the way we live changes, so will the way we work. Many jobs we take for granted will disappear, and most of today's students will end up in jobs that haven't even been invented yet.

Nostalgist

Rewilder

Garbage designer

Auto transport analyst

2a Can you guess what the future jobs pictured in exercise **1b** might involve? Discuss with a partner.

b 3.1))) Listen to the podcast and check your ideas.

c Would you be interested in doing any of these jobs? Why/Why not?

3 3.2))) Listen to the last section of the podcast in exercise **2a** again and complete the extracts with the correct future form of the verbs in brackets.

1 ... I always wanted to be a train driver. After hearing that, I think I _WILL BE_ (be) an auto transport analyst! _are going to be_

2 ... younger generations _going to be_ (be) much more proficient.

3 I _'m taking_ (take) a course in app design ...

4 It _starts_ (start) next week ...

5 I _going to_ (certainly work) in design ...

6 Nostalgists _will be_ (be) interior ...

7 **A** Well, let me know if you do decide to become a nostalgist!

   B I _will do_ (do).

4 Match completed extracts 1–7 in exercise **3** to explanations a–g in the Grammar focus box.

> **GRAMMAR FOCUS** future forms (*will, going to*), present simple and present continuous
>
> There are several ways to talk about the future.
>
> **1 will and going to**
> • We use *will*
>   a when we want to **make a prediction based on what we know now**. ___ 6 !
>   b when we **make a spontaneous decision**. ___ 1!
>   c when we **agree, promise, plan or refuse** to do something, as well as when we **make requests**. 7
> • We use *going to*
>   d when we **talk about plans or intentions we already have**. 5 ?
>   e when there is some **evidence in the present** to support the prediction. ___ 2 ?
>
> **2 Present forms to talk about the future**
> • We use the present simple
>   f to talk about a scheduled or timetabled event. 4
> • We use the present continuous
>   g to talk about arrangements and fixed plans, especially when we give the time, date or place. 3
>
> → Grammar Reference page 140

5a Choose the correct option to complete each sentence. Sometimes both are possible.

1 I'm *starting / going to start* a new online course in a few weeks.

2 I'm *going to study / studying* web design, but I'm not sure where yet.

3 However much things change, we *are always going to need / will always need* teachers.

4 Jobs of the future *will need / are needing* technological skills.

5 The course *is going to start / starts* next week.

6 I hope I've passed my course. I *get / am getting* my results tomorrow morning.

7 Apparently a successful app designer can earn thousands a day! I think I*'ll change / change* my career.

8 I think my job *will change / is changing* in the future.

b Discuss the reason for your choices in exercise **5a** with a partner. If both forms are possible, explain any difference in meaning.

6a 3.3))) Listen to Bella talking about her career plans. Write down any phrases you hear which use future forms.

b 3.3))) Compare your notes with a partner. Listen again if necessary. Explain *why* she used each form.

PRONUNCIATION pronouncing the letter 'l'

7a 3.4))) Listen to the following two words being pronounced. Do you notice a difference in the way the letter 'l' is pronounced in each word?

light   will

b Work with a partner. Read the words aloud and divide them into two groups, depending on the sound of the letter 'l'.

caller   final   help   life   lost   slow   spell   told   we'll

c 3.5))) Listen and check your answers. Then listen again and repeat.

8 Work with a partner. How would you contract these sentences in spoken English? Practise saying them using the second pronunciation of the letter 'l'.

1 I will help you.

2 What will happen next?

3 You will be great at the job.

4 She will start her course soon.

5 Where will you go?

6 We will work harder.

9 Discuss with a partner. What do you think will happen to the following traditional jobs? Which ones will changes the most? How do you think they will change?

- construction worker
- teacher
- lawyer
- farmer

Vocabulary talking about learning, thinking and knowledge

10a Which, if any, of the opinions 1–3 do you agree with? Discuss with your partner.

drop out   know your stuff   pick up

1 'Plenty of successful business people [1]leave university before they qualify. It's probably more important to get practical work experience anyway. You can [2]learn a lot of stuff on the job. So long as you [3]have good practical skills and knowledge, employers won't care if you have a piece of paper to prove it.'

get on   lose touch   make the most of   think ahead

2 'Flexibility is very important. You need to [1]make plans about what experience or qualifications you may need in the future, and [2]get as much benefit as possible from any opportunities you get to learn something new. It's very easy [3]not to stay in contact with changes in your area of work, but if you want to [4]be successful, you can't let that happen.'

do your best   give up   stick at it

3 'Getting a range of experience is all very well, but employers also need to see that you can [1]carry on with something, even when it's difficult. So if you're not enjoying a job, [2]try as hard as you can to find something you *do* like about it; don't [3]stop until you're really sure it isn't for you.'

b Replace the underlined phrases in exercise **10a** with the less formal idioms from the boxes with a similar meaning, making any necessary changes.

11 Choose three idioms in exercise **10a** and tell your partner about a time when you did these things. What did you learn from the experience that will help you in your future life?

12 **TASK** In what ways are you investing in your future? Turn to page 127 and complete the sentences.

▶ VOX POPS VIDEO 3

3.2 Best ways to invest your time

Vocabulary & Reading collocations with *time* and *money*

1 Work with a partner. Put the collocating verbs and phrases into the correct place in the diagram.

> ~~be short of~~ choose the right fritter away get your …'s worth
> have … to spare invest kill run out of set aside
> ~~take your~~ throw your … around waste while away

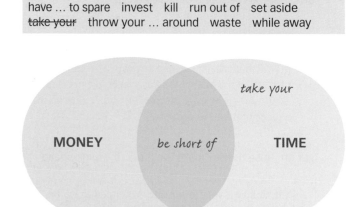

2a Complete the sentences using one of the collocations from the diagram in exercise **1**. If there is more than one possible answer, discuss any difference in meaning with your partner.

1 Apps such as Candy Crush or Fruit Ninja are a good way to _____ when you're bored.
2 If you _____, ready-made meals for the microwave are just as good as home-cooked food.
3 Don't _____ worrying about what other people have.
4 It's important to _____ for the people you care about.
5 Don't _____, try to save it for something really worth buying.
6 The best way to _____ is in your education.
7 If your education is expensive, make sure you _____ by working as hard as you can.

b Which of the statements in exercise **2a** do you (dis)agree with? Discuss with a partner.

c Which do you think is more valuable, time or money? Explain why.

3a Read the introduction to an online article. What is the article going to tell you – a, b or c?

a Why we shouldn't waste time.
b How to use your time more effectively.
c How to save more money.

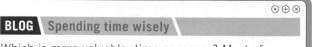

BLOG Spending time wisely

Which is more valuable, time or money? Most of us would probably say 'time'. So why do we waste hours watching boring TV programmes, or kill time playing games on our phones and tablets?

We think it's impossible to make more time. But, like money, we can choose to spend our time wisely or we can fritter it away.

b Read sections 1 and 2 of the article and check your answer to exercise **3a**.

1 Health

Until we actually get ill, most of us take our health for granted. We say we're too busy to go to the gym, or to cook a healthy meal, or to get enough sleep.

But, just to take an example, one in three adults today will have developed diabetes by the time they're sixty. Don't be one of them. Invest time in your health.

2 Time audits

According to Stephen Covey, in *The 7 Habits of Highly Effective People*, we tend to spend most of our time either dealing with things which must be done immediately, or doing things which don't really need to be done at all (like watching TV). Instead, we should be thinking about what we will be doing in five years' time, not just what we need to do by tomorrow.

These plans may not be urgent, but that doesn't mean that they aren't important. If you are always dealing with the day to day emergencies, you'll never manage to achieve anything bigger.

4a Work with a partner. Student A, read sections 3 and 4 of the article on page 127. Student B, read sections 5 and 6 on page 133.

b Tell your partner about the two sections you read. Then decide together on the two best ideas in the whole article.

Grammar & Reading talking about the future (2)

5 Read the Grammar focus box and, with the same partner, add two further examples of each verb form from the article in exercise **3a** and the two sections in Communication.

> **GRAMMAR FOCUS** future continuous and future perfect
>
> - We use the **future continuous** to talk about an action in progress at a certain future time.
>   *will + be + verb + -ing*
>   *This time next year, I'll be living in another country.*
>   a _____
>   b _____
> - We often use the future continuous with phrases such as *this time next year/in two years' time* to talk about what will be happening at a specific time.
> - We use the **future perfect** to talk about an action completed by a certain time in the future.
>   *will + have + past participle*
>   *By this time next year, I will have finished writing my book.*
>   c _____
>   d _____
> - We often use the future perfect with phrases such as *by this time next year/in five years' time* to talk about a point by which the action will already be complete.
>
> → Grammar Reference page 141

6 Read the last part of the article in exercises **3a** and **3b** and complete it with the future continuous or future perfect form of the verbs in brackets.

> ⊙ ⊕ ⊗
> **How to set goals for your future**
>
> Don't just think about work. Also think about what you **1**_____ (achieve) by this time next year in terms of your relationships with friends and family, travel, health, earning (and saving) money.
>
> Make sure your goals are specific and measurable. Everyone could say: 'By this time next year, I **2**_____ (earn) more money.' This doesn't help. You need to know exactly how you are going to do this. Break each goal down so that you know exactly what you **3**_____ (do) each week to achieve your goal.
>
> I also have an overall plan for the year. For example, last year was all about travel. I wrote in my plan, 'by this time next year, I **4**_____ (visit) ten different countries'. And I did. This coming year, I **5**_____ (concentrate) on settling down to my new life in Canada.
>
> Most people overestimate what they can do in a day, but underestimate what can be achieved in a year. Plan properly and you'll be amazed at what you **6**_____ (achieve) by the end of the year.

7a **TASK** Think about your goals and action plans for the next twelve months.
  1 Write down three goals connected with family, learning, travel or anything else.
  2 Think of specific actions you can take for each goal and decide when you will do them.

b Tell your partner about your goals, specific actions you will be taking and what you will have achieved by certain points in the next year. How many goals or actions are similar to your partner's?

Reading & Speaking skimming a text using topic sentences

1a Read the idioms and discuss the questions with a partner.

have a heart of gold **a golden opportunity**

be as good as gold

1 What do you think the idioms mean?
2 Do you have any similar idioms in your language?

b Read the first paragraph of the article on the right and compare it with your ideas.

2 Read the information in the Unlock the code box about using topic sentences to help you read quickly.

> 🔓 **UNLOCK THE CODE**
> skimming a text using topic sentences
>
> Skimming is a technique for reading a text quickly to absorb the main ideas. One way to do this is by reading the topic sentences in each paragraph.
> - The topic sentence is the sentence which carries the main message of a paragraph, and it is usually (but not always) the first sentence of each paragraph (see highlighted sentence in the article). Understanding the topic sentence in each paragraph can help you to get an overview of what is in the text, which can make it easier to quickly skim read.
> - The topic sentence is often supported by a sentence (or sentences) with further related information, or reasons.
> - The topic sentence and/or the supporting sentence(s) may also be backed up by examples.

3 Now read the whole article and underline the topic sentence in each paragraph.

Beautiful, rare and useful. No wonder gold has captured our imaginations throughout the ages.

1 From ancient times, gold has been of great importance to mankind. Many languages reflect this, using gold as a way of describing anything which is beautiful or valuable. In English, kind people 'have a heart of gold', particularly well-behaved children are 'as good as gold' and a 'golden opportunity' is one not to be missed.

2 The Ancient Greeks believed that gold was a combination of water and sunshine due to its brightness, and the Inca Kingdom called it the 'tears of the sun'. Gold may not have come from the sun, but it probably did come from another planet. The fact that it is always found on or near the surface of the Earth is possible evidence that it may have been brought here by asteroids.

3 Although it is found on every continent, gold is extremely rare. It is estimated that if all the gold in the world was put together, it would make a block of only twenty square metres. Its rarity adds to its value.

4 Gold is particularly treasured in the Middle East, China and India, where more than three billion people prefer to keep their wealth in gold, rather than as money in the bank. As well as being an investment, gold jewellery also has an important cultural role. Half the gold that Indians buy each year is bought for a wedding or other celebration.

5 Gold also has a multitude of less traditional uses in industry. It is not affected by air or water, making it an excellent protective coating for machinery. It is also well suited for conducting heat or electricity.

4 Use the topic sentences you have identified to help you match paragraph headings a–f to paragraphs 1–5 in the article in exercise **3**. There is one heading you do not need.

a Not from this world?
b How gold is used in modern manufacturing
c Gold as a symbol or metaphor
d The importance of gold in certain countries
e Some medical uses for gold
f There is less gold than you might think

5a Make a list of 4–5 items in your house that you would choose to try and save in an emergency (not including people or pets).

b Compare your list with a partner. Are any of the items similar?

c Are your items mainly things with a monetary value or sentimental value?

Vocabulary & Speaking noun suffixes

6a Read the information in the Vocabulary focus box about noun suffixes.

VOCABULARY FOCUS noun suffixes

- Certain suffixes tell you that the word is a noun. Recognizing these suffixes can help you understand a word, as well as increase your vocabulary.

- Some of the most common noun suffixes are:

-ence (reference)	-ance (appearance)
-ery (bravery)	-ity (reality)
-tion (intention)	-dom (wisdom)
-ment (measurement)	

- Sometimes adding a suffix causes small changes in spelling, for example:

enter → entrance	converse → conversation
curious → curiosity	vary → variation
scarce → scarcity	jewel → jewellery

b Work with a partner. Find at least one noun in the article in exercise **3** with each of the following suffixes.

1 -ance _____   5 -ence _____
2 -ity _____   6 -ery _____
3 -ment _____   7 -dom _____
4 -tion _____

7a Complete the sentences using the correct form of the words in brackets.

1 Winning a gold medal is quite an _____ (achieve). *ACHIEVEMENT*
2 All her gold jewellery was taken in the *ROBBERY* (rob).
3 The gold necklace was part of her *INHERITANCE* (inherit).
4 The Incas were an ancient *CIVILIZATION* (civilize).
5 Thank you for your _____ (generous). *GENEROSITY*
6 The whole village received an *INVITATION* (invite) to the wedding.
7 Having enough money gives you the _____ (free) to do what you want. *FREEDOM*
8 Gold has a special _____ (signify) in some countries. *significance*
9 I have a _____ (prefer) for silver jewellery, rather than gold. *PREFERENCE*
10 I get a lot of _____ (enjoy) from shopping. *ENJOYMENT*

b **3.6**))) Listen and check your answers.

PRONUNCIATION word stress – nouns

8a Complete the table with the new words in exercise **7a**.

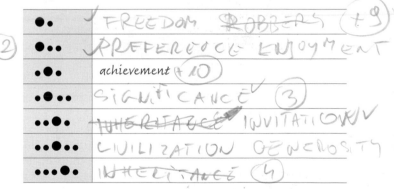

b **3.7**))) Listen and check your answers.

c We often stress the syllable before a suffix. With a partner, check the words in exercise **8a** and identify which words do *not* follow this pattern.

9 **TASK** Work with a partner. Student A, turn to page 127. Student B, turn to page 133. Take it in turns to give each other a word. For one point, turn it into a noun. For two points, put the noun into a sentence.

3.4 Speaking and writing

GOALS ☐ Say how likely something is to happen ☐ Write a balanced opinion essay

Speaking & Listening saying how likely something is to happen

1 Work with a partner. Read the predictions and discuss how likely you think it is that these things will happen.

Life in 2025

▸ People won't go on holiday any more but will enjoy virtual reality holidays where they feel as if they are on holiday, but are actually staying at home.

▸ When you go out for a meal, the restaurant will print out ice cream or pizza using a special 3D food printer.

▸ Because they use so much technology in their work lives, people will stop using technology to relax and instead learn old-fashioned skills, such as gardening.

2a **3.8**))) Listen to two friends, George (G) and Evie (E), discussing the predictions in exercise **1**. Write their initials next to a phrase below if they express an opinion on how likely it is to happen.

Virtual reality holidays
1 definitely won't   4 probably will
2 probably won't   5 definitely will
3 possibly will

Printed food in restaurants
6 probably won't   8 probably will
7 possibly will   9 definitely will

Technology-free leisure
10 definitely won't   13 probably will
11 probably won't   14 definitely will
12 possibly will

b **3.8**))) Listen again and complete extracts 1–7 from George and Evie's discussion.
1 G I wouldn't be surprised if it happened.
2 E … I still doubt people would be satisfied with a virtual holiday.
3 E I expect they'll just travel more within their own countries.
4 G … I think it's bound to happen.
5 E There's no chance of me eating something like that!
6 E Oh, that's sure to happen.
7 G Well, yes, I suppose it might happen …

c Complete the Language for speaking box with the phrases in exercise **2b**.

LANGUAGE FOR SPEAKING likelihood

- Definitely won't happen
  a bound   no chance
- Probably won't happen
  b surpris   doubt
- Possibly will happen
  c chance   suppose
- Probably will happen
  d suppose   wodn' sum
  e expect
- Definitely will happen
  f sure
  g doubt

PRONUNCIATION intonation – expressing certainty

3a **3.9**))) Listen to the phrases from exercise **2b**. Does the intonation make the speaker sound certain (C) or uncertain (U)?
1 C   2 C   3 C   4 U   5 C   6 C   7 U

b **3.9**))) Listen again and repeat, paying attention to the intonation.

4a **TASK** Make at least one prediction about each of the following areas.
- transport   • communication   • food
- home entertainment   • housing

b Work with a partner. Share your predictions. Respond to each other's predictions using the phrases in the Language for speaking box.

FRIDAY (handwritten)

Reading & Writing a balanced opinion essay

5 Look at the following essay question. Work with a partner and make a list of 2–3 arguments or examples to support each view.

> Some people believe that, in the future, we will have more and more leisure time as computers replace many of the tasks we do at home and work. Others believe that we will have less leisure time as employers will expect us to be available and connected to the internet at all times.
>
> Discuss both these views and give your opinions.

6a Read the essay. How many of your arguments are mentioned?

1 **¹Without doubt**, computers and the internet are becoming more and more important in all our lives. In the future, the development of technology is bound to have an impact on our lives and leisure time. However, it is uncertain whether technology will mean that we have more or less leisure time. *(handwritten: General statement / Thesis statement)*

2 **²Some people argue that** computers will start to do more and more for us in the home and at work. We have already seen examples of this with the invention of cleaning robots **³such as** the Roomba, and smart devices which enable us to turn appliances on or off from a distance. *(handwritten: ARGUM TOPIC)*

3 **⁴Others feel, however, that** although computers may help us with our daily tasks, this will not necessarily mean that we have free time. They argue that employers may simply expect us to have time to do more work. **⁵In addition**, wearable technology may mean that we are expected to be available to our employers at all times.

4 **⁶Personally**, I doubt that we will have more leisure time in the future. Back in the 1970s, it was predicted that more technology would mean that people in the future would have a five-day weekend. This has certainly not happened yet, and I don't expect it to happen in years to come. **⁷In fact**, it seems that the more technology we invent, the harder we are expected to work and the more we are expected to produce. *(handwritten: Conclusion)*

5 **⁸In conclusion**, while employers may not expect us to be constantly available in the future, I believe that they will continue to demand more of us.

b Read the essay again and match paragraphs 1–5 to sections a–e.

_3_ a arguments to support the second belief
_1_ b introduction (in your own words)
_2_ c arguments to support the first belief
_4_ d your opinion
_5_ e conclusion

7 Add the phrases in bold in the essay to the Language for writing box.

> **LANGUAGE FOR WRITING** writing a balanced opinion essay
>
> **Introduction**
> *(handwritten: without doubt)*
> In recent years, …   These days, …
>
> **Giving both sides of the argument** *(handwritten: other)*
> *(handwritten: Some people)*   *(handwritten: However)*
>
> **Giving extra details and examples**
> For example/instance, … *(handwritten: such as)*
> *(handwritten: In fact)*   Additionally, …
>   Moreover, …
>
> **Giving your own opinion**
> *(handwritten: personally)*   In my opinion, …
>
> **Introducing the conclusion**
> To conclude, …   To sum up, …
> *(handwritten: In conclusion)*

8a **TASK** You are going to write an essay. Look at the following essay question and plan out what you are going to write in the style of the five paragraphs given in exercise **6a**. Try to think of a main idea and some supporting information or examples for each paragraph. Write your essay in about 250 words.

> In recent years, the number of people travelling by air for business and pleasure has increased dramatically. Some people believe that air travel will continue to grow and that it will become easier, faster and cheaper. Others, however, believe that due to environmental pressures, flying is likely to become too expensive for most people.
>
> Discuss both these views and give your own opinion.

b Work with a partner. Read your partner's essay and comment on:

1 content – did they have some good ideas for both sides of the argument?
2 organization – did they follow the structure given?
3 language – did they use some of the phrases in bold from the essay?

(handwritten: SUMMARY)

3.5 Video

The future of work

1 Look at the photos. Which one is closest to the environment that you work in, or expect to work in one day? What are the advantages and disadvantages of each place?

2a Match the words and phrases in the box to definitions a–e.

> agile working work environment workforce
> working hours working practices

- a the group of people who work for an organization
- b the way that work is usually done in an organization
- c everything that forms part of the employees' relationship with work – colleagues, light and space, company rules, etc.
- d flexibility in when or where you work
- e how long you work and at what times of day

b With a partner, discuss how you think people's work environments, working hours and working practices have changed in recent years, or may change in the future.

3 ▶ Watch the video to **02.09** and compare what the speaker says with your ideas.

4 ▶ Watch again. Complete each statement with the correct topic from the box.

> careers creative environments social media
> technology writing in code

1 _____ has affected some industries negatively, but made others better and more profitable.

2 _____ is something that more people can do nowadays.

3 Younger people are more used to _____.

4 Now that many businesses use _____, there is a concern that workers may take advantage of this.

5 Young people starting _____ need to find jobs they enjoy.

5 **TASK** Work in small groups. Read the following description of a work environment. Make a list of possible good and bad points and discuss your reasons.

> The team is made up of people in several different countries, including some on the other side of the world. We meet daily online and describe what we have been doing and anything which is stopping us progressing. There is no need to go into an office, as we can work anywhere.

Review

1a Complete the advice about money. The first letter is given.

🏠 HOME	✏️ BLOG	🎬 FILM	▶️ TV	🎵 MUSIC	↗️ FASHION

● Top ways to spend less

1 Unless you have plenty of money to s_____, never go shopping without a list.

2 Use cash for small purchases so you notice how much money you are frittering a_____ on newspapers and coffees.

3 Save more. If you s_____ aside a certain amount of money each month, you will have less available, so you'll spend less.

4 I_____ in a short course to learn how to do simple repairs around the house. You'll save a fortune.

5 Don't t_____ your money around unnecessarily. You don't need to impress anyone.

6 If you join a gym, make sure you get your money's w_____. Don't keep paying a monthly fee if you never actually go.

b Which do you think is the best piece of advice in exercise **1a**? Discuss with a partner.

2 Choose the correct options to complete the sentences.

1 'This is so heavy.' 'Don't worry, I*'ll help* / *'m helping* / *help* you carry it.'

2 We need to get up really early because the plane *leaves* / *is going to leave* / *will have left* at 7 a.m.

3 If you get there late, all the best seats *will go* / *are going to go* / *will have gone*.

4 Stand back from the edge, the train *leaves* / *is leaving* / *will leave* soon.

5 Don't ring me at 7.30, I *will be watching* / *will watch* / *am watching* my favourite TV programme then.

6 What subject *are you going to study* / *do you study* / *are you studying* when you go to university?

3a 3.10))) Listen to the beginning of six sentences. Write what you hear and complete the sentences with your own ideas.

b Compare your sentences with a partner and explain what you wrote.

4 Match the two halves of these eight collocations.

1	pick something	a	at something
2	think	b	most of something
3	stick	c	ahead
4	do your	d	out of school
5	lose touch	e	up quickly
6	make the	f	your stuff
7	drop	g	with someone
8	know	h	best

5a Complete the sentences with nouns made from a root word in box A and a suffix in box B. Change the spelling if necessary.

A | able assist brave encourage real wise

B | *-ance* *-dom* *-ery* *-ity* *-ment*

1 The firefighter received an award for her _____.

2 People usually work better if they are given _____.

3 He has a lot of _____ in the subject, but doesn't work very hard.

4 **A** Thank you for your _____.
   B I was glad to help.

5 I dream of being a pop star, but in _____ I know it isn't very likely.

6 Older people have greater _____ because of their life experience.

b 3.11))) Listen and check your answers. Mark the main stress on the word you add to each sentence.

6a Put phrases a–g in order, from most likely (1) to least likely (7).

a	It's sure to …	e	It's bound to …
b	I expect it'll …	f	I suppose it might …
c	I wouldn't be surprised if …	g	I doubt that …
d	There's no chance of it …		

b Talk to your partner. How likely do you think the predictions are to actually happen?

• Patients will talk to doctors online unless the illness is serious.

• You will be able to upload the content of your brain to a computer.

• Money will disappear and all payments will be digital.

Creativity

4.1 Inventive ideas

Listening & Grammar using the passive

1 Work with a partner. Read the introduction to an article and look at the photos of four of the entries a–d. What do you think they are? How do you think they work?

Dyson Award

Twenty new inventions created by engineers and designers across the world have been shortlisted for the James Dyson Award. 650 projects were entered by imaginative scientists from eighteen different countries. The winning entry, which will be announced in November, will receive a prize of £30,000.

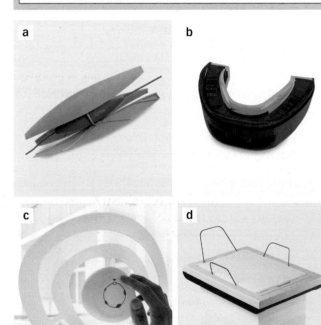

a

b

c

d

2a **4.1)))** Listen to descriptions of the entries and match photos a–d to entries 1–4.

b **4.1)))** Listen again. List two advantages of each invention.

3a Work with a partner. Look at the underlined verb forms in the introduction to the article and answer the questions.
   1 What tense is each verb form?
   2 What structure do they all use?

b Add these extracts from the listening to the correct section of the Grammar focus box. One extract is used twice.
   1 This invention has been designed to take up as ...
   2 When something is being printed, Stack moves ...
   3 ... two out of every three players on a team had been injured that year.
   4 ... the information is sent to a computer.
   5 If a player is moving more slowly than usual, for example, it will be measured ...
   6 The third invention ..., Xarius, was created by a German team.
   7 It can be attached to almost anything ...

GRAMMAR FOCUS passive forms

We make passive verbs with *be* + past participle. Passive verbs have the same tenses as active verbs, e.g.

a Present continuous: __2__   e Past perfect simple: ___
b Present simple: ___   f Future forms: ___
c Past simple: ___   g Modals: ___
d Present perfect simple: ___

We use passive forms to describe what happens to someone or something.

- If we want to say who or what does the action, we use *by*.
- Often the person or thing that does the action is not known, or is obvious or unimportant.
- Some verbs have two objects, which means there are two possible active and passive structures.
   The designs were shown to the judges.
   OR *The judges were shown the designs.*
   h _____
   OR *A computer is sent the information.*

→ Grammar Reference page 142

4a Complete the article with the correct passive forms of the verbs in brackets. In some cases more than one tense may be possible.

The Airdrop

The problem of drought-affected farmers
¹_____ (may/solve) by a recent
Dyson Award winner, Edward Linacre. Linacre
²_____ (inspire) by Australia's worst
drought in a century when he invented Airdrop.
Using his system, water ³_____
(can/collect) from the air. Linacre says the idea
⁴ _Was given_ (give) to him by the Namib   P.S.
Beetle, which survives in the desert by collecting tiny
amounts of moisture. Linacre ⁵ _has been_
recently _asked_ (ask) to develop his   PP S
device by the Chinese government and companies
in the Middle East, but, for now, he wants to keep
working on it himself. Up until now, the system _developed_
⁶_has been dev_ (develop) in his mum's backyard.
In the future, it ⁷_will be taken_ (take up) to a
more industrial level.   F.S

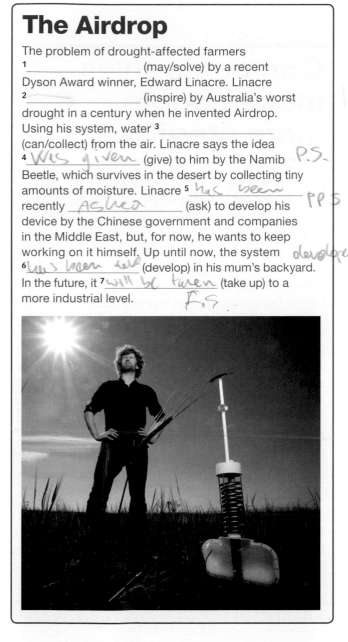

b 4.2))) Listen and check your answers. If any of your answers are different, discuss with your partner whether they are also possible.

PRONUNCIATION weak forms: _to be_

5a 4.3))) Listen to passive phrases from the article in exercise **4a**. What do you notice about the pronunciation of the forms of the verb _to be_?

b 4.3))) Listen again and repeat the phrases.

6 Rewrite each sentence to make two possible passive sentences. THE ENTRANTS
  1 They had given all the entrants an application form.
  2 They will give the winners a £10,000 prize.
  3 The Chinese government has sent Edward Linacre an offer.
  4 Looking at the Namib Beetle gave Linacre the idea for his invention.

Vocabulary & Speaking   how things work

7 Work with a partner. Match the verbs in the box to definitions 1–12.

attach   control   design   fix   generate   measure
monitor   place   protect   recharge   reduce   treat

  1 produce or create something (e.g. energy)
  2 give medical care
  3 be able to make something do what you want
  4 keep something safe
  5 put something in place so it will not move
  6 to fill with electrical power again
  7 fasten or join something to something
  8 find the size, weight, quantity, etc. of something
  9 make something less or smaller
  10 put something carefully in a particular position
  11 plan how something will be made
  12 check or test something regularly

8a With your partner, use the verbs in the box in exercise **7** (in the passive form where appropriate) to describe one of the inventions in exercises **1** and **2**, and explain how it works, using the vocabulary.

b Use your ideas to write a short paragraph about the invention.

9a TASK Work in groups of three. Student A, turn to page 127, Student B, turn to page 133. Student C, turn to page 135. Tell each other about your invention in your own words.

b Decide which invention is the most useful.

▶ VOX POPS VIDEO 4

Vocabulary & Speaking — describing your impressions

1 Work with a partner. Look at the three photos (above and on the right) and discuss the following questions.

1 Do either of you work in an office which looks anything like these? If not, would you like to? Why/Why not?

2 Do you think that working somewhere like this would make you more creative? Why/Why not?

2a With your partner, add the words in the box to the lists, making groups with similar meanings.

> conventional   innovative   inventive   odd   practical
> remarkable   silly   striking   user-friendly

weird: _odd_
original: _INNOVATIVE   INVENTIVE_
impressive: _REMARKABLE_
functional: _USER-FRIENDLY_
childish: _SILLY_
unimaginative: _____

b Are there any small differences in meaning between the words in each group in exercise **2a**? Discuss with your partner.

3 With a new partner, describe your impressions of each office in the photos, using the words from exercise **2**.

4a Read the newspaper article. Make a list of things the article mentions which might make people more creative.

b Compare the things you found with a partner. Which idea(s) do you think are most/least likely to work? Why?

Can companies make people more creative?

A lot of companies want their employees to be innovative and creative, but how can inventiveness be encouraged? We've all seen those pictures of striking, original or even truly weird offices, with ping-pong tables, swings, slides, even beds. But do they actually lead to greater creativity? It's hard to say. Having fun with colleagues on a slide might make you feel more relaxed and full of imaginative ideas, but then again, it might just be a silly waste of time.

Companies such as Google think that <u>if they can get you to bump into your colleagues</u> all the time, you'll do more sharing of ideas. <u>They have their employees eat lunch at long tables</u> so that they will meet and chat to more people. All this chatting might spark some ideas, but on the other hand, maybe a nice quiet office and some peace to think might actually be more user-friendly.

Another approach that some companies take is to try to make sure that you have nothing else to worry about other than coming up with new and impressive ideas. At Google, for example, breakfast, lunch and dinner are all provided free and <u>you can get your hair cut</u>, <u>get your bike repaired</u>, <u>have your car washed or serviced</u>, even <u>get your washing done</u>, without having to leave the building. Again, these could be seen as perks, but they could also just be a way of getting you to stay longer at work.

Ultimately, while companies like these could be fun places to work at, people actually often come up with the best ideas in spite of their environment, rather than because of it. J. K. Rowling famously wrote the first Harry Potter books while living on virtually no money, with a child to support. As Steve Jobs, the founder of Apple, once said about the difficult years of his company: 'We had nothing to lose and everything to gain.' Perhaps to be truly creative you need to be a bit less comfortable so you're 'hungry' to succeed?

■ **perk** something extra that you get from your employer in addition to a salary

`Grammar` using causative *have* and *get*

5a Look at the underlined sections of the article. Do these verb forms refer to actions you do yourself, or actions someone does for or to you?

b Check your ideas by reading the Grammar focus box, then add some of the underlined examples to the box.

> **GRAMMAR FOCUS** causative *have* and *get*
>
> • When we arrange for somebody else to do something for or to us, but we don't say who does it, we use
>
> *have* + object + past participle
>
> a _____
>
> OR
>
> *get* + object + past participle (slightly more informal than using *have*)
>
> b _____
>
> We can also use these structures when something has happened to us, and we didn't want it to happen.
>
> *I had my handbag stolen last night.*
>
> • When we arrange for somebody else to do something for us, or for somebody else to do something we want, and we *do* say who does it, we use
>
> *get* + person + infinitive with *to*
>
> c _____
>
> OR
>
> *have* + person + infinitive without *to*
>
> d _____

→ Grammar Reference page 143

6a Rewrite each sentence in three different ways, using the structures in the Grammar focus box.

> ## Perks of being a Google employee
>
> **1** A chef will cook breakfast for you.
> *You can get/have your breakfast cooked for you by a chef.*
> *Google will have a chef cook your breakfast for you.*
> *Google will get a chef to cook your breakfast for you.*
>
> **2** A doctor will give you free health checks.
> _____
> _____
> _____
>
> **3** Someone will do your dry-cleaning for you, for free.
> _____
> _____
> _____
>
> **4** Someone will fix your car for you.
> _____
> _____
> _____

b What perks would make you most want to work for a company? Discuss with a partner.

I'd like to have my car washed frequently.

7 Work with a partner. Which of these things do you think are more likely to make someone more creative? Put the list in order, from most likely (1) to least likely (6).

- playing music quietly
- hearing colleagues' phone conversations
- having the heating turned down
- having a messy desk
- feeling tired
- having a nap

8 **4.4**))) Listen to a radio programme about how people work and compare it with your ideas. Does anything surprise you? Discuss with your partner.

4.3 Vocabulary and skills development

Listening & Speaking omitting consonant sounds

1   Work with a partner. Look at the photos of 'yarn-bombing' and discuss the following questions.

1   Have you ever seen anything similar before?
2   Do you find it attractive or amusing? Why/Why not?
3   What do you think the point of it is?

2   **4.5** 》 You are going to listen to a podcast about yarn-bombing. But first, read and listen to the information in the Unlock the code box.

🔓 UNLOCK THE CODE
omitting consonant sounds

When people are speaking fluently some consonant sounds tend to be left out. This can make it difficult to understand what the speaker is saying.

/t/ and /d/

• When a word ends with a consonant cluster (two or three consonant sounds together) ending in the sound /t/ or /d/ and the next word begins with a consonant sound, the final /t/ or /d/ tends to disappear.

I'm not going sounds like 'I'm noh going' /ˌaɪmˌnɒˈɡəʊɪŋ/.
He stopped kicking the ball sounds like 'He stop kicking the ball' /hiˌstɒpˈkɪkɪŋðəˈbɔːl/.

• We **don't** usually leave out /t/ or /d/ before a vowel sound or /h/.

First of all /ˈfɜːst(ə)vˌɔːl/
She seemed happy /ʃiːˌsiːmdˈhæpi/

• We **don't** usually leave out /d/ before the sounds /r/, /w/, /l/ and /s/.

She seemed relieved /ʃiːˈsiːmdˌrɪˈliːvd/

3a **4.6** 》 Listen to the following sentences and cross out the /d/ or /t/ in bold if you don't hear it pronounced.

1   It looks a bit weir**d** to me.
2   Wha**t** does it mean?
3   What does i**t** mean? ✓
4   I'**d** like to knit something like that. ✓
5   I'd like to kni**t** something like that. ✓
6   I**t** looks amazing! ✓
7   I'**d** rather see this than graffiti. ✓
8   They shouldn'**t** put it on statues.
9   It doesn'**t** do any harm.

b   Compare your answers with a partner, and check your findings against the rules in the Unlock the code box.

4   **4.7** 》 Listen to a short podcast about yarn-bombing and answer the following questions.

1   What is the first example the speaker gives of yarn-bombing?
2   What has a yarn-bomber done in Paris?
3   At what time of day is yarn-bombing often carried out?
4   What do the yarn-bombers do with the photos they take?
5   What three reasons does the speaker give for why people yarn-bomb?

5   Work with a partner. Choose a public building or statue that might look good if someone covered it in knitting. Explain to another pair why you chose it.

Vocabulary & Listening   easily confused words

6a Choose the correct options to complete the following extracts from the listening in exercise **4**.

1 And in Mexico City, *other / another* yarn-bomber artist, Magda Sayeg …

2 Magda Sayeg has *specially / especially* designed a perfectly fitting cover for a city bus.

3 Yarn-bombing is very *quiet / quite*.

b Read the information in the Vocabulary focus box about easily confused words.

VOCABULARY FOCUS   easily confused words

Some pairs of words are very easily confused.

1 Sometimes the difference is grammatical:

affect/effect

• **Affect** is a verb and **effect** is a noun. The meanings are related.
It affected me badly./It had a bad effect on me.

Other examples: **advise** (verb)/**advice** (noun), **practise** (verb)/**practice** (noun)

2 This could be because the words sound very similar to each other or have a similar spelling:

specially/especially

• Use **specially** to say that something is done for a special reason.
I made this specially for you.

• Use **especially** to emphasize something. You can replace *especially* with 'in particular'.
It is popular all over the world, especially in the United States.

Other examples: **quite** (adverb)/**quiet** (adjective), **lose** (verb)/**loose** (adjective)

3 Sometimes words are confused because they are close to other words:

manage/control

• Use **manage** to say someone can successfully deal with a difficult situation.
She always manages to get all her work done on time.

• Use **control** to show you have power over someone or something – you decide what happens.
He finds it hard to control his children.

Other examples: **fault/mistake**

---

7 Choose the correct options to complete the sentences.

1 The *affect / effect* of the knitting is quite striking.

2 I knitted something *specially / especially* for his birthday.

3 She made a *fault / mistake* and the knitting ended up with a big hole in it.

4 Magda Sayek *manages / controls* a large team of knitters.

5 The knitted covers are usually quite *lose / loose* so it's easy to fix them to the object.

6 It doesn't take a lot of *practice / practise* to knit simple patterns.

7 As some local governments don't like it, yarn-bombers often have to be *quiet / quite*.

8 The best *advise / advice* to yarn-bombers is to do it at night.

PRONUNCIATION   easily confused words

8a **4.8**)) Listen and circle the word you hear.

1 specially / especially   3 lose / loose

2 quite / quiet   4 advise / advice

b **4.9**)) Now listen to the pairs of words and repeat. Practise the difference between the two words.

9a **TASK** With a partner, choose what you think are the five most confusing pairs of words in exercise **7** and say why.

b Write one sentence for each pair of words. Do not include the word itself but leave a gap for your partner to guess the correct word.

c Read the sentences aloud. Can your partner guess which word should go in the gap?

4.4 Speaking and writing

GOALS ■ Write a summary ■ Give opinions and try to change someone's opinion

Writing   writing a summary

1 Read the following quote. Do you agree with it? Why/Why not?

> 'People don't need to learn things by heart any more. They can go on to their phones and find out things instantly, they don't have to remember. Education needs to focus on creativity and problem-solving, not learning facts.'

2 Read the blog post. What would the blog post author think about the quote in exercise **1**? How do you know?

| HOME | BLOG | ABOUT ME | CONTACT | ◀ ⚪ ✉ |

In defence of rote learning

a   It is often said these days that the 'Google generation' has access to so many facts online that memorization is a waste of time. <u>Learning by heart, or 'rote learning', is seen as not only pointless, but also mindless</u>. People argue that it doesn't require any intelligence or creativity.

b   Creativity and problem-solving are very fashionable in education. But <u>how can people use their minds creatively if there's nothing actually memorized and stored in there? How do you create something from nothing?</u>

c   And, in fact, far from being a waste of time, memorization actually helps the brain to develop. Research shows that people who were required to learn things by heart at school are better able to focus on their work as adults.

d   Sure, you can use a calculator these days, but <u>isn't it actually quicker and easier to know your multiplication tables?</u> If you just know these basic things, that frees up your brain power for bigger and better things.

e   Think about it. How would you feel about having surgery with a doctor who had just had to look up how to do it on Google? <u>Expertise is developed through hours of learning, practice and memorization</u>.

3 Match summaries 1–5 to paragraphs a–e in exercise **2**.

1   Having to look up facts is a waste of time when you could just learn them.

2   Practice and memorization are essential if you want to be an expert.

3   Rote learning is often considered to be unnecessary and uncreative.

4   People need background knowledge, as well as the ability to be creative.

5   Learning things by heart benefits the brain.

4a Look at the possible summaries below. Which is the best overall summary of the blog post in exercise **2**? Why?

A
Many people think that rote learning is unnecessary and uncreative, but people need background knowledge before they can be creative. Learning things by heart makes the brain grow and, in the long run, saves a lot of time looking things up. It's also essential for anyone who wants to master a skill.

B
Many people think that memorization is a waste of time when any facts you could possibly need are easily available online on such sites as Wikipedia. It is argued that the 'Google generation' need to learn problem-solving and creativity, rather than facts and figures. However, there are many good reasons why learning things by heart can be beneficial.

b Compare your ideas with the following tips for writing a summary. Can you find good or bad examples in the two summaries in exercise **4a**?

1   A summary should include all or most of the main ideas in the text (not minor details).

2   You should use your own words where possible.

3   You should not add your own opinion or any extra information.

5 Read the information in the Language for writing box about paraphrasing in summaries.

> **LANGUAGE FOR WRITING** paraphrasing in summaries
>
> - Paraphrasing can involve replacing words and phrases with synonyms, e.g. *memorization* could be replaced with *rote learning* or *learning by heart*.
> - However, it is also often necessary to change the grammatical structure of the sentence.
> - An active sentence could be made passive, e.g. *People often say that …* could be replaced with *It is often thought that …*
> - Or a verb phrase could become a noun phrase, e.g. *learning by heart helps the brain to develop* could become *brain development is encouraged by memorization*.

6 How are the underlined phrases or sections from the blog post in exercise **2** paraphrased in summary A in exercise **4a**? Discuss with a partner.

7a **TASK** Read the short article from a website. Write a summary, in 50–60 words, of the key points of the article.

b Look at your summary carefully. Have you covered all the key points in exercise **4b**?

> NEWS ⟩ EDUCATION
>
> According to a new international study, education does not have to be a choice between rote learning or learning to think creatively. In fact, it seems that rote learning can eventually help learners to be better at problem-solving.
>
> 'Learning some knowledge and memorizing it is not a bad thing, it is a good thing,' argues Sir Michael Barber, a top education adviser who worked on the study. 'It is the basis on which you can do problem-solving. And the more knowledge you have, the more knowledge you are able to learn in the future, because it gives you a framework.'
>
> The study ranked countries on their educational performance, finding that Asian countries, such as South Korea, Japan, Singapore and Hong Kong, all did extremely well. All these countries are known for their reliance on rote learning and often criticized for it.
>
> However, the study also found that these countries did extremely well in problem-solving tests, indicating that the more traditional methods used also enabled students to think for themselves.

Speaking & Listening giving opinions and trying to change someone's opinion

8 What makes a good teacher? Is it more important for them to be creative, or motivating, or strict? With your partner, decide on the five most important qualities.

9 **4.10**))) Listen to two friends discussing the same question as in exercise **8**. Do they use any of the same adjectives you thought of? What else do they think is important?

10a Complete the phrases with words from the box.

> hand   look   personally   point   say   see   seems

1 Well, I have to _Say_ that …
2 Well, you've got a _point_, but …
3 Yes, but on the other _hand_ …
4 No, but _look_ …
5 _personally_, I think …
6 As I _see_ it, …
7 It _seems_ to me …

b Put the completed phrases in exercise **10a** into the correct category in the Language for speaking box.

> **LANGUAGE FOR SPEAKING** giving opinions and trying to change someone's opinion
>
> | Giving opinions | Trying to change someone's opinion |
> |---|---|
> | 1 | 2 |
> | *From my point of view, …* | 3 |
> | 5 | 4 |
> | 6 | *Yes, but don't you think …?* |
> | 7 | *Yes, but if you look at it from a different angle, surely …* |

11 **4.10**))) Listen again and check your answers.

PRONUNCIATION intonation – softening language

12a **4.11**))) Listen to the way that the speakers use intonation to soften the first part of what they say. Which is the closest intonation pattern, a ⤵ or b ⤴.

1 **Yes**, but on the other hand …
2 **No**, but look, …
3 **Well**, you've got a point, but …

b **4.11**))) Listen again and repeat, paying attention to the intonation.

13 Work with another pair. Decide on the five most important qualities of a teacher together, and put them in order of importance.

4.5 Video

La Belle Époque

1 Work with a partner. Look at the photos of Paris. What do you recognize in them?

2 Describe the photos using some of these words.

creativity elegance optimism peace prosperity

3 ▶ Read the questions. Then watch the video and find the answers.

1 What are the people in the painting at the beginning of the video doing?

2 What two flags are flying on top of the Académie Nationale de Musique?

3 How many hot-air balloons can you see at the 1900 World Fair?

4 What famous statue is there a model of inside the Musée d'Orsay?

5 What Italian city is the name of the metro station with a yellow sign?

6 What is the name of the department store at the end?

4 ▶ Watch again. Complete the summary.

> Built to commemorate the hundredth anniversary of the
> **1** _____, the Eiffel Tower is 324 metres tall and, for
> more than **2** _____ years, it was the tallest tower in
> the world.
> At the 1900 World Fair, people were able to see some of
> the latest inventions, such as films in which, for the first
> time, people were **3** _____. The World Fair also
> popularized '**4** _____ Nouveau', a popular style of
> design.
> The Musée d'Orsay was originally a **5** _____,
> and it was opened in 1900. It became a museum in
> **6** _____ and now contains many famous Belle
> Époque paintings.
> The underground metro also opened in 1900,
> on **7** _____, and is still used by nearly **8** _____
> passengers every year.

5a **TASK** Work in small groups. Prepare a presentation about one of these people living and working in Paris during the Belle Époque.

- Marie Skłodowska-Curie
- Claude Monet
- Gustave Eiffel
- Édouard Michelin
- Auguste Escoffier

b Give your presentation to another group, or to the rest of the class. Explain why this person was important.

Review

1 Complete the texts with the correct passive form of the verbs in brackets. In some cases, more than one tense may be possible.

The lives of millions of babies ¹_____
(could/save) by a new invention from British student
James Roberts. His low-cost inflatable incubator
²_____ (design) specifically for use
in the developing world and it ³_____
(can/manufacture) and transported for just £250.
Incubators ⁴_____ (usually/price) at
closer to £30,000.

Suncayr, which ⁵_____ (invent) by a
Canadian team of engineers last year, will show you
when you need to reapply your sunscreen. You just
write or draw something on your skin with a special
pen, then put on your sunscreen. When you
⁶_____ (no longer/protect), the drawing
will change colour, letting you know that it's time for
more sunscreen ⁷_____ (apply).

2a Rewrite each sentence using the structure in brackets.

1 Someone stole my bag last year. (have something done)
2 If I have a problem, I can easily find someone who will help me. (get someone to do something)
3 I go to the hairdresser for a haircut every six weeks. (get something done)
4 I don't know how to decorate, so I always hire a decorator. (have someone do something for you)
5 In the UK, you have to get a mechanic to check your car every twelve months. (have something done)
6 I'm very persuasive. I can usually make someone change their mind. (get someone to do something)

b Change three of the sentences in exercise **2a** so they are true for you. Discuss your sentences with a partner.

3a Underline the word which is different from the others.

1 control   fix   attach   stick
2 place   put   position   protect
3 monitor   generate   measure   check
4 reduce   enlarge   treat   increase
5 fix   generate   recharge   power

b Work with a partner and explain your answers.

4a **4.12**))) Listen to definitions 1–6 and write the number of the word being defined.

a conventional ___   d silly ___
b innovative ___   e striking ___
c remarkable ___   f user-friendly ___

b Choose three of the words in exercise **4a** and tell your partner about something or someone you would describe in those ways and why.

5a Complete the sentences with the correct word from the box, in the correct form.

affect / effect   fault / mistake   lose / loose
manage / control   quiet / quite

1 It was so _____ in the classroom that you could hear people breathing.
2 I am always _____ my keys. I need to tie them to my handbag or something.
3 I couldn't _____ myself any more and burst out laughing.
4 The accident wasn't my _____, the other driver should have kept further away from me.
5 His problems at home seem to be _____ his work.

b With a partner, write six sentences using the other word in each pair.

6a **4.13**))) Listen to three people talking about the following statement. Write down any phrases you hear which are used for giving opinions or trying to change someone's opinion.

It is far more important to enjoy your job than to earn a lot of money.

b Compare your list with a partner. Listen again if necessary. You should have five phrases. Can you add any others you know to give opinions or change someone's opinion?

Mind

5.1 As if it were yesterday ...

GOALS ■ **Talk about childhood memories** ■ **Use verbs with *-ing* and infinitive**

Vocabulary & Speaking talking about childhood memories

1 Work with a partner. Discuss the questions.

 1 What is your earliest childhood memory?

 2 How old were you?

 3 How well can you remember what happened?

2 Look at the sentences. Which describe a clear memory (C), which describe an unclear memory (U) and which describe no memory at all (N)?

 1 I can **vaguely** remember it. *So clear* U

 2 I have a **vivid** memory of it. C

 3 I've **no** memory of it **whatsoever**. N

 4 I can't remember the **precise** details. *some* U

 5 I can **just about** remember it. U

 6 I have no **recollection** of it. *suppomend* N

 7 My memory of it has begun to **fade**.

 8 I remember it **as if it were yesterday**. *fresh* C

 9 I can **recall** it very clearly. C

3a Complete the article with some of the bold words from exercise **2**.

When do childhood memories start to fade?

Most adults struggle to ¹ ___RECALL___ events from their first few years of life and now scientists have <u>identified</u> exactly when these childhood memories ² ___FADE___ and are lost forever. According to a new study into 'childhood amnesia' (the loss of early childhood memories), it occurs at around the age of seven. Most three-year-olds have a ³ ___just about___ memory of events from over a year earlier and these memories survive while they are five and six, but by the time they are over seven most children have little or no ⁴ ___recollection___ of these earlier years.

At seven, children can analyse events more clearly and have a better <u>understanding</u> of time and place. This means they <u>store</u> memories in a more effective way and in more ⁵ ___vivid___ detail, and it is easier to <u>access</u> these memories in later life. However, memories involving deep emotion can survive childhood amnesia.

b Work with a partner. Look at the underlined words in the article and try to guess their meaning from context.

4 Discuss the questions.

 1 When do childhood memories fade and why?

 2 What causes this to happen?

 3 What type of memories are less likely to fade?

5a **5.1**))) Listen to two people describing a childhood memory. Complete the first row of the table with brief notes.

	Irene	Tobias
What happened?		
How old were they?		
Which details do they remember vividly?		
Which details don't they remember?		

b **5.1**))) Listen again. Complete the rest of the table in exercise **5a**.

6 **TASK** Work in small groups. Tell each other about your childhood memories, using the language in exercise **2**.

Grammar & Speaking using verbs with -ing and infinitive

7a Look at the extracts from the listening in exercises **5a** and **5b**. Put the verbs in brackets in the -ing form or infinitive with or without *to*.

1 My father **let** me _sit_ (sit) on his shoulders.
2 I **remember** _feeling_ (feel) disappointed because Princess Elizabeth … didn't look like a princess.
3 I tried to **get** the horse _to slow_ (slow) down.
4 I **made** myself _fall_ (fall) off the horse.
5 In my panic, I didn't **remember** _following_ (follow) the teacher's instructions.

b **5.2**))) Listen and check.

8 Read and complete the Grammar focus box with the verbs in bold in exercise **7a**. There is one verb you do not need.

> **GRAMMAR FOCUS** using verbs with -ing and infinitive
>
> - After some verbs we use **-ing** forms; after others we use **infinitives**.
>   *The other children had to **avoid riding** over me.*
>   *I **pretended to be** excited.*
> - Some verbs are followed by **object + infinitive with to**, e.g. tell, want, ¹ _get_ .
>   *The riding teacher **told us to sit** up straight and **not to lean** forward.*
> - Some verbs are followed by **object + infinitive without to**, e.g. ² _let_ , ³ _make_ , help.
>   *He **helped me get** onto the horse.*
> - Some verbs are followed by + **-ing or infinitive with to** with a change of meaning, e.g. ⁴ _remember_ , forget, stop, regret.
>   *I'll never **forget falling** off that horse.*
>   *I **forgot to follow** the teacher's instructions.*

→ Grammar Reference page 144

9a Look at the pairs of sentences. With a partner, decide which structure, -ing or infinitive, is used to talk about things people did. Which talks about things people are/were supposed to do?

1 a I remember feeling disappointed.
  b Remember to sit up straight when the horse is trotting.
2 a I'll never forget seeing the fireman's face at the window.
  b Don't forget to lock the door.
3 a I regret telling you that story.
  b We regret to tell you the trip has been cancelled.

b In the following sentences, which structure says an activity has stopped, 1 or 2? Which gives the reason for stopping?

1 The car stopped to let the horse go by.
2 The horse stopped eating grass and looked up.

10 Choose the correct options to complete the text.

I'll never forget ¹ *to be / being* locked in the bathroom when I was two. I remember ² *to hear / hearing* my mother outside the door. She was trying to explain how to unlock it, but she couldn't get me ³ *to do / doing* it. I was too young to understand and I was crying too much. In the end, she called the fire brigade. When one of the firemen climbed up a ladder and broke through the bathroom window, it made me ⁴ *cry / crying* even more. He picked me up, opened the door and handed me to my mother. I only stopped ⁵ *to cry / crying* when, later, he let me ⁶ *try / to try* on his helmet. Although I was only two, I can recall it vividly. The fact that the story has been told so many times has probably helped me ⁷ *to remember / remembering* it.

11 **TASK** Work with a partner. You are going to practise using verb patterns in a conversation. Student A, turn to page 128. Student B, turn to page 132.

5.2 Bored!

Vocabulary & Speaking emotions and behaviour

1 Work with a partner. Make a list of five situations that make people very bored. Rank them from most boring (5) to least boring (1).

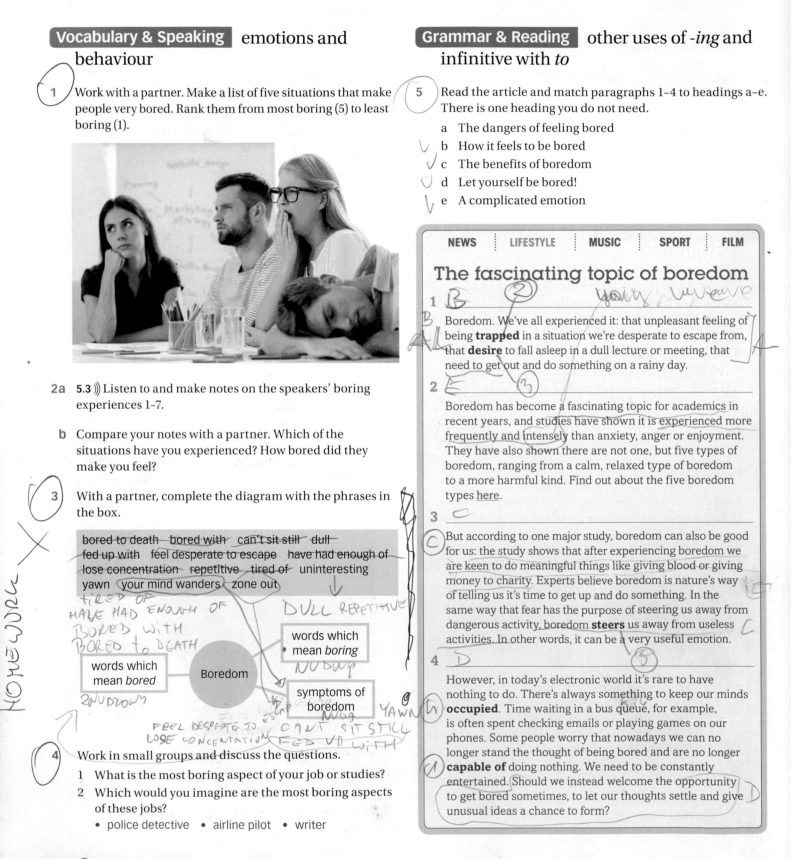

2a 5.3)) Listen to and make notes on the speakers' boring experiences 1–7.

b Compare your notes with a partner. Which of the situations have you experienced? How bored did they make you feel?

3 With a partner, complete the diagram with the phrases in the box.

bored to death bored with can't sit still dull
fed up with feel desperate to escape have had enough of
lose concentration repetitive tired of uninteresting
yawn your mind wanders zone out

words which mean *bored*

words which mean *boring*

Boredom

symptoms of boredom

4 Work in small groups and discuss the questions.

1 What is the most boring aspect of your job or studies?
2 Which would you imagine are the most boring aspects of these jobs?
   • police detective • airline pilot • writer

Grammar & Reading other uses of -ing and infinitive with to

5 Read the article and match paragraphs 1–4 to headings a–e. There is one heading you do not need.

   a The dangers of feeling bored
   b How it feels to be bored
   c The benefits of boredom
   d Let yourself be bored!
   e A complicated emotion

NEWS | LIFESTYLE | MUSIC | SPORT | FILM

The fascinating topic of boredom

1

Boredom. We've all experienced it: that unpleasant feeling of being **trapped** in a situation we're desperate to escape from, that **desire** to fall asleep in a dull lecture or meeting, that need to get out and do something on a rainy day.

2

Boredom has become a fascinating topic for academics in recent years, and studies have shown it is experienced more frequently and intensely than anxiety, anger or enjoyment. They have also shown there are not one, but five types of boredom, ranging from a calm, relaxed type of boredom to a more harmful kind. Find out about the five boredom types here.

3

But according to one major study, boredom can also be good for us: the study shows that after experiencing boredom we are keen to do meaningful things like giving blood or giving money to charity. Experts believe boredom is nature's way of telling us it's time to get up and do something. In the same way that fear has the purpose of steering us away from dangerous activity, boredom **steers** us away from useless activities. In other words, it can be a very useful emotion.

4

However, in today's electronic world it's rare to have nothing to do. There's always something to keep our minds **occupied**. Time waiting in a bus queue, for example, is often spent checking emails or playing games on our phones. Some people worry that nowadays we can no longer stand the thought of being bored and are no longer **capable of** doing nothing. We need to be constantly entertained. Should we instead welcome the opportunity to get bored sometimes, to let our thoughts settle and give unusual ideas a chance to form?

6 Match words in bold in the article in exercise **5** to definitions 1–5.

1 able to do something
2 unable to escape
3 a strong wish
4 busy doing something
5 moves something in a particular direction

TRAPPED
DISIRE
OCCUPIED

7 Work with a partner. Discuss the questions.

1 According to the writer, why can boredom be seen as useful? Do you agree?
2 Do you think we find it harder to deal with boredom than we used to? Why/Why not?

8 Find the words in the box in the article in exercise **5** and add them to the correct list in the Grammar focus box.

after capable keen nothing opportunity thought

GRAMMAR FOCUS other uses of *-ing* and infinitive with *to*

-ing form	infinitive with to
1 **adjectives + preposition + -ing form**, e.g. fed up with, tired of, _capable_ of *I'm **tired of doing** the same thing every day.*	4 **adjectives + infinitive with to**, e.g. about, desperate, easy, likely, 4 _keen_, surprised, rare, willing *How long are you **willing to wait**?*
2 **nouns + preposition + -ing form**, e.g. the chance of, difficulty in, a feeling of, the idea of, the purpose of, the 2 _thought_ of, a way of *I hate the **idea of having** nothing to do.*	5 **nouns + infinitive with to**, e.g. decision, desire, need, motivation, 5 _opportunity_ plan *She made a **decision to retire**.*
3 **before, since, while,** 3 _after_ **+ -ing form**. *I've not been bored **since changing** my job.*	6 **anything, anyone, anywhere,** 6 _nothing_ etc. and **something + infinitive with to** *I need **something to do**.*

→ Grammar Reference page 145

9a Read the article, ignoring the gaps. Which type(s) of boredom do you experience?

NEWS | LIFESTYLE | MUSIC | SPORT | FILM

The five types of boredom

'**Indifferent boredom**' is the boredom you feel while 1 _watching_ (watch) a boring TV programme, for example. It is a pleasant feeling which gives you the opportunity 2 _to zone_ (zone) out after a hard day's work.

'**Calibrating boredom**' is when your mind wanders from the present situation. You have thoughts about 3 _doing_ (do) something different but not the motivation 4 _to act_ (act) on them.

'**Searching boredom**' is when you are fed up with 5 _having_ (have) nothing to do and actively search for something 6 _to occupy_ (occupy) yourself. This can result in risky or illegal behaviour, but also creativity.

'**Reactant boredom**' is caused by feeling trapped in a situation. You have a desire 7 _to do_ (do) something but can't because you're stuck, e.g. in a long queue or dull lesson.

'**Apathetic boredom**' is similar to depression. This is the most worrying boredom type. You have no interest in 8 _trying_ (try) anything new and are incapable of 9 _finding_ (find) enjoyment in life.

b Complete the article with the correct form of the verbs in brackets.

10a **TASK** Work with a partner. Read the two blog article titles. What do you think the articles will say?

Do animals get bored?

Why do we yawn when we're bored?

b Work with a partner. Student A, turn to page 128. Student B, turn to page 133.

5.3 Vocabulary and skills development

GOALS ■ **Understand linkers** ■ **Understand phrasal verbs with *out* and *up***

Reading understanding linkers

1a How much do you know about the brain? With a partner, decide which of the activities below are normally performed by the left side of the brain and which by the right. Write *L* or *R*.

1 thinking logically *R*
2 spelling *L*
3 understanding jokes *R*
4 hearing the rhythm of music *R*
5 controlling the right half of your body *L*
6 recognizing objects *R*
7 appreciating the melody of music *R*

b 5.4)) Listen and check your answers.

2 Read the article. Which sentence, a, b or c, best describes the purpose of the article?

a To help you discover whether you are right or left-brained.
b To explain the truth behind a common myth. *(circled)*
c To give advice on how to develop your right-brain skills.

3 Read the information in the Unlock the code box on linkers.

> 🔒 **UNLOCK THE CODE**
> understanding linkers
>
> Linkers are used by writers and speakers to help show the connection between what has been said and what is going to be said. Use them to help you predict what comes next in a text.
>
> Linkers have different functions, e.g.
>
> - Making things clearer: *that is to say …* or *to put it another way …*
> - Giving examples: *for example, …, e.g. …, thus …*
> - Showing cause or reason: *because of …, owing to …, since …*

4 Complete the table with the highlighted linkers in the article.

Making things clearer	in other words
	FOR INSTANCE
Giving examples	FOR INSTANCE
	SUCH AS
	FOR INSTANCE
Showing a cause or reason	due to

Right brain, left brain?

'Is your desk organized?' 'Do you turn your head to the right when asked a question?' 'Are you good at word puzzles?' These questions are designed to help you work out whether you are right-brained or left-brained –
5 in other words, whether you are creative and thoughtful (right) or logical and analytical (left). Google 'right brain, left brain', and hundreds of online quizzes containing this kind of question will pop up.

It's a shame, then, that it's all a load of nonsense.

10 Recent research carried out at the University of Utah shows no evidence that one side of the brain dominates the other, i.e. that a person can be left-brained or right-brained. In fact, neuroscientists never accepted this idea in the first place.

15 So why is this theory so common? It all started in the 1960s when Nobel Prize winner Roger Sperry discovered that different halves of the brain controlled different activities. However, the media and popular psychologists decided to take Sperry's findings a step further. They
20 came up with the idea that some people use the right side of their brain more while others use the left side more. This resulted in numerous self-help books, management training courses and apps promising to help convert people from left-brained to right-brained thinkers.

25 Here's the truth: you use both parts of your brain all the time. Take language skills, for instance. While the left side deals with linguistic processes, such as understanding the meaning of words and sentences, the right side understands intonation and recognizes different voices.
30 Likewise, with mathematical ability, your left side helps you count whereas the right side enables you to estimate numbers.

Despite all the evidence against it, the belief that one part of the brain is dominant survived for years. This is
35 probably due to the fact that human beings love labels and categories. We have a need to simplify the truth. For this reason, the right-brained/left-brained theory is unlikely to go away any time soon.

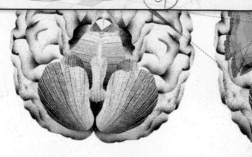

5 Read the whole article in exercise **4** and answer the questions with a partner.

1 According to popular psychology, what do *right-brained* and *left-brained* mean?

2 Why does the writer say that the right-brained/ left-brained theory is 'a load of nonsense'?

3 How do the left and right brain work together to help us a) understand language and b) do maths?

4 What is the writer's prediction for the future of the right-brained/left-brained theory? Why?

Vocabulary & Speaking   phrasal verbs with *out* and *up*

[handwritten: vlowa! Ewing!]

6 With a partner, find these phrasal verbs in the article in exercise **4** and try to guess their meaning. *[handwritten: to figure out/understand, Figure, calculate]*

- work out (line 4) *[handwritten: explain srut]*
- pop up (line 8) *[handwritten: appear scolenly]*
- carry out (line 10) *[handwritten: to creat srut]*
- come up with (line 20) *[handwritten: wymysla!]*

7 Read about phrasal verbs with *out* and *up*. Match the verbs in exercise **6** to the meanings in the Vocabulary focus box.

> **VOCABULARY FOCUS** phrasal verbs with *out* and *up*
>
> Some particles, e.g. *on*, *out*, *up*, can express a particular meaning when they are used in a phrasal verb.
>
> - *up* can mean
>   1 begin to happen and/or appear (sometimes unexpectedly), e.g. *set up*, *take up*.
>   2 create and construct something, e.g. *dream up*, *think up*.
> - *out* can mean
>   1 search for something, such as information or the answer to a difficult problem, then find it or discover/prove something, e.g. *find out*, *figure out*.
>   2 finish doing, disappear, use completely, e.g. *die out*, *phase out*.

[handwritten: ① occur scolenly]

8a Match the sentence halves. *[handwritten: unexpecty happend]*

1 Something urgent has **come up** *[F]*
2 You don't need to book the restaurant *[E]*
3 She said she missed the meeting because she was ill, but *[D]*
4 He got top marks in his exam, but *[C]*
5 Someone from the IT department **sorted out** my computer problems, *[A]* *[handwritten: fix srut]*
6 I **ran out of** time in the exam *[B]* *[handwritten: → no more]*

a and it's been working fine since then.
b and couldn't finish my essay.
c it **turned out** he had cheated. *[handwritten: change against]*
d I think she was **making** it **up**. *[handwritten: imagyn/create]*
e – you can just **turn up**. *[handwritten: come up]*
f so I'm afraid I have to rush off.

b With a partner, try to guess the meaning of the phrasal verbs in bold from the context in exercise **8a**. Then match them to the meanings in the Vocabulary focus box.

9a TASK Complete the questions with a phrasal verb from exercises **6** and **8a**.

1 Are you good at _making up_ stories?
2 Do you tend to use a calculator or do you _sorted out_ maths problems in your head? *[handwritten: worked]*
3 Have you ever _pop up_ petrol? *[handwritten: RUN OUT OF]*
4 Have you ever bought something which _TURNED OUT_ to be a waste of money?
5 Do you mind if friends _TURN UP_ at your home without calling first?

b Ask and answer the questions with a partner.

▶ VOX POPS VIDEO 5

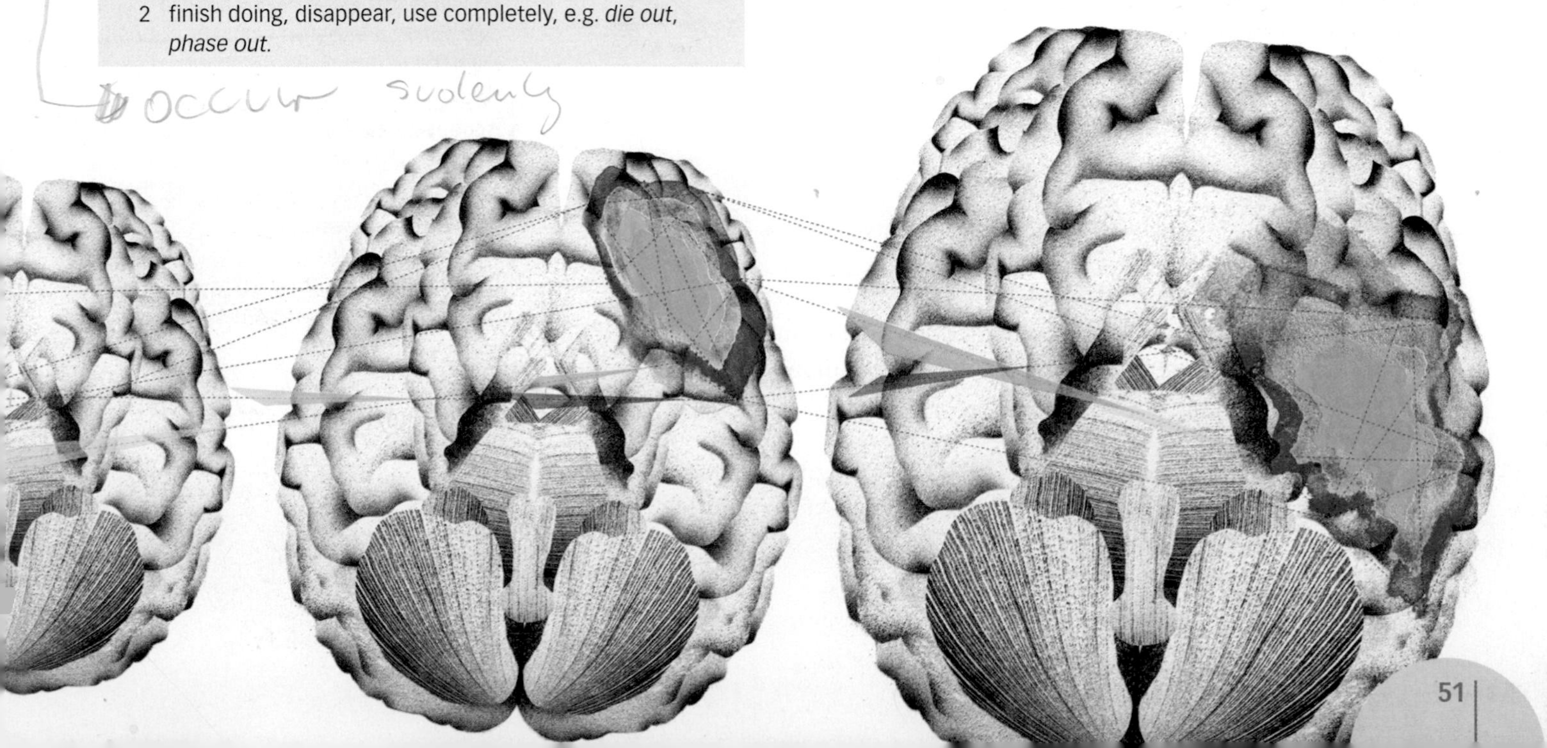

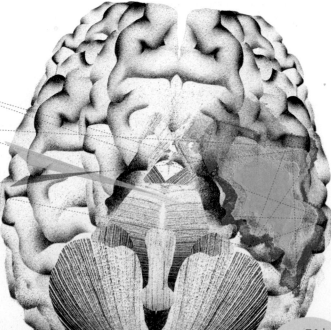

5.4 Speaking and writing

GOALS ■ Language to give solutions ■ Write an article giving advice

NIEPOSLUSZNY

Speaking language to give solutions

1a Work with a partner. Match problems 1–5 to problem types a–e.

1 Your sink is blocked.   a technical
2 Your friend has a bad nosebleed.   b behavioural
3 Your child is disobedient.   c practical
4 Your mobile phone is faulty.   d logistical
5 You need to get a large group   e health
   of people from A to B.

b Which of the problem types are you good at solving? Which ones would you search the internet to find a solution for?

2a 5.5))) Listen to three business partners discussing a problem.
1 Which photo illustrates the problem, a or b?
2 What solutions do they choose?

b 5.5))) Listen again. Which other solutions were suggested? Why were they rejected?

3a Complete the sentences with words from the box.

| alternative consideration effective if no point think way worth |

1 One _way_ (alternative) would be to install some security cameras.
2 We need to take cost into _consideration_
3 I don't _think_ that's an option ...
4 Would it be _worth_ putting in some of those fake cameras?
5 I think a better _alternative_ forward would be to put in some of _way_ those lights.
6 ... that would be a/an _effective_ solution.
7 Do you think there would be any _point_ in changing the lock ...?
8 ... what _if_ we also paint the walls with anti-climb paint?
9 ... there's _no_ harm in doing that.

b 5.6))) Listen and check.

PRONUNCIATION phrase stress

In English, fixed phrases have their own rhythm or stress patterns. To be understood and to sound natural it is important to get these patterns right.

4a 5.7))) Listen to some phrases from the listening in exercise **3b** and mark the main stresses.

b 5.7))) Listen again and repeat.

5a **TASK** Work in groups of three. Turn to page 128 and choose one of the situations. Brainstorm a list of four solutions.

b Role-play your meeting. Take it in turns to put forward suggestions. Think about the advantages and disadvantages of each suggestion and choose the best two.

c Report the results of the meeting back to the class.

LANGUAGE FOR SPEAKING
working out solutions to problems

Coming up with solutions
What if we ... + present/past?
Would it be worth ... + -ing?
Would there be any point in ... + -ing?
Do you think there'd be any point in ... + -ing?
One option/alternative would be + infinitive
We need to take ... into account.
We need to take ... into consideration.

Accepting suggestions
That would be an effective solution.
I suppose there's no harm in doing that.

Rejecting suggestions
I'm not convinced.
I don't think that's/That isn't really an option.
I think a better way forward would be to ...

Writing an article giving advice

6a With a partner, discuss how you would solve the following problem.

> You have been wearing a ring for several years. It is now too tight and uncomfortable to wear. You want to get it enlarged, but you can't get it off your finger.

b Read the online advice article. Are any of your ideas mentioned? According to the writer, which solution is most likely to work?

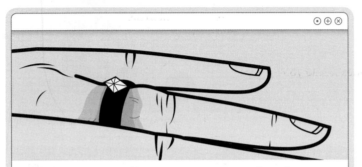

How to remove a stuck ring

First cool your finger by putting your hand in cold or iced water. This will help reduce the swelling in your finger. If using iced water make sure you remove your hand after ten minutes, otherwise you might damage your fingers.

Once your finger is cold, cover it in something slippery, such as hand cream, baby oil or even butter. It's better not to use a strong soap in case it irritates the skin.

Gently twist the ring from side to side. You should twist rather than pull, but be careful not to twist too hard or else your finger may swell even more, which will make it even harder to remove the ring.

If this doesn't work, try using a piece of string, or even better, dental floss. This is the method used in hospitals. It's not advisable to do this on your own. Get someone else to do it for you. Wrap the dental floss tightly around your finger, as far as your knuckle. Wind it tightly, but avoid winding it so tightly that your finger turns blue. Then unwind the dental floss. As you unwind it the ring will move up your finger until you can pull it off. Whatever you do, don't put the ring back on until it has been resized!

c Look at the highlighted phrases in the online advice article in exercise **6b** and find:

1 two which give advice to do something.
2 four which give advice *not* to do something.
3 three which introduce reasons why you shouldn't do something.

7 Look at some advice for changing a light bulb. Rewrite the sentences with the words in brackets.

1 It's essential that you turn the power off. (sure)
2 Wait a few seconds before touching the old bulb. It might be hot. (case)
3 Push the new bulb in gently so that it doesn't break. (else)
4 Don't turn the switch on again until you've finished replacing the bulb. (whatever)
5 For safe disposal of the old bulb, wrap it in the packaging from the new bulb. (advisable)

LANGUAGE FOR WRITING an article giving advice

Giving advice to do something
Make sure you …   *Remember to…*
It's advisable to …   *Don't forget to …*
You should …

Giving advice not to do something
It's not advisable to …   *Whatever you do, don't …*
Make sure you don't …   *Be careful not to …*
Try not to …   *Avoid … (+ -ing)*

Introducing reasons
… as/because it could …   *… in case it (+ present tense)*
… otherwise/or else it might

8a **TASK** Work with a partner and discuss how to solve the problems below.

- You want to remove a (harmless) spider from the ceiling without killing it.
- Your car is stuck in mud.
- You are struggling to open a jar of gherkins.

b Choose one of the problems, or your own idea, and write an online article giving advice about what to do and what not to do to solve it. Use the Language for writing box to help you.

5.5 Video

Boredom

1a Match 1–5 to a–e to make compound nouns.

1	spread	a	chart
2	production	b	sheet
3	attention	c	line
4	instant	d	span
5	pie	e	gratification

b Complete each sentence with a compound noun from exercise **1a**.

1 He has a very short _____. He can't concentrate on anything for more than few minutes.

2 A/An _____ consists of a circle divided into sections.

3 I find inputting data into a/an _____ so tedious.

4 We live in an age of _____, where we want things immediately and get restless if we have to wait.

5 I once had a really repetitive job working on a/an _____ in a bottling factory.

2 Use the compound nouns and other words in exercise **1b** to describe the photos. Which photo seems most boring to you?

3 ▶ Watch the video. What is said about the following things?

1 what the presenter's job involves

2 working hours in the 1950s compared to now

3 the word 'boredom'

4 people's attention span nowadays

4 Watch again. Complete these sentences according to what the presenter says.

1 The boundaries between our home and work life …

2 Although we're working less, we …

3 Thanks to faster internet speeds and mobile technology, we …

4 This culture of instant gratification has …

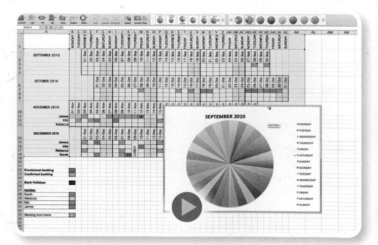

5a **TASK** Read the sentences below. Mark each one, agree (✓), disagree (✗) or depends (?), so they are true for you.

1 I hate having nothing to do.

2 I get bored easily.

3 I need instant gratification.

4 I often end up working at home in the evenings.

5 I find it hard to switch off from my work/studies.

6 I can rarely focus on just one thing, like a book.

b Compare your answers with a partner. How similar are you?

Review

1a Complete the questions with the correct form of the verbs in brackets.

1 Do you remember _____ (be) five years old?

2 Have you ever forgotten _____ (pay) for something?

3 Would you let someone _____ (smoke) in your home?

4 What do you do to help you _____ (stay) awake when you're feeling tired?

5 Are you good at making people _____ (laugh)?

6 If your partner was vegetarian, would you stop _____ (eat) meat?

b Work with a partner. Ask and answer the questions.

2 Complete the article with the correct form of the verbs in the box.

> attract   do   launch   learn   listen   open   pay   sell

Would you be willing ¹ _____ money to attend something called The Boring Conference? You may be surprised ² _____ that every year since ³ _____ in 2010 in London, this conference has been a huge success.

The one-day conference is a celebration of subjects which are often considered dull, but when examined more closely, reveal themselves to be deeply fascinating.

When blogger, James Ward, first had the idea of ⁴ _____ the conference, he never imagined it would be capable of ⁵ _____ so many visitors. Past conference-goers have had the opportunity ⁶ _____ to ten-minute talks on topics as diverse as sneezing, toast, barcodes and vending machines.

If you're looking for something different ⁷ _____ this spring, try The Boring Conference, but tickets are likely ⁸ _____ out fast, so get organized!

3a Match words 1–6 to meanings a–f.

1 vaguely   a gradually disappear

2 fade   b remember

3 recollection   c exact

4 recall   d memory

5 precise   e clear, detailed

6 vivid   f not clearly

b Work with a partner. Describe how clearly you can remember these things.

- your first bedroom
- the first concert you went to
- your last day at secondary school

4 **5.8))** Listen to the definitions of seven words and phrases. Which definitions are correct and which are incorrect?

5a Complete the phrasal verbs in the conversation.

A I thought you were playing tennis with Jack after work today.

B That was the plan, but he didn't ¹ _____ up.

A That's the third time he's let you down! What excuse did he ² _____ up with this time?

B Oh, something had ³ _____ up at work. It's hard to ⁴ _____ out whether he's telling the truth or ⁵ _____ it up.

A You never know, it may ⁶ _____ out to be true. So have you rescheduled?

B No, I haven't. I'm ⁷ _____ out of patience with him, to be honest.

b With a partner, practise reading the conversation aloud.

6a Choose the correct options to complete the sentences.

1 One *alternate* / *alternative* would be to ask him to leave.

2 A better *route* / *way* forward would be to speak to him directly.

3 Would it be worth *getting* / *get* a second opinion?

4 Do you think there would be any point *in* / *on* speaking to her boss?

5 What *if* / *that* we stop her pocket money?

6 We need to take cost *in* / *into* consideration.

b Work with a partner. Choose a problem below or think of your own. Role-play a discussion about how to deal with it.

- a disobedient child
- a difficult colleague
- a lazy, messy flatmate

Community

6.1 Crossing cultures

GOALS ■ Talk about cultures and communities   ■ Understand and use articles

Vocabulary & Reading cultures and communities

1   Look at the photos. Where do you think they were taken? Why? Discuss your ideas with a partner.

2   Read the online magazine article and check your ideas.

3a Look at the highlighted vocabulary in the article and find four plural words which describe *groups of people*.

b   Match the four words from exercise **3a** to definitions 1–4.

1   People who belong to the same family as someone who lived a long time ago. *ANCESTORS*

2   People who have come into a foreign country to live there permanently. *CITIZENS*

3   People who are legally accepted as members of a particular country. *IMIGRANTS*

4   People related to you who lived a long time ago. *DESCENDANTS*

| NEWS | PHOTOS | VIDEO | TRAVEL | ENVIRONMENT |

As you pass through a nine-metre-tall red *torii* gate into the Liberdade neighbourhood and see the Japanese street lamps and signs, you might assume you were in ¹Tokyo. But you'd be wrong. Liberdade is actually the centre of ²the biggest Japanese community ³in the world (outside Japan) and it's in São Paulo, Brazil. More than 1.5 million people with Japanese ancestors live in Brazil, 60,000 of them in Liberdade.

The first settlers arrived over a hundred years ago to work in the coffee plantations, but soon started to move to the cities, particularly São Paulo. ⁴Immigrants need to adjust to new things, but it was difficult for the Japanese settlers at first, as they encountered such a different language, food and climate. However, the community is now very well established, and Liberdade, including ⁵the Museum of Japanese Immigration, is one of São Paulo's main attractions. Every weekend, the area is full of people buying flowers, clothes and Japanese-style food. Many popular Japanese festivals also take place in the area. For example, ⁶*Hanamatsuri*, a ceremony where sweet tea is poured onto the feet of a statue. ⁷The ceremony is then followed by ⁸a parade through the streets with flowers and a large model white elephant. Or the festival of stars, *Tanabata Matsuri*, where people wear typical Japanese costumes and decorate the streets.

WEDDING

4 Work with a partner. Explain the difference between the other pairs or groups of words highlighted in the article.

1 custom/costume
2 festival/ceremony/parade
3 neighbourhood/community
4 adjust/establish

5a Choose the correct options to complete the questions.

1 What aspects of the Liberdade *neighbourhood* / *community* make it seem like Tokyo?
2 Why did the first Japanese *immigrants* / *descendants* first come to Brazil?
3 Why was it difficult for them to *establish* / *adjust* at first? *ADAPT*
4 According to the article, which event includes a *parade* / *ceremony* through the streets?
5 Give an example of another Japanese *festival* / *costume* mentioned in the article.
6 Give an example of a Welsh *costume* / *custom* mentioned in the article. *TRADITION*

b Now read the whole article in exercise **2** again and, with a partner, answer the questions in exercise **5a**.

Another fascinating example is the Welsh community **9**in the Chubut Valley, Patagonia, **10**Argentina. Welsh immigrants first arrived in the area over 150 years ago, but although they now consider themselves to be very firmly Argentinian citizens, many of their 50,000 descendants still speak Welsh and maintain traditions and customs, such as serving Welsh teas and writing poetry.

CASA DE TE
Plas y Coed
LA MAS ANTIGUA Y TRADICIONAL

Grammar articles

6 Complete the Grammar focus box with the underlined phrases and words from the article in exercise **2**.

GRAMMAR FOCUS *a/an*, *the* and – (no article)

- We use *a/an* (indefinite article):
  a when something is one member of a class
  b when we mention something for the first time
- We use *the* (definite article):
  c when it's the only one of something, or the only one in a place
  d when we think it's clear which one we're talking about (often because it's the second time we've mentioned it)
  e with superlative forms
  f with rivers, valleys, certain mountains (e.g. *the Matterhorn*), ranges of mountains, oceans, seas, plural country names or groups of islands (e.g. *The Baltic States*, *The Maldives*) and deserts
  g with the names of theatres, cinemas, hotels, galleries and museums
- We use no article:
  h to generalize about something (with plural or uncountable nouns, including abstract nouns)
  i with most country names, continents, states, lakes and mountains
  j with towns/cities, neighbourhoods and streets

→ Grammar Reference page 146

7 Choose the correct options to complete the information about a Welsh festival in Patagonia.

An *eisteddfod* is **1** *a* / – Welsh festival of **2** – / *the* literature, music and performance. But it is not only held in **3** *the* / – Wales. An *eisteddfod* has been held in **4** *the* / – Patagonia since **5** *a* / *the* group of Welsh immigrants arrived in the valleys of **6** *the* / – Andes in the second half of **7** *the* / *a* nineteenth century.

8 **TASK** Work with a partner. Student A, turn to page 129 and Student B, turn to page 134.

▶ VOX POPS VIDEO 6

6.2 Alone or together?

GOALS ■ Talk about housing and living   ■ Use determiners and quantifiers

Vocabulary & Speaking   housing and living

1a Work with a partner. Make a list of five advantages and five disadvantages of either living alone *or* living with a partner and/or family.

b Join another pair who chose to make the other list and compare your ideas. Discuss your ideas as a group.

2 Complete the texts about two different trends, using the words in the boxes.

> globally growth households independently
> resident shift

According to recent research, the number of people living alone is shooting up dramatically. ¹ *globally* there's been a rise from 153 million people in 1996 to nearly 300 million this year. It's more popular to live ² *independently* in some countries than in others. Sweden has the highest percentage, with 47% of homes having just one ³ *resident*, and the UK and Germany also have quite high percentages. But this is definitely a global trend, and for many countries it represents a dramatic cultural ⁴ *shift*. In fact, the nations with the fastest ⁵ *growth* in one-person ⁶ *households* are China, India and Brazil.

> facilities private properties resources separately
> supported socially

In many countries, particularly in Northern Europe, but increasingly elsewhere, there is a big move towards something called *co-housing*. This is where people live ⁷ *socially* in ⁸ *separately* houses, but the ⁹ *properties* are grouped into a small community with some shared ¹⁰ *resources* such as heating, gardens, a laundry and entertainment space. In other words, it's not that different from an old-fashioned village, where everyone ¹¹ *supported* each other, spent time together ¹² _____ and shared certain ¹³ _____, like the village hall.   *facilities*

3 Work with a partner. Discuss the following questions.

1 Why do you think there has been a global growth in one-person households? Is this happening in your country?

2 Is community important to you? Do you, or would you like to, see your neighbours socially?

3 What might be the advantages of sharing resources, such as electricity and facilities, with other residents in your neighbourhood? Might there be any disadvantages?

4 6.1))) Listen to a radio programme about the trends mentioned in exercise **2**. Decide if these statements are true (T) or false (F).

1 **Many** more people now live alone than before.   T

2 **Both** Emma and Harry live with family.   F

3 **A number of** people in the Lilac co-housing project don't share their house.   T

4 **Neither** Harry nor Emma feels lonely.   F

5 According to Harry, **too many** people have rooms they don't use.   T

6 **Every** house at the Lilac co-housing project has its own garden.   F

5 Would you prefer to live like Emma or like Harry? Why? Discuss with a partner.

Grammar using determiners and quantifiers

6 Look at the words in bold in exercise **4** and choose the correct options to complete the Grammar focus box.

GRAMMAR FOCUS determiners and quantifiers

- We can use **many**, **a number of**, **hundreds of**, **several**, **few**, **a few**, with [1] countable / uncountable / countable and uncountable nouns.

- We can use **much**, **a great deal of**, **a large quantity of**, **little**, **a little** with [2] countable / uncountable / countable and uncountable nouns.

- We can use **a lot of**, **lots of**, **some and any** with [3] countable / uncountable / countable and uncountable nouns.

  Note that **a few** and **a little** emphasize the positive (*A few houses have been built already*) and **few** and **little** emphasize a small number (*Little has been done to improve the situation*).

- **Too many** is used with [4] countable / uncountable / countable and uncountable nouns and **too much** is used with [5] countable / uncountable / countable and uncountable nouns to mean 'more than we need' or 'more than is a good idea'.

- **Enough** is used with [6] countable / uncountable / countable and uncountable nouns to mean 'as many/much as we need'.

- We can use **all** with [7] singular / plural nouns and verbs. We use **every** and **each** with [8] singular / plural nouns and verbs.

  All the houses have their own gardens.
  Every house has the same front door, but each one is a different colour.
  There are houses on each side of the street.
  (NOT every side of the street)

  Note that we use **every** for all of the people or things in a group of three or more, and **each** to mean every individual person or thing.

- We use **both**, **either** and **neither** to talk about two people or things.

  Both is used with [9] singular / plural nouns, **either** and **neither** are used with [10] singular / plural nouns.

→ Grammar Reference page 147

7 Choose the correct option to complete each sentence. Sometimes both options are possible.

1 How *much* / *many* houses are there in the community?
2 *Every* / *Each* house is the same size.
3 *Little* / *Few* people could live completely alone on an island.
4 Do the houses cost *a great deal of* / *a lot of* money?
5 *All* / *Every* the houses have three bedrooms.
6 *Neither* / *Both* of the bedrooms is very large.
7 There aren't *enough* / *many* car parking spaces.

8a 6.2)) Listen and write down the five sentences that you hear.

b How is *of* pronounced? Notice the links between the words in each phrase.

c 6.2)) Listen again and repeat.

9 Look at the design for the Lilac co-housing project. What do you think are the best/worst aspects about it? How would you change it?

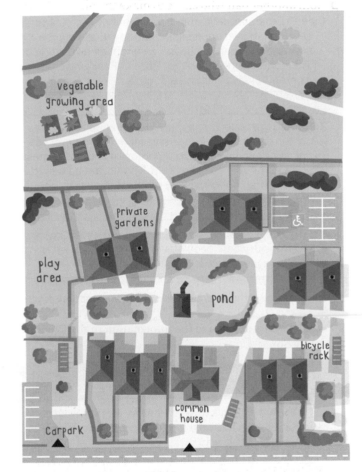

10 Work with a partner and design a new community. This could be co-housing or an estate of completely separate properties. What facilities and resources will you include?

11a TASK Tell another pair about your community. Then write ten sentences comparing the two communities, using the language from exercise **6**.

In our community there are a few ..., but in Sonia and David's community there are lots of ...
Both the communities ...

b As a group of four, use your sentences to present the two communities to the class, and discuss the similarities and differences.

6.3 Vocabulary and skills development

Listening & Speaking understanding fluent speech

1 Match photos a–c to descriptions 1–3. What do all three have in common?

online community

1 P2PU is an online learning community where users set up their own courses and study groups. All the courses are open to anyone and no fees are charged. The abbreviation stands for Peer to Peer University, as members learn from each other.

2 People interested in cosplay (dressing up in costumes as superheroes and other characters) use online communities to post photos of their costumes so other people can see them. They can also talk to, and arrange meetings with, other cosplayers.

3 With over a million members worldwide, BookCrossing is a website where people list where they have left books they enjoyed for other people to pick up and read.

■ **peer** someone of the same age or same position in society as you

2 **6.3**)) Read and listen to the information in the Unlock the code box.

> 🔓 **UNLOCK THE CODE**
> putting in extra sounds to link vowels
>
> If one word ends in a vowel sound and the next word begins with a vowel sound, we often add a consonant sound /j/, /w/ or /r/ between the vowels.
>
> /j/: If the vowel sound at the end of the first word is /iː/ or /aɪ/, we use /j/ to link the words.
>
> /j/ /j/
> I didn't realize he would be English. I only speak a little Spanish.
>
> /w/: If the vowel sound at the end of the first word is /uː/, /aʊ/ or /əʊ/, we use /w/ to link the words.
>
> /w/ /w/
> Who is living there?   The class is now over.
>
> /w/
> He wanted to go outside.
>
> /r/: If the word ends in 'r' or 're', some varieties of English don't pronounce the 'r', making the last sound a vowel, for example car /kɑː/. When the word is linked to a word beginning with a vowel, the /r/ sound reappears.
>
> /r/
> The car is ready.

3a Work with a partner. Look at the following sentences and questions and mark where you think there might be an extra /j/, /w/ or /r/.

1 How do I make a P2PU course?
2 All the courses are open to anyone.
3 Users can set up their own courses.
4 ... so other people can see it.
5 ... with over a million members worldwide.
6 Leave it for another person to find.

b **6.4**)) Listen and check your ideas.

c **6.4**)) Listen again and repeat.

4 **6.5**))) Listen to a short podcast about online communities and complete the sentences with 1–2 words from the listening.

1 _Online_ communities are expanding more rapidly than any other.
2 BookCrossing members are usually people _who enjoy_ sharing the experience of reading.
3 People with a/an _rare illness_ can benefit from advice from others who are suffering from the same disease.
4 Distance learning is much better when you can talk to and see _each other_ online.
5 Cosplayers may use the internet _to organize_ face-to-face conventions.
6 Neighbours who join StreetBank might lend their neighbours barbecue _equipment_ or help their neighbours to _do up_ their houses. _improved / decorated_

5 The podcast talks about the benefits of online communities. With a partner, make a list of five disadvantages. Share your ideas with the class.

Vocabulary high-frequency verb collocations

6a Complete the sentences with the correct form of the words in the box. One word is used twice.

do	get	give	have	make	set	take

1 Online or virtual communities are used to _getting_ people with similar interests together.
2 Many people who _have_ an unusual medical condition can now chat with others who have the same condition.
3 Being able to communicate online _makes_ all the difference to the learning experience.
4 Cosplay conventions are places where everyone can _get_ dressed up.
5 Cosplayers _take_ dressing up very seriously.
6 BookCrossers talk about _setting_ their books free.
7 StreetBank neighbours _give_ their neighbours permission to borrow things.
8 Bad advice from people online can _do_ a lot of damage.

b Check your answers by reading the information in the Vocabulary focus box.

> **VOCABULARY FOCUS** high-frequency verb collocations
>
> The following high-frequency verbs are often used in expressions, but do not add much/any meaning. The main meaning lies in the words that collocate with the verb.
>
> The most common such verbs are:
>
> **do:** *do you good, do a lot of damage, do nothing*
>
> **get:** *get to know someone, get into an argument, get an illness, get together*
>
> **give:** *give someone an idea/a fright/a headache, give someone permission, give a speech/talk/lecture, give something some thought*
>
> **have:** *have an argument/chat, have problems/difficulties, have an accident, have a lie-down*
>
> **make:** *make yourself understood, make the most of something, make sure of something, make all the difference*
>
> **put:** *put into practice, put in charge, put pressure on, put the blame on*
>
> **take:** *take the blame, take control, take something seriously, take a look*
>
> **set:** *set free, set a limit, set a date, set a good/bad example*

7 Rewrite the underlined part of each sentence using the word in brackets and one of the verbs from the Vocabulary focus box. _make sure_

1 He needed to <u>be certain of</u> his facts. (sure)
2 Have you <u>decided when your wedding will be</u> yet? (date) _set a date_
3 He couldn't <u>get anyone to understand him</u>. (understood) _make himself understood_
4 She <u>said it was all his fault</u>. (blame) _take the blame_
5 She <u>thought about it carefully</u>. (thought (n)) _give it some th_
6 I'm tired, so I'm going to <u>lie down for a while</u>. (lie-down) _have a lie-down_

8a Choose five more collocations from the box and write sentences like those in exercise **7**, using another phrase or synonym.

b Give the sentences to your partner. Can they guess the collocations correctly without looking at the box?

6.4 Speaking and writing

Speaking & Listening starting a conversation with a stranger

1 Which do you think are the best/worst places to make new friends? Work with a partner and put the following suggestions in order from best to worst. Explain why.

- at a party *1*
- at work *2*
- online *6*
- on public transport *4*
- playing a sport *5*
- studying together *3*

2 6.6))) Listen to three short conversations between strangers. Where do the conversations 1–3 take place?

1 DON'T KNOW
2. work
3. public transport
see

3a Work with a partner. Look at the conversation starters in the Language for speaking box and tick the ones used in the conversations in exercise **2**.

LANGUAGE FOR SPEAKING starting a conversation with a stranger

1 ✓ Lovely weather, isn't it?
Are you a friend of (Nicola's)?
4 ✓ I'm sorry to bother you, but …
✓ Excuse me, is anyone sitting there?
I hope you don't mind me asking, but (haven't we met somewhere before)?
3 ✓ Is it always this busy?
2 ✓ Sorry, but I couldn't help overhearing …
So, how do you know Jonathan?
Have you lived round here/worked here/been in this class long?
Excuse me, do you mind if I …?

b 6.6))) Listen again to check your ideas.

4a 6.7))) Listen again to each conversation starter and write the reply you hear.

b How else could you respond to each conversation starter? For each one used in the listening, write a new reply which would help to keep the conversation going.

5 TASK Work with a partner. Choose a different conversation starter from the Language for speaking box and write a short conversation.

6 Act out your conversation for the class, or another pair. Can they guess where your conversation is taking place?

Reading & Writing describing data

7 Who do you spend time with most days, or every day? Discuss with a partner.

- classmates
- neighbours
- family
- work colleagues
- friends

8a Look at the chart below about people in England. What are the key things you notice?

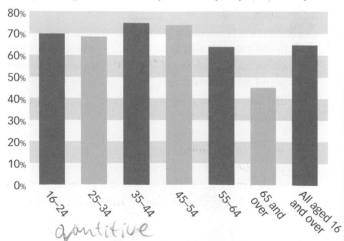

Spending time most days or every day with family

gantitive

b Do you think the data would be different in your country? Discuss with a partner.

9 Read the following description of the data. One sentence is factually wrong – can you identify which one?

> _Outline_ ⊖ ⊕ ⊗
>
> The chart shows what percentage of people in England spend time with their family daily, or almost every day. It is organized by age groups, from 16–65 and over.
>
> On average, looking at all the age groups together, about 65% of people see their family every day, or nearly every day. The age groups which see their relatives most often are those aged 35–44, with about 75% seeing them daily, closely followed by those aged 45–54, with about 74%.
>
> Younger people also meet up quite often with their families, especially those in the 16–24 age bracket. About 60% of these see their family most days. As they get older this percentage drops slightly to about 68%, before rising again at age 35.
>
>
>
> Perhaps the most noticeable feature of the data is the fact that people seem to spend less time with their family as they go into middle age and, most strikingly, older age. Fewer than half of those aged over 65 are with their families every day.

10 Work with a partner. Decide whether the following pieces of advice for writing a description of data are a good idea or not.

1 Always start by saying what the graph or chart shows. ✓
2 Use your own words rather than copying the exact words on the chart. ✗
3 Describe every single figure shown on the chart. ✓
4 Group information together to make paragraphs. ✓
5 Give your opinion about why the data is the way it is. ―

11 Look at the following words and phrases in the description in exercise **9**. Then look at the whole description and try to find another word or a phrase which is a different way of saying the same thing.

DAILY 1 every day   3 see their family   5 age group _generation_
ALMOST EVERY DAY 2 nearly every day   4 striking   6 45% LESS

12a TASK Look at the following chart. Discuss the questions with a partner.

1 What does the chart show? Can you put this in your own words?
2 What two different things does the chart compare and contrast?
3 What are the most noticeable features of the chart?

Participation in selected activity groups, by gender, 2010-2011

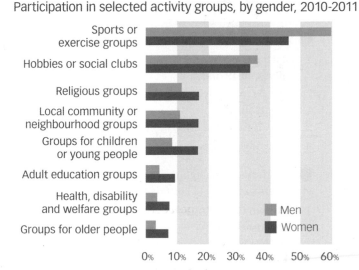

b How could you group the information to make 4–5 paragraphs?

c Now write a description of the chart in exercise **12a** in about 150 words.

LANGUAGE FOR WRITING describing data

The chart/graph shows/demonstrates/illustrates …
In the chart/graph we can see …
It is noticeable/evident/clear that …

The amount of time (uncountable nouns) …
The number of people (countable nouns) …

However, …
In contrast, …
… is much/significantly/noticeably more … than …

On average, …
Overall, …

By far the most …
Perhaps the most striking/noticeable feature of the data is …
A key feature of the data is …

13 Read your partner's description and check it against the advice from exercise **10**.

6.5 Video

Communal living

1 Work with a partner to divide the words and phrases in the box into three categories of your choice.

> bay   counter culture   dock   hippie   houseboat
> look out for each other   neighbourly   tight-knit
> vibrant hub of art, music and politics   waterfront

2 With your partner, decide how the words and phrases in exercise **1** might relate to the three photos.

3 ▶ Watch the video and answer the questions.

  1 In what ways has San Francisco changed since the 1960s and 1970s?
  2 Why do many people prefer to live across the bay, in Sausalito?
  3 What is the most affordable housing in Sausalito?
  4 What advantages are there to living there?

4 ▶ Watch the video again. Decide if the following statements are true (T) or false (F).

  1 Tourism is causing more and more people to move to San Francisco.
  2 The cost of houses in both Sausalito and San Francisco is increasing.
  3 There are now several hundred houseboats in Sausalito.
  4 The houseboats were first converted in the 1940s.
  5 The houseboats do not have electricity or running water.
  6 There is still a strong sense of community and neighbourliness.

5a **TASK** Work in small groups. Read the definition of 'gentrification'. How have the Sausalito houseboats been gentrified?

> **gentrification** (*n*) the process of changing an area or neighbourhood so that it is suitable for people of a higher social class than before

b Make a list of at least five reasons why gentrification of a neighbourhood might be a good thing, and at least five reasons why it might not. Think about the different people it will affect either positively or negatively.

c Compare your lists with another group. Do you generally think gentrification is a good thing or not?

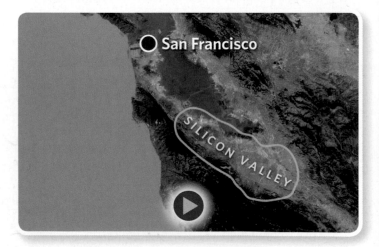

San Francisco

SILICON VALLEY

Review

1a Look at the photo and discuss with a partner. What do you think is happening?

b Complete the article with *a/an, the* or – (no article).

It's such ¹ _____a_____ simple idea that you wonder why no one has ever thought of it before. Young students from ² ___–___ Brazil want to learn English, and elderly Americans living in retirement homes are often lonely and want someone to talk to. So why not bring them together?

³ ___A___ Brazilian language school has done just that. ⁴ ___the___ school set up a programme for young Brazilians and older Americans living in ⁵ ___–___ Chicago to meet and chat online. ⁶ ___the___ lessons are recorded as private YouTube videos, so that the students' teachers can evaluate their progress.

The students have improved their English, but perhaps ⁷ ___the___ biggest gain has been the opportunity to bridge the gap between generations.

c What do you think about this way of learning English? Discuss with a partner.

2 Choose the correct options to complete the statements.

1 *Many / Much* people in the UK now live alone – three times the number in 1971.

2 And relatively *few / little* people now live in households of six or more people.

3 Although *many / a great deal of* people believe that more elderly people now live alone, in fact, the biggest increase in one-person households has come from those aged 16–59.

4 The *number / quantity* of over-sixties living alone has remained about the same, at 17%.

5 Almost *every / each* home now has a colour television, up from 74% in the 1980s.

6 And in 1972, only *few / a few* homes had washing machines, but now 96% do.

3 Choose the word which is different from the others in each group.

1 traditions   customs   costumes

2 recollection   memory   concentration

3 festival   community   parade

4 immigrant   descendant   ancestor

5 vivid   dull   uninteresting

6 ceremony   neighbourhood   community

4a Match 1–8 to a–h to make phrases.

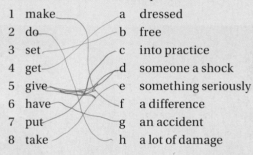

1 make   a   dressed
2 do   b   free
3 set   c   into practice
4 get   d   someone a shock
5 give   e   something seriously
6 have   f   a difference
7 put   g   an accident
8 take   h   a lot of damage

b Choose three phrases from exercise **4a** and write a sentence or two about a time when you did this or this happened to you.

5a **6.8**))) Listen to six definitions. Which words are being defined? Write the number next to each word.

facilities _2_   independently ___   shift _6_
globally _3_   resident _1_   private _5_
growth ___   separately ___   properties ___
household _4_   supported ___   socially ___

b Work with a partner. Can you provide definitions for the other words in exercise **5a**?

6a Put the words in the right order.

1 help / overhearing / sorry / I / but / couldn't ...

2 but / sorry / I'm / bother / to / you ...

3 you / friend / are / Nicola's / of / a ?

4 know / how / you / so / do / Jonathan ?

5 me / anyone / there / is / excuse / sitting ?

6 it / weather / lovely / isn't ?

7 asking / hope / you / mind / don't / but / I / me ...

b Work with a partner. Think of at least four situations in which you might use some of these ways of starting a conversation.

c Choose one sentence and role-play a short conversation with your partner.

7

Rules

7.1   Finders keepers?

noun

GOALS	■ Talk about crime and justice	■ Use present modal verbs

Vocabulary   crime and justice

1a Look at the photos. Can you think of two things all the objects might have in common?

b **7.1**))) Listen to four short news items and check your ideas.

2 **7.1**))) Listen again. Which story do you find the most surprising? Why?

3a Look at the following extracts from the listening. What word class is each of the underlined words? A noun, a verb or an adjective?

> *verb   adj.*
>
> *A bag containing $200,000 **worth** of diamonds has been returned to its grateful owner.*
>
> *It is estimated that the coins are **worth** around $10 million.*
>
> *verb   adj.*

b Work with a partner. Look at the following extracts and decide what part of speech in brackets each underlined word is. Then write a new sentence using the underlined word as the other part of speech.

1 He has received a <u>reward</u> from the dealer. (verb or noun?)
   noun
   He was rewarded for his honesty.

2 A scrap metal dealer has made a <u>profit</u> of more than $32 million. (verb or noun?)
   noun

3 He found a news <u>report</u> about the eight Fabergé eggs still missing. (verb or noun?)
   verb

4 They <u>claim</u> ownership of the coins found on their property. (verb or noun?)

5 They have still had to hand the coins over to an <u>official</u> while a decision is made. (noun or adjective?)
   noun

6 The police now <u>suspect</u> that the thieves must have abandoned the valuable paintings. (verb or noun?)

Finders keepers?

'Finders keepers, losers weepers' goes the old playground chant. And it seems that a lot of people use the saying to justify keeping money and other valuables that they find. But really, is it that simple?

A local couple have recently been given an eleven-month suspended sentence for claiming the money on a winning lottery ticket which they found on the floor of a shop. [1]They also have to give the money back. The couple assumed that the money was theirs to keep, but in most countries it is actually illegal to keep any lost property you come across unless you are unable to find the owner.

It does depend on the circumstances, of course. Often, if you find a small amount of money, legally, [2]you don't have to

🔗 ▶ ✉

4a Read the blog post at the bottom of the page, then choose the sentence which best summarizes the writer's view.

 a If people are stupid enough to lose something, it's their own fault if someone else keeps it.

 b If something doesn't belong to you, it is almost never OK to keep it.

b Do you agree with the writer's view? Discuss with a partner.

5 Match the highlighted words in the blog post to meanings 1–8.

 1 things that people have left in a public place by accident
 2 against the law
 3 give or be a good reason for something
 4 the facts and events that affect what happens in a particular situation
 5 a court sentence – where you will go to jail only if you commit another crime within a specified time
 6 by chance, not planned
 7 left and no longer wanted or needed
 8 small things that you own which are worth a lot of money

6 Complete the sentences about the couple who found the gold coins, using vocabulary from exercises **3** and **5**.

 1 According to the _____, the coins are two hundred years old, so the owner must be dead.
 2 The coins were lost or _____ two hundred years ago and were only found _____.
 3 The coins may be from a bank robbery or something else _____.
 4 In these _____, the coins ought to be in a museum.
 5 It wouldn't matter if the coins were only _____ a small amount, but they're very valuable.
 6 The couple should get a _____ instead of getting to keep the coins.

report it, as it would be very difficult to find the owner. ³And you can usually keep anything which the owner has clearly abandoned. But if you find anything which ⁴could be identified, ⁵you can't just keep it.

However, even if legally ⁶you don't need to find the owner, shouldn't we do the right thing anyway? Another story I read recently told of some students who found $40,000 stuffed into an old sofa. The sofa had been given to a charity shop, so perhaps they had a right to keep the money. But they found the original owner and discovered that her children had accidentally lost the money by giving the sofa away while she was in hospital. The students had no idea that she kept her life's savings in it, and that in fact she and her family needed the money badly.

So, is 'finders keepers, losers weepers' fair enough? No, in my opinion, it's just theft.

Tags: blog, opinion, money

Grammar present modal verbs

7 Read the Grammar focus box and add underlined examples 1–6 from the blog post in exercise **4a**.

GRAMMAR FOCUS present modal verbs

Strong obligation
Use *have to/must* to talk about things that are necessary or are an obligation.
You must try to be tidier.
a _____

Lack of obligation/necessity
Use *don't have to/don't need to/needn't* where there is no obligation or necessity.
We needn't get any more milk – we have plenty.
b _____
c _____

Prohibition
mustn't can't
Use *mustn't/can't* to say something is not allowed.
You mustn't ever leave that door unlocked.
d _____

Permission
Use *can/may* to ask for or give permission and say something is allowed.
May I leave the room?
e _____

Possibility and probability
Use *could/might/may* to talk about things that are possible or probable.
I think that might belong to Julie.
f _____

→ Grammar Reference page 148

8 With a partner, discuss which *two* options are possible in each sentence. Does the meaning change between the possible two options?

 1 The law about keeping lost property *might / can / could* be different in different countries.
 2 You *can't / mustn't / have to* keep a lottery ticket if you find one.
 3 If you find a small amount of money, you *don't have to / mustn't / needn't* hand it in.
 4 You *are unable to / should / could* go back and look for your wallet, it *can / might / may* still be there.
 5 You *may / mustn't / can* leave your bag here, it will be safe.
 6 I *ought to / have to / can* be more careful with my valuables in future.

9 **TASK** Work with a partner. Turn to page 129 and follow the instructions.

GOALS ☐ Use verbs and prepositions ☐ Use past modals of deduction

Vocabulary & Reading using verbs and prepositions

1 Work in small groups. Discuss the following questions.

1 Approximately how many times a day do you check your phone? What do you look at? Do you think people use their phones too much these days? Why/Why not?

2 Are you (or would you be) happy to deal with work emails outside work (e.g. before or after work or in the holidays)? Why/Why not?

2a Look at the headline of the news article. With your partner, make a list of reasons for and against this ban.

b Now read the article and compare it with your ideas.

3a Match verbs 1–6 to the prepositions in the box. There may be more than one possibility.

for to on against from

1 protect *from*   3 protest *against*   5 insist *on*

2 react *to*   4 expose *to*   6 criticize *for*

b Now find the verbs in exercise **3a** in the news article and check your answers.

4 Choose the correct options to complete the sentences.

1 Employers have been accused *for* / *of* taking advantage *of* / *from* their employees.

2 Employers' expectations have been blamed *for* / *on* increasing working hours.

3 As a result, the government has prohibited employers *in* / *from* contacting workers outside office hours.

4 However, the new rules will not apply *on* / *to* all jobs.

5 Lawyers whose clients count *against* / *on* them at all times, will still be available out of hours.

BUSINESS | EUROPE

Major European companies ban work emails outside working hours

Some of Germany's biggest companies have brought in rules to protect their workers from being disturbed by work email outside office hours. Firms such as the car manufacturers Volkswagen have reacted to growing levels of employee stress and burnout by installing software to prevent emails from reaching employees at home.

In France, workers have protested against the way that the use of electronic devices has been exposing workers to much longer (unpaid) hours than the official thirty-five-hour working week. In response, the government has recently introduced laws which insist on employers switching off email contact after 6 p.m.

But some employers and employees have criticized the new rules for not taking account of modern-day flexible working practices. Many parents, for example, prefer to leave work early to pick up their children and then check emails later in the evening. The fact that you can be contacted on email might actually mean that a lot of people are able to leave the office earlier than they would have done ten or fifteen years ago.

Margaret Smyth, Berlin

5 Look at the online article. Have you experienced anything similar at work or school? Discuss in pairs.

> ⊙ ⊕ ⊗
>
> ## Does your boss have strange or unfair rules for the office?
>
> A government minister has reportedly made a list of rules for her staff which have been leaked to the media. The guidelines are supposed to include a rule that staff stand up when she arrives, and that people do not use the corridor next to her office while she is eating, as the noise is distracting.
>
> Have you ever had a boss who insisted on strange or unfair rules?

6 Now read some of the comments on the article. Could there have been any good reasons for these rules? Discuss your ideas with a partner.

> ⊙ ⊕ ⊗
>
> *I used to work somewhere where the company insisted on us parking our cars all facing the same way.*
>
> *We were expected to eat lunch sitting at our desks.*
>
> *We had to start work very early. There were always team meetings at 7.30 a.m.*
>
> *We were forbidden to use cups without lids.*

7 **7.2**))) Listen to two people discussing the comments in exercise **6**. Compare what they say with your ideas.

Grammar   past modals of deduction

8 Look at the extracts from the listening and, for each one, decide if the person …

a   is almost certain something happened or was true.
b   finds it hard to believe what happened.
c   is guessing about what happened.

1   It must have been a way of making the car park look tidier or something!
2   It might have been a safety issue.
3   It could have been something like that.
4   They can't have stopped them having a lunch break.
5   They may have needed people to stay in order to answer the phones.
6   It might have been in a hot country.
7   Someone must have spilt a drink over a computer!

9 Now read the Grammar focus box and add examples from exercise **8** to each section.

> **GRAMMAR FOCUS** past modals of deduction
>
> We can use **must/can't/might/could** + **have** + **past participle** to make deductions about a past event or situation.
>
> • Use *must have* + past participle when you are almost certain something happened or was true.
>
>   a ___ , ___
>
> • When you are almost certain something is not true, or did not happen (or you can't believe it happened), use *can't have* + past participle.
>
>   b ___
>
>   Note that we do *not* usually use *mustn't have*.
>
> • When you are guessing about what happened, or you think something possibly happened or was true, use *might/could/may have* + past participle.
>
>   c ___ , ___ , ___ , ___

→ Grammar Reference page 149

10 Rewrite sentences 1–7, replacing the underlined words with a phrase using a suitable past modal of deduction.

1   It isn't possible that they worked such long hours.
2   Perhaps they had a long lunch break.
3   I'm sure they hated their jobs.
4   I'm pretty certain he was fired.
5   Maybe he resigned.
6   Perhaps he was made redundant.
7   They definitely weren't friends.

PRONUNCIATION *have* in past modals

11a **7.3**))) Compare your answers in exercise **10** with those in the listening. Notice the weak form of *have*.

b **7.3**))) Listen and repeat.

12a **TASK** Work with a partner. Look at the following extract from a newspaper story and make deductions about what happened.

> *The manager insisted that we had to wear make-up if we wanted to keep our jobs.*

Think about the following questions: What was the job? Why did the manager insist on make-up? Did the employee complain?

b Now turn to page 129 and read the newspaper story. Were your deductions correct?

GOALS ■ Understand ellipsis ■ Understand the meaning of prefixes

Reading & Speaking understanding ellipsis

1a Look at the illustration and the title of the article, which is an idiom. What does it mean? Discuss with a partner.

b Read the first paragraph of the article and compare with your ideas.

2 Before you read the rest of the article, read the information in the Unlock the code box about understanding ellipsis.

> 🔓 **UNLOCK THE CODE**
> understanding ellipsis
>
> Ellipsis is when one or more words are left out of a phrase or sentence because the writer assumes that they aren't necessary for understanding.
>
> - In **noun ellipsis** we often don't repeat a noun (or pronoun or noun group) which has already been mentioned.
>
>   *Julia has six years' experience, but Mike (has) only two (years' experience).*
>   *She bought a ticket but (she) didn't use it.*
>
> - In **verb ellipsis** we either don't repeat a verb form, or use only the auxiliary.
>
>   *The weather has been excellent and the food (has been) delicious.*
>   *They are not working as hard as I feel they should (work).*
>
> Understanding ellipsis will help you understand the flow of a text.

3 Work with a partner. Use the words and phrases in the box that replace what you think has been left out through ellipsis.

do well he I member of staff say was

1 He tried several times, but failed.
2 I knew he would do well, but I wouldn't. *Do well*
3 He fired two members of staff and promoted a third.
4 What you *don't* say is as important as what you do.
5 His ideas were imaginative and his work excellent.
6 I applied for promotion, but didn't get it.

Opinion

The carrot or

What motivates you more? The carrot (incentive or promise of reward) or the stick (threat of punishment)? Or maybe something else altogether?

When we try to make things better, whether a workplace, an organization or a whole system, like the banking system, or the health service, we usually try to either reward people by giving them incentives or control them through making rules.

But there are problems with both approaches. If people have to follow the rules and can't use their own judgment, they will sometimes make decisions which we can clearly see are unfair or wrong. And if we rely on incentives, we end up with people who are only concerned about their own self-interest. The incentives encourage them to 'game' the system, rather than to make decisions based on everyone's best interests.

Rules and incentives are not enough. We also need what psychologist Barry Schwarz refers to as 'practical wisdom'.

4 Now read the rest of the article and answer the questions. In most cases this will require you to understand ellipsis.

1 What three examples does the writer give of places which we might want to improve? *Workplace, organisation*
2 According to the writer, what is the problem with simply following rules?
3 What do incentives discourage people from doing?
4 What happens if you have moral skill but you don't have moral will? *when they have to tailor the rules*
5 How does Schwarz think the priorities of bankers have changed?
6 What three things does Schwarz think we need to improve in our systems and institutions? *people can make wrong decisions, unfair.*

the stick?

3
There are two parts to practical wisdom. Firstly, people need to be able to try things out and see them fail, which is never going to happen when they have to follow rules rigidly. Schwarz calls this 'moral skill'. The second part of practical wisdom is 'moral will', or the ability to do what is right for others as well as for yourself. And, says Schwarz, that can't be learnt when people are only motivated by incentives, because incentives make us self-centred.

If you have moral skill but not the will to do the right thing, you end up using your skills to manipulate people. For example, Schwarz argues that in the old days bankers wanted to make money, but they also wanted to serve their clients and communities. They made sure people weren't taking on more debt than they could manage, that they were saving for a rainy day. But by focusing on incentives, banking lost its moral will.

If we want institutions and systems which truly look after our best interests, we have to have rules and incentives and encourage the development of practical wisdom.

6

5 What rules and incentives does your place of work or study have? Tell your partner. *booking, whole system, webservice*

Vocabulary the meaning of prefixes

6a Look at the examples from the article. What other words can you think of which use the prefix in bold?

> 'people who are only concerned about their own **self**-interest'

> 'incentives make us **self**-centred'

b Read the information in the Vocabulary focus box about the meaning of prefixes.

> **VOCABULARY FOCUS** the meaning of prefixes
>
> Some prefixes have a very clear meaning which can help you to understand the meaning of the whole word.
> - *self-* (done to or by yourself): *self-awareness* = understanding yourself
> - *bi-* (two): *bilingual* = speaking two languages
> - *inter-* (between or from one to another): *intercontinental* = between continents
> - *mono-* (one): *monoplane* = a plane with one wing
> - *multi-* (many): *multicoloured* = with many different colours
> - *semi-* (half, or partly) *semicircle* = half a circle
>
> Check the use of hyphens in a good dictionary.

7 Complete the sentences using the root word in brackets and a suitable prefix.

1 People who speak more than one language tend to earn more than people who are _mono_ (lingual).
2 When it comes to chocolate, I have absolutely no _self_- (control). I can't help eating it.
3 Although he is seventy, he's still only _semi_ (retire); he works two days a week.
4 The company set up an _inter_ (nation) competition, with entries from all over the world.
5 It is 200 years since the school opened, so they are celebrating their _multi_ (centenary).
bi

8a **TASK** Work with a partner. Look at the words in the box and try to guess the meaning, using the prefixes to help you.

> biannual interconnect monotone multimillionaire
> self-destructive semi-human

b Write a short text using as many of the words in the box as possible. Compare your text with your partner's.

▶ VOX POPS VIDEO 7

7.4 Speaking and writing

Speaking & Listening agreeing and disagreeing

1 Read the three news extracts. What do all the news stories have in common?

World News

HOME **NEWS** POLITICS BUSINESS ENTERTAINMENT SPORT

Smart parking meters in Madrid will charge more for more polluting cars

Under a new law which aims to reduce pollution in the capital, electric cars will park for free and hybrids will get 20% off 💬 234 comments

China's polluters to face large fines under law change

China's legislature votes to revise 25-year-old environmental law to include harsh penalties for polluters

Proposed new traffic laws target distracted drivers across the UAE

There is no law against wearing sunglasses while driving at night, putting your make-up on, or sending a text message at the wheel – but that is about to change 💬 676 comments

2a **7.4** ⟫) Listen to three friends talking about one of the news articles in exercise **1**. Which one? How many of the speakers agree with the change in the law?

b **7.4** ⟫) Work with a partner. Listen again and make notes of the arguments in favour of the change in the law (Student A) and against (Student B).

Student A	Student B
• _____	• _____
• _____	• _____

c Talk with your partner and compare your notes. Which side of the argument do you agree with? Why?

3 **7.4** ⟫) Listen again and complete the phrases in the Language for speaking box.

LANGUAGE FOR SPEAKING agreeing and disagreeing

Agreeing
I'm ¹_____ you there. (more informal)
I completely agree.
True enough.
Yes, that's spot on. (more informal)
Absolutely!
I don't think anyone would disagree with that.
That's just what I was thinking.
I couldn't agree more.

Disagreeing
That's not really how I ²_____ it.
You can't be ³_____! (more informal)
Come ⁴_____ it! (more informal)
I'm not sure I quite agree.
I can't agree with you there.
I beg to differ.
I'm not sure about that.

PRONUNCIATION agreeing or disagreeing strongly

4a **7.5** ⟫) Listen to the phrases in the Language for speaking box and mark those which are expressed strongly (i.e. with emphasis).

b **7.6** ⟫) Listen to the strong phrases. Notice the stress and how the intonation rises and falls.

c **7.6** ⟫) Listen again and repeat.

5a Work with a partner. Choose one of the other headlines in exercise **1** (or another new or proposed law you know about) and make a list of arguments in favour (Student A) and against (Student B).

b Discuss the law together, making your arguments for or against. As friends, you can be quite informal and emphatic.

c Now have the same conversation, imagining that you are two work colleagues who don't know each other very well. How does your language change?

6 Look at the dictionary definition of 'campaign' and discuss the following questions with your partner.

> **campaign** *verb* campaign for/against sb/sth – to take part in a planned series of activities in order to make something happen or to prevent something happening

1 What kind of things do people campaign about? Give 3–5 examples.
2 Have you ever taken part in a campaign? If so, tell your partner about it. If not, why not?

Writing   writing a persuasive letter/email

7 Look at the following campaigns on a website. Which, if either, would you support? Why/Why not?

| HOME | CAMPAIGNS | NEWS | JOIN US | DONATE |

CAMPAIGN

Reduce street homelessness

We need to pressure the government to do more to help get homeless people off the streets and into safe accommodation, where they can start to rebuild their lives.

CAMPAIGN

Stop cuts to support for disabled people

The government is planning to make huge cuts in public spending on support for sick and disabled people, putting tens of thousands of people into poverty. Send an email to your MP to argue against these cuts.

8a Read this email sent in support of one of the campaigns in exercise **7** and add the underlined phrases to the correct section in the Language for writing box.

> ✕ Sent: TUESDAY 12.29
>
> Subject: street homelessness
>
> Dear Mr Smith,
>
> <u>I am writing to ask you to support our campaign to</u> end street homelessness.
>
> Although there have been some improvements, <u>it is obvious that</u> too many people are still having difficulty in finding a safe place to spend the night.
>
> <u>Without sufficient hostel places we cannot</u> protect the often young and very vulnerable. <u>Unless something is done</u>, the numbers of those suffering from cold, hunger and even attacks by members of the public will continue to grow.
>
> <u>I urge you to add your support to this campaign</u>.
>
> <u>I look forward to your reply</u>.
>
> Yours sincerely,
>
> Claire Hall

LANGUAGE FOR WRITING writing a persuasive letter/email

A persuasive letter or email will usually be quite formal because the writer is hoping to make the reader see that this is an important matter, and because the writer wants to be taken seriously.

Introducing the topic
I am writing to express my deep concern about …
a _____

Introducing your argument
I feel strongly that …
b _____

Consequences of not taking action
This issue must be addressed or …
c _____
d _____

Request for action
I hope you will feel able to add your support to this campaign.
e _____

Closing
f _____
I thank you in advance for your support in this important matter.

b Check your answers with a partner.

9 **TASK** Using the other campaign, or something else you feel strongly about, write your own persuasive email.

10 Read your partner's email. Can you suggest any ideas or language which would make it more effective?

Video

Against the law?

1   Work with a partner. Match words from box A to words from box B to make collocations.

> **A** | common legal major minor prison

> **B** | crime misdemeanour sentence sense statute

2   Work with a partner. All the actions in the list below are crimes somewhere in the world. Do you think they should be crimes? If so, are they major crimes or minor misdemeanours? What punishment should they receive (if any) – a caution, a fine, a prison sentence?

   • driving while sleeping
   • selling cabbage on a Sunday
   • building sandcastles on the beach
   • forgetting your wife's birthday
   • making funny faces at police dogs
   • feeding the homeless

3   ▶ Watch the video about strange laws around the world. Which of the laws in exercise **2** are mentioned?

4   ▶ Watch the video again. Decide if the following statements are true (T) or false (F).

   1   British Members of Parliament can wear armour to work if they wish.
   2   The Italian police felt that flip-flops weren't smart enough to be worn in public.
   3   Different states in the USA have different laws.
   4   The law about police dogs wasn't intended to include funny faces.
   5   In 1644, the English government banned Christmas.
   6   Eating mince pies is still illegal in England.

5a   **TASK** Work in groups. Choose one of the following activities and work together to think of some logical reasons why they might have been banned.

   • buying chewing gum (without a medical prescription)
   • wearing a suit of armour in the Houses of Parliament
   • building sandcastles on the beach

 b   Compare your ideas with another group. Decide on the best or most likely reasons.

6a   With your group, make up a silly or strange law. Think of a logical reason for enacting this law. Tell the class about it and try to persuade them to pass the law.

 b   As a class, vote on which new law you are going to pass.

Review

1a Complete the second sentence so that the meaning is similar to the first, using a present modal.

   1 It is a good idea to have insurance when you travel.
       You _____ have insurance when you travel.
   2 It is essential to take your passport when you go abroad.
       You _____ take your passport when you go abroad.
   3 It isn't necessary to change money nowadays; just use a cashpoint.
       You _____ change money nowadays; just use a cashpoint.
   4 It isn't a good idea to leave a large tip in restaurants.
       You _____ leave a large tip in restaurants.
   5 You are not allowed to smoke in restaurants.
       You _____ smoke in restaurants.

  b Work with a partner. Are all the statements in exercise **1a** true for you? If not, change them using a different modal.

2a **7.7** 》) Listen to five situations and complete the replies in any way that makes sense to you.

   When she saw him, she screamed loudly.
   'She can't have expected to see him.'
   1 She must have _____
   2 He could have _____
   3 It must have _____
   4 He might have _____
   5 It can't have _____

  b Compare your ideas with your partner. Did you have similar ideas?

3 Complete the questions with the words from the box.

| abandoned accidentally circumstances illegal |
| lost property profit reward valuables |

   • Have you ever offered or received a/an ¹_____ for finding some ²_____?
   • Where do you think is the safest place to keep ³_____, such as jewellery?
   • In what ⁴_____ do you think it is acceptable to keep something that you find?
   • Have you ever ⁵_____ taken something that belonged to someone else? If so, what did you do with it?
   • Should it be ⁶_____ for airlines to make a/an ⁷_____ out of selling luggage which has been lost or ⁸_____?

4a Complete the text with suitable prepositions.

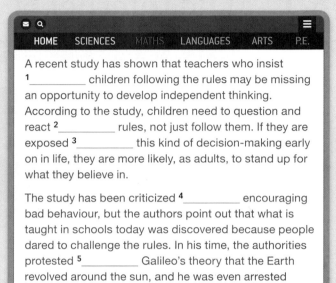

   A recent study has shown that teachers who insist ¹_____ children following the rules may be missing an opportunity to develop independent thinking. According to the study, children need to question and react ²_____ rules, not just follow them. If they are exposed ³_____ this kind of decision-making early on in life, they are more likely, as adults, to stand up for what they believe in.

   The study has been criticized ⁴_____ encouraging bad behaviour, but the authors point out that what is taught in schools today was discovered because people dared to challenge the rules. In his time, the authorities protested ⁵_____ Galileo's theory that the Earth revolved around the sun, and he was even arrested ⁶_____ it. But time has, of course, proved him right.

  b Do you agree that breaking the rules can be a good thing? Why/Why not? Discuss with a partner.

5a **7.8** 》) Listen to six definitions and complete the words being defined.

   1 multi_____   4 bi_____
   2 mono_____   5 semi-_____
   3 inter_____   6 self-_____

  b Work with a partner. Try to think of at least one more word that uses each of the six prefixes in exercise **5a**.

6a Choose the correct option to complete each expression for agreeing or disagreeing.

   1 *True / Clever* enough.
   2 Yes, that's *mark / spot* on.
   3 That's *even / just* what I was thinking.
   4 That's not really how I *see / know* it.
   5 You can't be *serious / silly*.
   6 I *ask / beg* to differ.

  b Complete the sentences in any way which is true for you.
   It should be illegal to …
   Under no circumstances should people be allowed to …

  c Discuss your sentences in a small group. Use the phrases in exercise **6a** to agree and disagree with each other.

Old and new

8.1 The Internet of Things

The Internet of Things is here ... and it's about to change your world!

Vocabulary & Listening   smart technology

1a Work in small groups and discuss the questions.

1 How would your life be different without the internet?

2 What, in your view, is the best thing about the internet? What is the worst thing?

b Look at the picture above and discuss the questions with a partner.

1 Have you heard of the Internet of Things? If so, how would you explain it? If not, what do you think it means?

2 Why do you think it is happening now?

2 **8.1**))) Listen to the first part of a radio interview with a technology expert and check your answers to exercise **1b**.

3a **8.2**))) Listen to the next part of the interview. Tick the topics that are mentioned.

- business investment opportunities
- devices in the home
- health and fitness
- cars
- animals
- trees

b **8.2**))) With a partner, make notes about how the people below could benefit from IoT. Listen again and check.

a car owners   b farmers   c people with diabetes

4a In the last part of the interview the disadvantages of IoT are discussed. What do you think the presenter and technology expert will talk about? Discuss with a partner.

b **8.3**))) Listen and check your predictions. Make notes on the details you hear.

5 How do you feel about the Internet of Things? Do you think the benefits are greater than the risks? Why/Why not?

6 Complete each group of collocations with a noun from the box.

broadband   data   device   fault   privacy   security   technology

1 hack a _DEVICE_ / control a _DEV_ remotely / a smart _DEV_ / an internet-connected _DEVICE_

2 personal _DATA_ / send and receive _DATA_ / access _DATA_ / protect _DATA_

3 high-speed _broadband_ / install _BROADBAND_ / wireless _BROADBAN_

4 high _security_ / a threat to _security_ / a _security_ issue / _sec_

5 a technical _FAULT_ / develop a _FAULT_

6 advances in _technology_ / the latest _tecn_

7 protect your _privacy_ / respect someone's _privacy_ / a threat to _privacy_

7 Work in groups and discuss the questions.

1 How many handheld smart devices (e.g. smartphone, tablet) do you own? Which do you use most? Why?

2 Do you have a broadband connection in your home? How fast and reliable is it?

3 Has your computer or any other device you own ever been hacked?

4 How do you feel about companies using your personal data to advertise their products to you?

5 Have you read any news stories about internet-based security attacks?

Grammar & Speaking relative clauses

8 Read the information about identifying and non-identifying relative clauses. Then, with a partner, look at sentences 1–6 from the listening in exercises **2** and **3** and decide if the relative clauses (underlined) are identifying or non-identifying. Write *IR* or *NIR*.

> *An identifying relative clause tells us which person, thing or place you are talking about. The sentence makes no sense without it.*

> *A non-identifying relative clause gives extra, non-essential information. The sentence makes sense without it.*

1 It's a phrase <u>we hear a lot nowadays</u> …
2 My guest on today's programme is Duncan Bates, <u>whose award-winning blog covers the latest news in the world of technology.</u>
3 IoT is the technology <u>that allows any physical object … to communicate with other objects</u> …
4 … IoT is an area <u>in which huge amounts of money are being invested</u> …
5 … you could have a … car <u>whose inbuilt computer could go online when it develops a fault</u> …
6 The pump, <u>which is attached to your body,</u> monitors the insulin levels in your blood.

9 Study the relative clauses in exercise **8**, then match sentences 1–6 to rules a–e in the Grammar focus box. One sentence matches to more than one rule.

GRAMMAR FOCUS identifying and non-identifying relative clauses

- In identifying relative clauses:
  a you can use *that* instead of *who* or *which*, e.g. _____.
  b you can leave out the relative pronoun when it is the object of the relative clause, e.g. _____.
- In non-identifying relative clauses:
  c use commas to separate the clause from the rest of a sentence, e.g. _____ and _____.
  d *Whose* is used in both types of relative clause to talk about possession, e.g. _____ and _____.
  e Prepositions can come before their relative pronoun in formal English. Prepositions are followed by *which*, not *that*, for things, e.g. _____.
  In informal English the preposition comes at the end of the sentence.
  IoT is an area I'm interested in.

→ **Grammar Reference** page 150

10a Complete the sentences with *who*, *whose* or *which*.

1 What we really need is a smoke detector _____ knows the difference between burning toast and a real fire.
2 Do you know anyone _____ has a smart fridge?
3 I don't like the idea of living in a world in _____ everything _____ I do is monitored.
4 I have a smart coffee machine, _____ is connected to my alarm, _____ means my coffee is ready as soon as I wake up.
5 Songdo, _____ is a 'smart city' in South Korea, has 60,000 residents _____ homes all have ultra high-speed broadband.
6 A Japanese company has recently introduced a smart toilet _____ you can control using a smartphone app.

b With a partner, decide which of the relative pronouns in exercise **10a** can be replaced with *that*.

c Which pronouns can be omitted completely?

PRONUNCIATION pauses in relative clauses

11a 8.4))) Listen to the sentences. Notice how the commas affect the pronunciation.

Identifying: *Cars which are internet-connected can book themselves in for a service.*
Non-identifying: *My car, which is internet-connected, can book itself in for a service.*

b 8.5))) Listen and write five more sentences, then insert the commas.

c Read aloud the sentences in exercise **11b**. Pay attention to the pronunciation of the relative clauses.

12 TASK You are going to discuss the benefits and potential risks of some internet-connected things. Student A, turn to page 129. Student B, turn to page 134.

▶ **VOX POPS VIDEO 8**

GOALS ■ Describe people ■ Use participle clauses

Vocabulary & Reading describing people

1 Work with a partner. Discuss the questions.

1 What do you understand by the term 'generation gap'?

2 How different are your attitudes and opinions from those of other generations in your family? Think about the following.

- bringing up children
- importance of social status
- new technology
- saving and spending money
- other cultures and nationalities
- fashion
- manners
- music
- working hard

2 Look at the names of the different generations, as used by demographers and the media. Which are you?

1 **Baby Boomers**   Born 1946–1964
2 **Generation X**   Born 1965–1980
3 **Generation Y**   Born 1981–2000
4 **Generation Z**   Born after 2000

3 Match profiles A–D to generations 1–4 in exercise 2.

A _____1_____

Born shortly after World War II, this generation had more opportunities in life than their parents. Optimistic and willing to work long hours, they tend to define themselves by their professional achievements. They are often **well educated** and can be quite competitive in the workplace. Outside work they 1_____B_____, seek enjoyment in life.

B _____3 / Y_____

This generation, joining the workforce at the start of this millennium, is also known as the 'millennial' generation. They have different priorities from their parents, caring less about earning large salaries 2_____A_____. They have a (perhaps unfair) reputation for being **self-centred**, **arrogant** and believing they deserve the best in life. Some think this comes from constantly being told since birth 3_____E_____. This generation is more **open-minded** than previous ones in their attitudes to other cultures and nationalities.

C _____4 / Z_____

Sometimes referred to as *Generation Net*, this generation never experienced a world without the internet. Because of the internet they are very **well informed** about world events. They are also even more **tech-savvy** than previous generations, with children as young as two being able 4_____D_____. This generation, having lived through an economic recession, probably won't take money for granted.

D _____2 X_____

Sandwiched between Baby Boomers and Generation Y, this generation shares many of their characteristics. They 5_____B_____ they value a work-life balance. A higher divorce rate and an increase in working mothers meant many from this generation grew up often being alone. They therefore tend to be independent, **family-focused** and have a **realistic** attitude to life. They also tend to be **critical** of authority.

4 Complete the profiles in exercise **3** with phrases a–e.

   a and more about work-life balance *2*
   b like to be active and *1*
   c tend to be hard-working, but *5*
   d to operate smartphones and tablets *4*
   e that they are special *3*

5 Work with a partner. Although stereotypical, are the generation profiles true for people in your country/people that you know? Give examples.

6 Match five of the adjectives in bold in the profiles in exercise **3** to definitions 1–5.

   1 knowing a lot *WELL INFORM*
   2 knowing a lot about computers, etc. *TECH-SAVVY*
   3 having studied at college or university *WELL EDUCATED*
   4 willing to accept ideas and situations different from your own *OPEN-MINDED*
   5 expressing your negative opinion about something you think is wrong *CRITICAL*

7a With a partner, complete the table with <u>all</u> the adjectives in bold in the profiles in exercise **3**.

Positive	Negative	It depends
WELL EDUCATED	*ARROGANT*	*SELF-CENTRED*
OPEN-MINDED		*REALISTIC*
WELL INFORMED		*CRITICAL*
TECH-SAVVY *FAMILY-FOCUSED*		

  b Add these words to the table in exercise **7a**.

traditional R

> conventional   easy-going   irresponsible   loyal
> self-confident   stubborn

8a Write six adjectives from the completed table in exercise **7a**, three that apply to you and three that don't.

  b Work with a partner. Tell your partner how you see yourself. Give examples.

> *I would say I'm quite …   I can be a bit … sometimes.*
> *People tell me I'm …*

  c How similar or different are you? Tell the class.

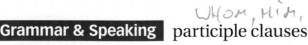
WHOM, HIM,

Grammar & Speaking participle clauses

9 The highlighted words in the profiles are **participle clauses**. Read the Grammar focus box and answer the questions.

Which of the highlighted participle clauses …

   1 replace relative clauses?
   2 have an active meaning?
   3 have a passive meaning?

GRAMMAR FOCUS participle clauses

A **participle clause** begins with a **present participle**, e.g. *coming, eating*, or a **past participle**, e.g. *gone, taken, born*.

- Participle clauses allow us to include more information in a single sentence. Compare:

  This generation is sandwiched between Baby Boomers and Generation Y. It shares many of their characteristics.
  Sandwiched between Baby Boomers and Generation Y, *this generation shares many of their characteristics.*

- Some participle clauses can replace relative clauses:

  Generation Y, **told since birth that they are special,** *(= who have been told that they are special) can sometimes be self-centred.*

- The present participle has an **active** meaning. The past participle has a **passive** meaning.

  People **growing up after World War II** *(= who grew up after …) had more opportunities than their parents. Generation Z,* **also known as Generation Net** *(= who are also known as …), were born in this millennium.*

- We use *having* + present participle with verbs with an active meaning to make it clear we are talking about the past.

  Generation Z, **having lived through an economic recession,** *won't take money for granted.*

→ Grammar Reference page 151

10 Complete the sentences with the present or past participle form of the verbs in brackets.

   1 It's not strange nowadays to see two-year-olds _____ (operate) smartphones.
   2 Generation X, _____ (call) 'Gen X' for short, was born between 1965 and 1980.
   3 Generation Y, is the generation _____ (follow) Generation X.
   4 (Have) _____ grown up in the Digital Age, Gen X and Y are tech-savvy.
   5 Gen X is the name of a famous British punk band, _____ (form) in 1976.

11 Rewrite the questions using participle clauses.

   1 What are some of the challenges which face those who work in a multi-generational workplace?
   2 In what ways are people who were brought up in the age of social media different from older generations?
   3 What are the factors which affect the beliefs and attitudes of a generation?
   4 How do you think people who are born after 2020 will be different?

12 **TASK** Work in groups. Select three of the questions and discuss them. Compare ideas with another group.

8.3 Vocabulary and skills development

GOALS ☐ Listen for stressed words ☐ Understand adjectives + dependent prepositions

tomatos

Listening listening for stressed words

1 With a partner, answer the questions about the food items in the box.

1 Which three do you eat or drink most regularly? How do you like to eat/drink them?

2 Which three do you have least often? Why?

3 Which can you see in the photos?

> aubergines avocados beef chillies citrus fruit coffee courgettes dairy products onions papayas peanuts pineapples potatoes rice sweetcorn tomatoes turkey vanilla wheat

VANILLA

2 **8.6**))) Underline the stressed syllable in the words in exercise **1** which have more than one syllable. Then listen and check.

3 **8.7**))) Read and listen to the information in the Unlock the code box about stressed words.

> 🔓 **UNLOCK THE CODE**
> listening for stressed words
>
> • It is very hard to hear every word in an extended piece of speech. This is because the unstressed words are spoken extremely quickly. Focus instead on listening out for the stressed words as these carry the main meaning.
>
> • Many unstressed words are grammar words (for example: articles, pronouns and auxiliary verbs).

4 **8.8**))) You are going to listen to a short extract from a talk about chillies. Complete the transcript of the talk with the stressed words that you hear.

> Chillies are ¹ _grown_ all over the world. They're from the same ² _family_ as tomatoes, ³ _potatos_ and ⁴ _aubergines_. Although they make your ⁵ _mouth_ ⁶ _burns_, they are also thought to have a number of ⁷ _health_ benefits. For example, they can help with ⁸ _stomach_ problems, ⁹ _beauty_ problems and can reduce the feeling of ¹⁰ _pain_ .

5a **8.9**))) You are now going to hear a short extract from a talk about vanilla. You will hear it twice. The first time, do not write anything, just listen to get the main idea. The second time, note down only the important, stressed words.

b Work in small groups. Use your notes to try to rebuild your text using grammar words.

6 With a partner, decide where you think the foods in exercise **1** first originated. Write the words in the correct place below. If you don't know, guess.

Foods from the New World (the Americas, Australia)	Foods from the Old World (Europe, Asia, Africa)
aubergines avocado chilies citrus fruit courgette papayas sweetcorn peanuts pineapples potatoes	beef, coffee dairy products onion rice ~~turkey~~ wheat tomato vanilla turkey

7 8.10))) Listen to a food historian talking about the origins of New and Old World food. Check your answers to exercise **6**.

8 8.10))) Listen again. Complete the sentences with one or two words.

1 The Columbian Exchange took place in the early _____ .

2 It is estimated that nowadays _____ of all the world's crops originally came from the Americas.

3 For three centuries the Europeans showed little interest in _____ or _____ because they thought they were _____ to eat.

4 When the potato crop in Ireland failed in the 1840s, _____ people died of hunger.

5 Quinoa, a type of grain from the _____ , is considered to be a _____ in many other parts of the world.

Vocabulary & Speaking   adjectives + dependent prepositions

9a Complete the extracts from the listening with a preposition from the box.

> about   as   in   of   on   with

1 These foods ... were first introduced to the rest of the world during a process **known** ___as___ the 'Columbian Exchange' in the early 16th century.

2 However, nobody ... as, initially, the Europeans weren't very **enthusiastic** ___about___ the new foods.

3 People were **suspicious** ___of___ them, thinking they were dangerous to eat.

4 Ireland had become so **dependent** ___on___ potatoes that when the potato crops ...

5 It's strange ... Columbian Exchange, Argentina – now so strongly **associated** ___with___ beef – had no cows, Mexican cuisine ...

6 In these parts of the world, quinoa is now considered a 'superfood', as it is extremely **rich** ___in___ protein.

b 8.11))) Now listen and check.

> **VOCABULARY FOCUS** adjectives + dependent prepositions
>
> • Some adjectives are almost always followed by a particular preposition. These are called 'dependent prepositions' and are followed by a noun (or pronoun) or the -ing form of a verb.
>
> *She's very keen on avocados.*
> *Is he capable of cooking a meal on his own?*

10 With a partner, try to guess the meaning of the adjectives + prepositions in bold in sentences 1–8. Then replace the words in italics with phrases a–h.

1 Many people *aren't* **aware of** the risks of eating too much sugar.

2 I *was* **impressed by** the food in the Chinese restaurant. I'd definitely go back.

3 My brother-in-law is *very* **fussy about** what he eats. He only eats burgers and pizza.

4 It is said that in a hot climate, drinking hot tea is **preferable to** cold water if you want to cool down.

5 The Europeans *were* **responsible for** taking new diseases to the New World.

6 Which countries *were* **involved in** the Columbian Exchange?

7 It's not very **characteristic of** my father to eat so little. He must be ill.

8 I'm not a vegetarian, but I'*m* **sympathetic to/towards** the vegetarian cause.

a more attractive and suitable than ~~for~~
b very much liked
c don't know about
d too concerned about
e typical of
f took part in
g understand and support
h can be blamed for

11a TASK Choose six of the adjectives and prepositions in exercises **9** and **10** and write sentences which illustrate their meanings.

b Work with a partner. Read your sentences aloud, but don't say the adjective. Your partner has to guess what the word is.

8.4 Speaking and writing

GOALS ■ Give your impressions of an event ■ Write a review

Speaking & Listening giving your impressions of an event

1a With a partner, describe the photos. What adjectives could you use?

b Have you ever been to an event like this, or similar? Tell your partner about it.

2 **8.12**)) Listen to a conversation between Anya and her friend Zac, who are at the festival. Answer the questions with Anya (A), Zac (Z) or both (B). Who ...?

1 enjoyed the combination of ancient and modern B
2 was slightly disturbed by the giant moving face A
3 found the event too crowded B
4 wasn't very impressed by the fish in the phone box Z

3a Complete the extracts from the listening in exercise **2** with words from the box.

> bit highlight just live liking particularly point that way

1 What I __just__ like is the contrast of old and new.
2 ... the colours are __just__ stunning ...
3 ... I really like the __way__ the buildings seem to come alive ...
4 ... the __highlight__ for me was that building with the giant face ...
5 I found it a __bit__ disturbing, though.
6 It's a bit too packed for my __liking__, ...
7 I didn't really see the __point__ of it.
8 ... I just wasn't __that__ impressed.
9 It didn't really __live__ up to my expectations, ...

b **8.13**)) Listen and check. Then practise saying the sentences.

4a **TASK** Think of an art exhibition, musical, play, concert, film or another event you have been to recently. Make a note of what you liked and what you didn't.

b Work in groups. Describe the event, using the language in the Language for speaking box.

> **LANGUAGE FOR SPEAKING** describing your impressions
>
> • **Positive impressions**
>   *It's (just) stunning/magical/breathtaking/fascinating.*
>   *It's really impressive/inspiring.*
>   *What I particularly liked/loved was ... + noun/noun clause*
>   *I like the way ... + verb clause*
>   *For me the highlight was ... + noun/verb -ing*
>   *It was well worth ... + verb -ing*
>
> • **Negative impressions**
>   *I wasn't that impressed by ...*
>   *I found it a bit dull/weird/disturbing/disappointing.*
>   *I didn't see the point of it.*
>   *It's a bit/much too ... for my liking.*
>   *It didn't really live up my expectations.*

a liking

Writing & Reading — writing a review

5 Work with a partner. Discuss the questions.

1 Do you enjoy going to the circus?

2 Are circuses an important part of your country's culture?

3 Why might some people disapprove of circuses?

6a Complete the online review of a circus show with words from the box.

> disappointed   impossibly   individual   kindly   magnificent
> talent   thrilling   wooden

HOME   WRITE   **COMMENT**   SEARCH   CONTACT

Review: **Gifford's Circus**

When I won tickets for Gifford's Circus in a competition, I wasn't convinced I'd enjoy it. In fact, I nearly gave the tickets away. Thank goodness I didn't, as it turned out to be one of the most [1]_____ shows I've ever seen! *thrilling*

The secret of its appeal is that it combines the charm of a small, old-fashioned circus with world-class [2]_____ *talent* from performers recruited from countries as far afield as [a] Russia, China and Ethiopia. The ninety-minute show [b] includes a huge variety of breathtaking displays: acrobats, gymnasts, fire-throwing jugglers and performing animals, all of which are accompanied by live music. What makes it unusual is that all the acts are linked by a story, so it's more than just a series of [3]_____, unrelated performances. *individual*

The fire-throwing jugglers went down very well with the audience, as did the man who added chair after chair to an [4]_____ tall tower on which he was balancing. I *impossible* could barely look!

For me, the highlight of the show was the animals: a [5]_____ horse ridden by the circus owner, dogs *magnificent* jumping through hoops and riding horseback, [c] and the most enormous turkey – and it really was huge! – strutting majestically round the ring. It was an extraordinary sight!

[d] Gifford's describes itself as a 'humane circus', and treats its animals [6]_____ *kindly*. Their dogs, for example, are rescue dogs, abandoned by their previous owners, and trained to perform using treats and rewards, not punishment. They certainly seemed well cared for.

The show is on until the end of the month. [e] If you get a chance to go, take it. You won't be [7]_____. A word *disappointed* of advice: take a cushion, as the seats are [8]_____ *wooden* benches.

b Read the review again. Put the following information in the right order, 1–5.

- An overall impression *1*
- Highlights of the show *4*
- Background information about the company *2*
- Recommendations *5*
- Contents of the show *3*

7 Read the rules about punctuation in the Language for writing box. Match the underlined phrases in the review to some of the rules. Some go with more than one rule.

> **LANGUAGE FOR WRITING** punctuation: commas, inverted commas, colons and dashes
>
> **Commas (,)** are generally used to reflect pauses in speech, e.g.
> 1 to separate words in a list: *There were jugglers, acrobats, gymnasts and a clown.*
> 2 to separate clauses in complex sentences: *Their dogs are rescue dogs, abandoned by their previous owners, and trained to perform using treats.* *List*
>
> **Inverted commas (' ' or " ")** are used:
> 3 around direct speech: *'This show is spectacular,' she said.* or when quoting from somewhere else: *One magazine review called it 'the greatest show on Earth'.*
>
> **A colon (:)** is used:
> 4 to indicate that what follows it is an explanation or expansion of what comes before it: *Bring the following documents: driving licence, insurance certificate and passport.*
>
> **Dashes (–)** are used, in pairs:
> 5 to separate an interruption from the rest of the sentence. *The show included acrobats, jugglers – these were the highlight for me – and performing animals.*
>
> If the interruption comes at the end of the sentence, only one dash is used.

8 Add punctuation to the sentences.

1 The words magical and thrilling are often used to describe Gifford's

2 We laughed clapped and cheered throughout the show

3 There are tickets left for the following performances Wednesday 6 p.m. Thursday 3 p.m. and Friday 12 p.m.

4 Next year if the circus returns next year I will definitely go again

9a **TASK** Write an online review for an event you have been to recently.

b Exchange reviews with a partner. Check the punctuation and grammar. Does the review make you want to attend the event?

8.5 Video

Traditional skills

1 Look at the words and phrases in the box. Which do you associate with traditional manufacturing processes and which with modern processes?

> ancient techniques   coal ovens   machinery
> mass-produced   rural   skilled craftsmen
> technologically advanced   urban

2 Look at the photos. What product is being made?

3 ▶ Watch the video. Which of these are mentioned?
a China's population
b China's shift from rural to urban society
c the invention of paper
d traditional paper-making methods
e other Chinese inventions
f modern paper-manufacturing methods

4 ▶ Watch again. Complete the summary with words from the box.

> computers   fabric   hand   notebooks   technologically
> washed

> Over the last 35 years, China has changed from a rural society to one of the world's most ¹_____ advanced societies, producing 90% of the world's ²_____. However, China is also responsible for the invention of paper. In Shiqiao village, paper is still made using traditional techniques. For example, tree branches are cut down by ³_____, bark removed and ⁴_____ in a local river. Next, there are a number of long, painstaking processes. The final product is a beautiful paper, thicker than mass-produced paper, with a texture similar to ⁵_____. It is used to make products such as ⁶_____ and lanterns. It is expensive but made to last for a long time.

5 **TASK** Work with a partner. Look at the reasons for buying handmade rather than mass-produced products. Put these reasons in order of importance for you.
a The object is unique.
b It is made to last, not be thrown away.
c It is made with devotion, care and skill.
d Traditional crafting skills are kept alive.
e You support local craftspeople, not large corporations.
f Mass-produced goods are often made by people working in poor conditions.

Review

1a Read the article and replace *who* and *which* with *that* where possible.

TECHNEWS ● ⊕ ⊗

Technology myths and truths

1 The most economical speed at which you can drive your car is 89 kilometres per hour.

2 The metal detectors which you walk through at airports can damage electronic devices like laptops.

3 Some of the fires which have occurred at petrol stations have been caused by the electromagnetic radiation which comes from mobile phones.

4 Aeroplane passengers who don't switch off their electronic devices during take-off and landing are putting lives at risk.

5 A phone battery lasts longer if you close all apps which are open.

6 Fibre-optic broadband, which is made of thin glass or plastic fibres, works faster than ordinary broadband.

b Work with a partner. Which relative pronoun in exercise **1a** can be omitted?

c 8.14 ⟫ Discuss which of the sentences in the article in exercise **1a** are myths and which are true. Then listen and check.

2 Complete the questions with the present or past participle form of the verbs in brackets.
Can you think of …
1 a word _____ (begin) with *arr-*?
2 a device _____ (invent) in the 21st century?
3 a vegetable _____ (introduce) to Europe from South America in the Columbian Exchange?
4 an adjective _____ (use) to describe a person who refuses to change their opinion or attitude?
5 a word _____ (mean) 'new'?

3a Which word does not collocate with the word in bold?
1 high-speed　wireless　remote　**broadband**
2 develop　protect　repair　**a fault**
3 install　send　receive　**data**
4 access　protect　respect　**privacy**

b Complete the questions.
1 Do you like to keep up to date with the l_____ technology?
2 What have been the biggest a_____ in technology in your field of work or study?
3 Have you ever experienced an online s_____ issue, e.g. a hacked email or bank account?

c Work with a partner and answer the questions in exercise **3b**.

4 Match the words to make adjectives to describe people.
1 open-　　　　a informed
2 well-　　　　b minded
3 tech-　　　　c confident
4 self-　　　　d savvy
5 easy-　　　　e going

5a Complete the phrases in the sentences with the correct prepositions.
1 I only recently became aware _____ …
2 I try not to get involved _____ …
3 It's important not to be too dependent _____ …
4 I'm not very sympathetic _____ …
5 Italy is often associated _____ …

b Complete the sentences in exercise **5a** so they are true for you. Compare your sentences with a partner.

6a Put the words in the right order.
1 violent / It / was / a bit / my / for / liking .
2 I / costumes / particularly / What / liked / were / the .
3 was / It / worth / seeing / well .
4 that / I / by / wasn't / it / impressed .
5 It / live / didn't / to / expectations / up / my .

b Work with a partner. Choose one of the following events that you have been to recently and describe your impressions of it.
• An academic event, e.g. a lecture/talk
• A cultural event, e.g. an exhibition, play or film
• A business event, e.g. a talk or conference

9.1 Dark days and white nights

GOALS ■ Talk about different climates and lifestyles ■ Use adjectives and adverbs

Vocabulary & Listening different climates and lifestyles

1 Work with a partner or in a small group and discuss the questions. *2h*

　1 Roughly what time does it get light and get dark in your country, or where you are living now?

　2 Does it change much throughout the year? *16h*

　3 What do you think it would be like to live somewhere where it was light for twenty-four hours in the summer and dark for twenty-four hours in the winter?

2a **9.1**))) Listen to Amna, who originally came from Pakistan, talking about life in the Norwegian city of Tromsø. Which does she prefer, long days or long nights? Why?

b **9.1**))) Listen again and make notes in the table below.

	Positive aspects	Negative aspects
Long nights		*dark all the time cold and snowy*
Long days		

3 If you moved to another country, would you (or do you) prefer to live somewhere very different to your home country, or quite similar? Why? Discuss with your partner.

4a Work with a partner. Divide the words in the box into adjectives and adverbs.

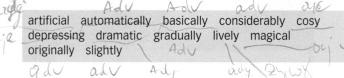

artificial automatically basically considerably cosy depressing dramatic gradually lively magical originally slightly

b Work with a partner. Student A, match the adjectives from the box in exercise **4a** to their definitions below. Student B, match the adverbs to their definitions.

Adjectives

1 full of energy and interest *lively*

2 wonderful, mysterious and exciting *magical*

3 making you feel sad and not enthusiastic *depressing*

4 noticeable, surprising or impressive *originally* *dramatic*

5 not natural *artificial*

6 warm and comfortable *cosy*

Adverbs

1 much or a lot *considerably*

2 in the most important ways *considerably basically*

3 slowly, over a period of time *gradually*

4 a little *slightly*

5 done or happening without thinking *automatically*

6 in the beginning *basically originally*

c Teach your partner any words he/she doesn't know.

5a **9.2**))) Work with a partner. You are going to listen and complete your phrases. Student A, see below. Student B, turn to page 134.

> 1 ... the sun _____ doesn't appear for twenty-four hours ...
> 2 ... people _____ assume that I must find it really difficult ...
> 3 I _____ come from Pakistan ...
> 4 ... not only is it _____ warmer than Norway, ...
> 5 ... the light _____ starts to come back ...
> 6 It only gets _____ darker for about an hour ...

b Now check your answers together.

6a Complete the sentences with words from the box in exercise **4a**.

1 I love the Golden Autumn in Poland, the colours of the trees are so _magical_   _Dramatic_

2 When I hear people talk about the rainy season, _automatically_ think of tropical islands.

3 If it's cold outside, I prefer being _cosy_ by the fire to going outside.

4 England is so green because it _slightly_ _Basically_ rains all the time.

5 There's nothing like the smell of freshly-cut grass. Much better than any _____ perfume.   _artificial_

b Choose three of the sentences in exercise **6a** and change them so that they are true for you or for where you live. Compare your sentences with a partner.

I love the monsoon season in Thailand – everything smells so fresh.

Grammar & Speaking   adjectives and adverbs

7 Read the Grammar focus box and complete the examples with six of the words from the box in exercise **4a**.

GRAMMAR FOCUS   adjectives and adverbs

Adjectives
- We use adjectives to describe people or things.
- Adjectives can be used in two main positions: _dramatic_
  1 before a noun: *a* ¹ _magical_ *landscape.*   _magical_
  2 after a verb (usually *be*, but also *seems, looks, feels,* etc.): *The room looks* ² _cosy_ .

Adverbs
- We use adverbs to say more about verbs: _considerably_   _slightly_
  1 to say how something happens or is done. *The weather has* ³ _gradually_ *improved since this morning. It's quite nice now.*   _gradually_
  2 to give your attitude towards something. ⁴ _basically_ *, I think it's a bad idea.*   _basically_
  3 to say when and where something happens. *I go **there weekly**.*
  4 to talk about the level or extent of something. *It's* ⁵ _considerably_ *hotter in the rainy season than in the winter – by about twenty degrees.*
  5 to tell us how often something is done. *I **rarely** go out at night.*

Common confusions
- Adverbs often end in *-ly*, but not always: *often, never, yesterday, now, everywhere, nearby.*
- There are also some adjectives which end in *-ly*: *friendly, likely, lonely, lovely, silly, ugly,* ⁶ _lively_ .
- Some words can be both adjectives and adverbs: *daily, early, hard, fast, weekly.*
  I get a daily paper.
  I go there daily.

→ Grammar Reference page 152

8 Choose the correct options to complete the sentences. Explain the reasons for your choices to your partner.

1 In tropical countries, the sun sets very *quick / quickly.*
2 Staying awake all night is *completely / complete* stupid.
3 In springtime, the flowers smell *wonderfully / wonderful.*
4 She spoke to me *very friendly / in a very friendly way.*
5 I feel much more *cheerful / cheerfully* when it's spring.
6 The rain fell so *hard / hardly*, it washed away the mountainside.

PRONUNCIATION dropped syllables

9a Work with a partner. Look at the adjectives in the box and mark how many syllables you expect to hear in each word.

comfortable different family favourite interesting miserable separate

b 9.3)) Now listen to the adjectives in exercise **9a** and mark how many syllables you really hear.

c 9.3)) In some words the syllable which comes after the syllable carrying the main stress can be dropped in normal speech. Listen again and repeat.

10a TASK Work with a partner. Choose a season in your country and answer the questions.

What adjectives could you use to describe …?

a how the natural world looks at that time of year
b how you or other people feel in that season
c the weather

b Prepare to talk about the season to your partner for 1–2 minutes. Think about …

- the positive and negative aspects of that season. Is it your favourite? Why/Why not?
- the kind of things you and other people like to do at that time of year.
- how it is different from the other seasons of the year.

c Give your presentation to a new partner. Listen to your partner and think of two questions to ask him/her at the end.

9.2 Sleep

Grammar & Reading · past and present habits

1a Work with a partner. Look at the photos and make a list of at least five places where people might sleep, apart from in a bed.

b Have you ever slept in any of the places in your list? Why? How restful was it? Tell your partner.

2 With your partner, decide if you think these statements are true (T) or false (F).

1 Going to sleep straight after learning something new will help you to remember it. T

2 Women are almost twice as likely as men to fall asleep while driving. F

3 Teenagers need as much sleep as small children. T

4 Nowadays, people sleep less since the invention of electric light. T

5 It is possible to train yourself to need less sleep. F

6 A fifteen-minute sleep is more refreshing than a cappuccino. T

3 Read the online article and check your answers to exercise **2**.

Home   News   Science   Technology   [Search]   ⊙ ⊕ ⊗

Some facts about sleep which may surprise you

Insomnia is almost twice as common in women as in men, but even those who feel they haven't slept a wink probably have had more sleep than they think. Nowadays we believe that we need to get eight hours' uninterrupted sleep; but in the Middle Ages, people would often get up for a while in the night, wide awake, to chat or even visit neighbours. However, it is true to say that having artificial light sources has meant that we tend to get less sleep overall than we used to.

According to recent research, nearly half of US adults admitted to falling asleep unintentionally during the day – at work, on public transport or, worryingly, while driving. Twice as many men as women admit to nodding off while driving. In many cultures, having a snooze (though not while driving!) is much more culturally acceptable than in the US, and it might help to make the roads safer. Apparently, a short nap is more refreshing than a cup of coffee.

Once parents stop managing their bedtimes, teenagers usually start going to bed much later. However, because their brains are still developing, they still need between nine and ten hours a night, as much as a six-year-old. Late-night studying, however, does have some advantages, as there is evidence that sleeping when you've just learnt something new will help your memory to retain it.

80% of people need between six and nine hours' sleep a night. But if you are used to sleeping like a log for nine hours, can you force yourself to get used to having only six? Apparently not, but you can catch up on missed sleep by having a lie-in, and it even works if you have the lie-in on the morning before you miss the sleep.

4   Complete the Grammar focus box by looking at the highlighted phrases and words in the article.

GRAMMAR FOCUS past and present habits

Past habits

- We use **1** _____ *used to* + bare infinitive for finished habits and situations: things that were true but are not true now.
- **2** _Would_ + bare infinitive is also used to talk about past habits and typical behaviour, but it cannot be used in this way with state verbs (e.g. *live, love, be*).

Present habits

- When we want to talk about present habits, we can't use *used to* + infinitive. We use the present simple tense and sometimes an adverb such as **3** _usually_ *usually*.
- We use **4** _be_ + *used to* + *-ing* to say that we **are** familiar with or accustomed to something.
- We use **5** _get_ + *used to* + *-ing* to say that we **are becoming** familiar with or accustomed to something – it isn't our usual behaviour yet.

Note that both these uses of *used to* in the present are adjectives + prepositions, not verb forms.

→ Grammar Reference page 153

5   Choose the correct options to complete the sentences. Sometimes both options are possible.

1   I have to get up at 6 a.m. for my new job. It's difficult because I'm not *used to getting up* / *used to get up* so early.

2   João has lived in Brazil all his life, so he's *getting used to* / *used to* it being hot at night.

3   I *used to love* / *would love* late nights, but now I seem to need my sleep more.

4   Don't ring me before 9 a.m., as I *usually* / *used to* get up late at the weekend.

5   When I first started working nights, it was difficult. But now I'm *used* / *getting used* to it. It isn't a problem any more.

6   When I was a child, I *used to* / *would* stay up late reading with a torch under the sheets.

Vocabulary sleep patterns

6   Complete the sentences using the correct form of the verbs in brackets.

1   If you aren't used to _sleeping_ (sleep) in a hammock, it can be uncomfortable.

2   I used to _wake up_ (wake up) a lot at night, but now I'm so tired I sleep really heavily.

3   I can't get used to _going_ (go) to bed when it's still light outside.

4   Did you use to _have_ (have) nightmares when you were a kid?

5   I found it difficult to get used to _sleeping_ (sleep) in my new bed.

6   She found it hard when she had a baby because she was used to _get_ (get) plenty of sleep.

7   Write an expression from the article in exercise **3** which has a similar (S) or an opposite (O) meaning to these idioms.

1   get up at the crack of dawn (O) _lie-in_

2   fast asleep (O) _wide awake_

3   falling asleep (S) _to nodding off_

4   be a light sleeper (O) _sleep like a log_

5   sleep soundly all night (O) _a wink_

6   have a nap (S) _having a snooze_

opposite
similar

8a Complete the idioms.

1   Given the choice, would you prefer to have a/an _lie_ in or to get up at the _crack_ ? of dawn

2   How quickly do you usually _go to_ off at night? sleep

3   Are you a _light_ sleeper, or do you sleep like a/an _log_ ?

4   When was the last time you had a night where you didn't sleep a/an _wink_ ?

5   Have your sleep habits changed? Did you use to _fall_ asleep more quickly?

6   Have you had to get used to a different amount of sleep? Do you ever have a/an _nap_ during the day?

b   **9.4**))) Listen to Maria talking about her sleep habits. Which question in exercise **8a** is she answering?

c   Ask and answer the questions in exercise **8a** with your partner.

▶ VOX POPS VIDEO 9

9.3 Vocabulary and skills development

Reading & Speaking understanding reference

1 Look at the list of commonly held beliefs about the moon. Do you think any of these are scientific facts? Why/Why not? Discuss with a partner.

  1 The 1969 moon landings were faked. At the time, science was not advanced enough to travel there, so the film simply cannot be genuine.

  2 Supermoons, when the moon appears bigger because it is closer to Earth, can cause tsunamis because the gravitational force is so much stronger. Such disasters would be more common if the moon was any nearer.

  3 The side of the moon which we cannot see is in permanent darkness because the rays of the sun cannot reach there.

  4 A full moon can make people go crazy. Police and hospital workers know that people are wilder when there is one.

  5 The Earth could not survive without the moon. It stops the Earth from tilting on its side, which would dramatically affect the weather.

2 9.5))) Listen and check your ideas.

3a Read the information in the Unlock the code box about reference.

> 🔓 **UNLOCK THE CODE**
> reference
>
> Texts are linked together by using words to refer back to earlier parts of the text.
>
> For example:
>
> 1 Pronouns, e.g. *he, she, her, him, this, that, these, those, one(s)* and possessives, e.g. *its, their, his, her,* etc. can refer back to nouns, phrases or sentences. *The same* can also be used in this way.
>
>   *Nor is it true that the other side of the moon is always dark. This is just a myth, its far side is lit by the sun just as often as the side we can see.*
>
> 2 A form of auxiliary verbs like *do*, e.g. *do, does, did, have done*, can refer back to a verb or a verb plus what follows it. *So* is often used instead of *it* to replace what goes after a verb.
>
>   *When the American team first landed on the moon, they planted a flag. In doing so, they accidentally started the myth that the moon landings were faked …*
>
> 3 Adverbs like *here, there* and *then* can be used to refer back to a situation.
>
>   *… the flag appeared to flutter in a slight wind – and clearly there is no wind there (on the moon).*
>
> 4 Nouns, for example, 'one' or 'ones', can be used to refer back to other nouns or situations. *Such a/an* (singular) or *such* (plural) can be used before a noun to mean *this kind of*.
>
>   *Sometimes there are tsunamis at the same time as a supermoon, but such occurrences are just a coincidence.*

b Work with a partner. Look at the sentences in exercise **1** and find examples of reference.

c Now read the article on page 91. What do the highlighted words and phrases refer to?

4 Read the article again and answer the questions. You will need to understand reference to do this.

  1 What did people tend to avoid doing on a full moon?

  2 What kind of nights do hunting animals prefer? DARK

  3 What have people feared for thousands of years?

  4 How did the Ancient Greeks explain the supposed impact of the moon on human behaviour?

  5 Do more people get injured or get in trouble at the time of a full moon? NO

  6 What three effects does the moon seem to have on human sleep patterns? ① 30% less deep sleep ② people took longer to get to sleep ③ stayed asleep for less time

Man and the moon?

In a world where electric street lights and car headlamps illuminate the night, it is easy to overlook the moon, to [1] forget that not so many years ago anyone who wanted to move about at night depended on a full moon to light their way. Travellers used almanacs to chart the phases of the moon and plan their journeys, farmers used the moon to harvest their crops and anyone committing a crime would think twice about doing so on a moonlit night.

Myths and legends tell of creatures that hunt under a full moon, but the fact is that most animals are actually less active when the moon is at its brightest. [2] Animals which fear being eaten feel safer in the darker nights, and predators are better able then to hunt unseen. Only humans and other primates seem to be naturally more active at full moon.

But while we can be reassured by the light, people also fear the effect of the full moon on human behaviour. This dates back many thousands of years. The Ancient Greeks knew the moon affected the tides and concluded that it had a similar [3] impact on the water in the human brain. And even today, many people [4] believe that hospitals and police stations are busier at the time of the full moon, despite plenty of research that has failed to confirm this.

However, a recent piece of research has shown that the moon *does* appear to affect our sleep. Brain scans taken when the moon was full showed 30% less deep sleep, and that on those nights people took longer to get to sleep, and [5] stayed asleep for less time.

It seems that deep in our brain, we may still have the remnants of an ancient body clock, designed to protect us by keeping us just a little more wakeful on moonlit nights.

Vocabulary — synonyms and antonyms

5a Read the Vocabulary focus box.

> **VOCABULARY FOCUS** synonyms and antonyms
>
> As well as using reference and substitution, writers also use lexical links to make a text easier to follow, and to avoid repetition.
>
> One very common way of doing this is to use synonyms (words with similar meanings) and antonyms (words with opposite meanings).
>
> *Supermoons, when the moon appears bigger because it is closer to Earth may cause tsunamis because the gravitational force is so much stronger. Such disasters would be more common if the moon was any nearer.*
>
> *Some people said the 1969 moon landings were faked. At the time, science was not sufficiently advanced for us to travel there, so the film simply could not be genuine.*

b Look at the article in exercise 4 again and find synonyms or antonyms for the underlined words or phrases 1–5.

6 Match each word in the box to synonym or antonym, 1–6.

> absence   cease   deliberate (adj)   evil   match (verb)   praise (noun)

1 stop	3 bad	5 presence
2 criticism	4 contrast	6 accidental

7 **TASK** Work in small groups. Sit in a circle if possible. One student should choose an item of vocabulary from exercises **5** and **6**. The next student has to say a synonym or antonym for that word. The next student provides another synonym or antonym for the same word. Continue until you run out of ideas, then start with a new word.

9.4 Speaking and writing

GOALS ■ Interrupt appropriately ■ Write a report

Speaking & Listening — interrupting appropriately

1a Work in small groups. Look at the photos. Which kind of evening entertainment do you prefer? Why?

b Discuss the questions with your group.

1 How often do you go out in the evening? What do you usually do?

2 How late do you usually stay out? Does it matter to you if you have to get up early the next day?

3 How good is the nightlife or evening entertainment in your town or city? How could it be improved?

2a Read the headline. How would you feel if you lived nearby? Pleased or annoyed? Why?

> **News 〉 Business**
>
> ## Regent Court to be redesigned as late-night food quarter
>
> Plans to create a food quarter in the street have been given the go-ahead despite objections by people living there. At a recent town council meeting …

b **9.6** 》 Listen to part of the town council meeting about the plans. Which of the following people do you hear giving their opinion? How do you know?

a A student aged about twenty

b The parent of two small children

c A restaurant owner

d A local councillor for the Eco Party

e The councillor who is chairing the meeting. The food quarter was his idea.

3 **9.6** 》 Listen again. Write three phrases you hear being used to interrupt people.

4a Divide the following ways of interrupting people into a) more formal, polite ways and b) more informal or direct ways.

- If I could just interrupt a second, …
- Excuse me for interrupting, but …
- I'd like to comment on that …
- Can I just say …
- Can I say something here?
- I'd like to say something, if I may.
- Just a second, …
- Hang on a minute …

b Check your answers in the Language for speaking box.

> **LANGUAGE FOR SPEAKING** interrupting
>
> **More formal/polite**
> *If I could just interrupt a second, …*
> *Excuse me for interrupting, but …*
> *I'd like to comment on that …*
> *I'd like to say something, if I may.*
>
> **Less formal/more familiar**
> *Can I say something here?*   *Hang on a minute, …*
> *Can I just say …*   *Can I just come in here?*
> *Just a second, …*

PRONUNCIATION polite intonation – interrupting

5a **9.7**))) Intonation also affects how polite an interruption sounds. Listen to five pairs of phrases and, in each case, write down whether you think A or B sounds more polite.

b **9.8**))) Listen and repeat the polite intonation.

6 **TASK** Work in groups of 4–5. Turn to page 130 and choose a role card each. Look at the arguments on your card and add any others you can think of.

7a Carry out a role-play of the town council meeting about the food quarter in exercise **2**. Each student must use *at least two* of the ways of interrupting people in the Language for speaking box during the role-play.

b Decide together who made the best arguments and say why.

Writing a report

8 Look at the report on a different meeting, written by a committee member giving recommendations, and label sections 1–4 with headings a–d.

  a Recommendations
  b Why the report has been written
  c Benefits of the proposed scheme
  d Drawbacks of the proposed scheme

9 Complete the Language for writing box with the underlined examples in the report in exercise **8**.

LANGUAGE FOR WRITING writing a report

Note that a report is usually written in quite formal language.

Introductory paragraph
1 _____
2 _____
3 _____

This report is intended to ….

Reporting what was said and what happened
… 4 _____ / 5 _____ / 6 _____ *that …*
7 _____

Giving recommendations
8 _____
9 _____
10 _____

The council might like to consider …
I would suggest that …

10 Work with a partner. Make a list of the benefits and drawbacks to the planned food quarter which were mentioned in your meeting.

11 **TASK** Use the information to write a report on your meeting using the report in exercise **8** as a model. You should write about 250 words.

Proposed new housing

TOPIC: REGENT'S COURT DEVELOPMENT   DATE: THURSDAY 9 APRIL

1 The purpose of this report is to give an account of the outcomes of the recent meeting about the scheme to build new housing on the parkland to the east of the town. Around fifty people attended the meeting, including many local residents. The report summarizes some of the main arguments made during the meeting and concludes with some recommendations.

2 Councillor Smith began the meeting by summarizing some of the reasons for proposing the new scheme. With several new companies opening up in the town,

he pointed out that there has been an influx of new people to the area and housing is now in short supply. This is affecting everyone in the town as housing is becoming less affordable. According to Mr Mackay, who represented the construction company, the new apartment blocks would include large outdoor play areas, which, he argued, would compensate for the loss of parkland.

3 However, when discussing the issue, the majority of local residents who attended felt that it was more important to keep the natural parkland. Ms Parker,

a councillor for the Green Party, also reminded the meeting that the parkland is a haven for wildlife, which would be displaced by the new buildings.

4 In conclusion, it was evident that there is quite a lot of negative feeling about the proposed scheme. I would recommend that further research is done into how the new housing could be made as green as possible, perhaps keeping a 'wild' area to support the local birds and insects. It might also be helpful to have a scale model made up for people to view at the council offices.

9.5 Video

A town in the shadows

1 Work with a partner. Use the words in the box to describe the photos.

> deep   mountain   narrow   rugged   snow-capped
> towering   valley   wooded

2 All the photos show Rjukan, in Norway. With your partner, discuss what it might be like to live here. What would be the best and worst things?

3 ▶ Watch the video about Rjukan. Choose the best summary of the video.

> **A** The video begins by looking at the effect of the weather on our physical and mental health. It then explains why Rjukan is so cold, and describes the impact of the world's largest hydroelectric power plant on the town, both historically and nowadays.

> **B** The video first discusses how the weather can affect our moods. It then explains the impact of Rjukan's geography on its citizens and tells us a little about the history of the town. Finally, it describes how the geographical problem has now been at least partially solved.

4 ▶ Watch again. What do the following numbers refer to?

1	–5	4	1913	7	17
2	1908	5	1928	8	20
3	104	6	2001	9	half a million

5a **TASK** Work in groups. Decide on the best thing and the worst thing about the town or city that you live in or that you are staying in.

b Compare your ideas with another group. Choose the best and worst things together. Think of a way to improve the worst thing.

c Present your ideas to the rest of the class. Explain the reasons for your choices.

Review

1 Choose the correct words to complete the text. In some cases, both forms are possible.

How to get used to working the night shift

People [1] *usually / used to* find it quite hard to switch from working during the day to working at night. Although you may [2] *be used to / used to* staying up late, it's completely different when you have to do it every night.

When I first started working nights, I [3] *would / used to* just nap during the day, but I soon realized that it's really important to get a proper sleep. Turn off the phone and if your family [4] *usually / are used to* make a lot of noise during the day, ask them to go out!

Make sure you eat really well. I [5] *used to / would* think that it was OK to eat junk food at night. The sugar helped me to stay awake. But I put on a lot of weight, and started to feel more and more tired.

Finally, don't forget your friends. If you [6] *usually / get used to* meet during the evening, you may miss out on social occasions, and it's easy to start to feel isolated.

2 Complete the sentences, using the correct form (adjective or adverb) of the words in brackets.

1 It is _dangerous_ (dangerous) to stand under a tree in a thunderstorm.
2 It _frequently_ (frequent) rains in the winter.
3 The music sounded _beautiful_ (beautiful).
4 Luckily, the weather was _absolutely_ (absolute) perfect.
5 I _rarely_ (rare) carry an umbrella.
6 It was raining a little when we left, but it stopped pretty _quickly_ (quick).

3a Complete the sentences with suitable words from the box in the correct form, adjective or adverb.

artificial/artificially   automatic/automatically
considerable/considerably   depressing/depressingly
magical/magically   original/originally

1 I hate _artificial_ flowers, they look false.
2 I find winter a bit _depressing_, I feel down when I don't get any sunshine.
3 It is _considerably_ hotter in Spain than in the UK.
4 I _automatically_ check if I have my keys before I leave the house; it's just a habit now.
5 It was a/an _magical_ moment when we told the kids about the holiday. They were so excited.
6 I think her family were _originally_ from Wales, but they've lived in England for many years now.

b 9.9))) Listen and write the three questions you hear. Then discuss them with a partner.

4a 9.10))) Listen and mark the dropped syllable in the words.

vegetable   every   camera   restaurant   mystery

b Practise saying the words with a partner.

5a Replace the underlined words in each sentence so that it has the same (S) or an opposite (O) meaning.

1 I didn't sleep a wink last night. (O) _I slept like a log._
2 When I checked, the children were wide awake. (O) _Fast asleep_
3 I know someone who always has a little nap at his desk after lunch. (S) _snooze_
4 He deliberately stepped on my foot. (O) _accidently_
5 The company ceased trading after they had lost money. (S) _stopped_
6 Criticism can encourage people to learn. (O) _Praised_

b Choose three of the words or phrases in exercise **5a** and write sentences about yourself or your experiences.

c Discuss your sentences with a partner.

6 9.11))) Listen to a conversation and complete the following more formal, or polite, ways of interrupting.

1 Excuse me _____, but ...
2 I'd like to _____ that ...
3 If I could just interrupt _____, ...

10 Senses

10.1 Can you believe your eyes?

GOALS ☐ Talk about looking and seeing ☐ Use adjectives in the correct order

Vocabulary & Reading words for looking and seeing

1a Look at the photo below and read the instructions.

Can you spot the predator waiting to pounce on you? If you haven't seen it yet, it's probably too late to escape! Turn to page 130 to see it more clearly.

b Work with a partner. Compare what you see with what your partner sees. Now do the same with the images below.

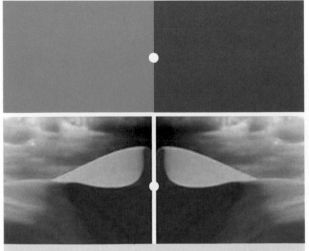

The two desert scenes are the same, but one is a mirror image. Stare at the white dot between the green and red squares for about 30 seconds. Don't even glance away. After 30 seconds, look at the dot between the two desert scenes. What do you notice?

2a Work with a partner. Look at the highlighted words in the instructions in exercises **1a** and **1b**. Can you explain the difference between them?

b Look at the words in the box and answer the questions.

> gaze   glance   glare   observe   spot   stare

1   Which word(s) mean(s) to look ...?
   a   at something for a long time
     _____, _____, _____
   b   in an angry way _____
   c   with some pleasure or enjoyment _____
   d   in a surprised or shocked way _____
   e   carefully; to learn something _____
   f   quickly at someone or something _____

2   Which word means to 'notice something suddenly'?
   _____

3   Which words take the preposition *at*?
   _____, _____, _____, _____

3a Work with a partner. Can you explain or guess how the illusions in exercise **1** work?

b Read the online article and check your ideas.

> In the black and white photo, the panther is hardly visible, but as soon as we add colour, it's easy to distinguish the predator from the background. Why? Because in the black and white picture you are only seeing the surfaces according to how much light they reflect. The colour lets you see the quality of light as well as the quantity and reveals the panther. In a real-life jungle situation, this might save your life, and the importance of colour vision might therefore explain why people are generally more fearful in the dark.
>
> The sense of sight, however, is about much more than what our eyes actually see. In fact, what we see is pretty meaningless – it's just patterns of light. We need the brain to interpret these patterns, and it tends to do this in ways that have proved useful in the past. This is usually helpful, but sometimes this means the brain actually creates an illusion by trying to make sense of information from the eyes.

4 Match the highlighted words in the article to meanings 1–6. Check your ideas with your partner.

1 the ability to see
2 makes something known that was unknown before
3 give your attention to, or look carefully at something
4 recognize the difference between two things
5 able to be seen or noticed
6 send back light

5 Choose the best options to complete the sentences.
1 The head teacher *observed / gazed at* the lesson.
2 People who are colour-blind often can't *focus / distinguish* red from green.
3 I didn't want him to catch me looking, so I just *glanced / stared at* his name badge.
4 Turning the light on *revealed / reflected* how dirty the kitchen was.
5 I've *spotted / glared at* quite a few people wearing ties.
6 There has been a *vision / visible* improvement in your work.

Grammar & Speaking order of adjectives

6 Work with a partner. Student A, turn to page 130 and describe the photo there. Student B, describe the photo below.

Illusions are fun, but they also tell us a lot about how the brain works, which is why neuroscientists, such as Beau Lotto, are carrying out research into illusions. The jungle photos and the red and green desert are both illusions he has used in his work. And what does the desert scene tell us? According to Lotto, it's evidence of how the brain uses past experience to interpret our world. When we focus on the green and red for a while the brain learns about greenness on the left and redness on the right and then applies it to the desert scenes … at least for a while.

Ultimately, what this means is that the world we think we see is not actually the world as it is. Everything we see is created by the brain, which means the ancient philosophers who held that the world is an illusion were, in some ways at least, completely right.

7 Look at the phrases describing parts of the photos in exercise **6** and try and put the words in brackets in the correct order.

1 … what looks like a/an (yellow / rubber / and / small / orange) boat …
2 … a/an (enormous / grey) crocodile waiting for them …
3 … its eyes are (orange / bright / very / and / threatening) …
4 … his back against a (concrete / low) wall …
5 … his usual (leather / long / black) boots …
6 … Robin is in a (green / red / and) costume …

8 **10.1** 》) Now listen to the full descriptions and check your answers.

9 Read the Grammar focus box and complete with the examples from exercise **7**.

GRAMMAR FOCUS order of adjectives

- If you want to use more than one adjective to describe something or someone, they are usually put in a particular order:

  opinion/value → size → age → shape → colour → origin/nationality → purpose → material/function/definition

  a beautiful round copper bowl
  1 _____ (size/colour)
  2 _____ (size/material)
  3 _____ (size/colour/material)

  Note that it is very unusual to use more than three adjectives together.

- When adjectives come after a verb, we usually put *and* before the last adjective. The order is less fixed after a verb, but we often put an opinion adjective last.

  He was tall, dark and handsome.
  4 _____

- Always use *and* between two colours.

  black and white
  5 _____
  6 _____

→ **Grammar Reference** page 154

10 Rewrite the sentences, adding more adjectives of your choice.
1 The forest was dark.
2 I sat down under a large tree.
3 The grass was soft.
4 There were some pretty flowers.
5 Suddenly, I saw a deer with brown eyes.
6 I was very still.

11 **TASK** Work with a partner. You are going to describe another photo. Student A, turn to page 130. Student B, turn to page 135.

10.2 Sense of humour

Grammar & Listening *if* + other conjunction clauses

1a **10.2**))) Listen to this joke, voted the funniest joke by a survey of several nationalities. Do you think it's funny?

b Work with a partner. Student A, turn to page 130. Student B, turn to page 134. Read your joke and practise telling it to yourself. Then tell your partner the joke.

c With your partner, put the three jokes in order according to how funny you think they are.

2a **10.3**))) Listen to the first part of a radio programme about humour and write down which nationalities might prefer each of the jokes in exercise **1**, according to the speaker.

b Do you find different things funny from your friends or from your family? Tell a partner.

3 **10.4**))) Listen to the second part of the programme and complete the following statements with one word from the listening.

1 The final line of a joke is known as a _____.
2 To have a good sense of humour you also need to be pretty _____.
3 To get a joke you need to understand language and have good knowledge of the _____.
4 Children can't tell or understand jokes properly until they reach the age of _____.

4a Use the hints in square brackets to complete each extract from the listening in exercises **2** and **3** with a conjunction from the box.

as soon as	if	in case	unless	until	when

1 _____ [condition] you joke about it, it doesn't make you as anxious, I suppose.
2 I'm very careful about telling jokes to people I don't know, _____ [because I might] I offend them.
3 ... there are quite a lot of jokes I don't tell _____ [except if] I know the people pretty well!
4 We usually laugh _____ [immediately after] we realize that we've been mentally going in the wrong direction.
5 ... _____ [each time] you tell a computer a joke, it won't laugh?
6 Even young children struggle with this _____ [up to the time] they get to about five.

b **10.5**))) Listen to the programme and check your answers to exercise **4a**.

c What is the difference in meaning between the following pairs of sentences? What do you notice about the verb forms in both clauses? Discuss with a partner.

1 If you joke about it, it makes you less anxious.
   I will feel less anxious if I make a joke about it.
2 I'm very careful about telling jokes to people I don't know, in case I offend them.
   I won't tell you that joke, in case it offends you.

5 Complete the Grammar focus box with the words in the box.

> conjunctions   unless   result   clause   future   in case
> any

GRAMMAR FOCUS conditional and conjunction clauses

- To talk about something which **always happens** as a
  ¹_____ of something else we usually use:

  If + present tense, present tense.
  If you joke about it, it doesn't make you as anxious.

  Note that present tense can mean ²_____ present tense, including present continuous and present perfect. We can also use present modal verbs in either ³_____.

  If you have offended someone, you can always apologize.
  If I'm telling a joke and no one laughs, I go bright red.

- Other ⁴_____ such as *unless, as soon as, when, in case* are used in a similar way, but with different meanings.

- To talk about **future possibilities** we usually use:

  If + present/future
  If I make a joke about it, I won't feel as anxious.

  Again, note that we can use **any** present tense in the *if*-clause and **any** ⁵_____ form (*going to, will,* future continuous, future perfect) in the other clause.

  If you don't laugh at my joke, I'm going to cry.

- Other conjunctions can also be used with a future meaning, but followed by a **present tense**.

  I'm not going to watch the show ⁶_____ *it's funny.*
  I'll start applauding **as soon as** *you've finished your speech.*
  I'll buy tickets now ⁷_____ *the show sells out.*
  I'll probably be sitting near the front **when** *you get there.*

- We can use *should* after *in case* to give the idea of 'by chance'.

  I'll buy tickets now in case the show should sell out.

→ Grammar Reference page 155

6 Complete the sentences using a different conjunction each time and the correct form of the verbs in brackets.

1 _____ they sell more tickets, the show _____ (be) cancelled.
2 I'm going to leave my phone on vibrate _____ someone _____ (need) to contact me during the show.
3 Ring me _____ the show _____ (finish). I'll be waiting to hear how it went.
4 The show won't start _____ the lights _____ (go down).
5 They won't be able to have the show outside _____ it _____ (rain).
6 It will be great to see the show _____ it _____ (come) here on tour.

Vocabulary & Speaking rating performances

7a Work with a partner. Decide if the adjectives in the box are positive or negative ways of describing something.

> annoying   childish   comical   distasteful   hilarious
> irritating   pointless   predictable   ridiculous   tedious
> thought-provoking   witty

b Group the adjectives in exercise **7a** into categories 1–5. Some words might belong in more than one category. What differences in meaning are there between the adjectives in each category?

1 might make you feel cross or upset	
2 funny or amusing	
3 boring or dull	
4 silly	
5 clever	

PRONUNCIATION word stress – adjectives (2)

8a Underline the stressed syllable in the adjectives in exercise **7a**.

b **10.6**))) Listen and check your answers.

9a **TASK** Think about a comedian, comedy actor or comedy series that you know quite well. It might be one you really like or one you really dislike. Prepare to tell your partner about him/her or the show. Use the following questions to help you.

- If it is funny, why is it funny? Is it witty, or is the humour more visual?
- If it isn't funny, why isn't it? Is it distasteful or just childish or predictable?
- Can you give an example of something which was or wasn't funny and explain why? Try to use some of the adjectives in exercise **7a**.
- Is it popular in your country? If so, what kinds of people enjoy it?

b Work with a partner. Tell your partner about it. If your partner has seen the person or show, he/she can comment, too.

▶ VOX POPS VIDEO 10

10.3 Vocabulary and skills development

Listening & Speaking understanding assimilation

1   Work with a partner. Which of the taste words in the box do you associate with the different foods shown in the photos? What other types of food can you think of which have these tastes?

> bitter   salty   sour   sweet

2   In recent years a fifth type of taste, umami, has become more recognized. What, if anything, do you know about umami? Try to answer the following questions with your partner.

1   What kind of taste is umami?
2   In which country was it originally identified?

3   **10.7**))) Listen to a short extract from a radio podcast and check your ideas.

4   **10.8**))) Read and listen to the information in the Unlock the code box.

🔓 UNLOCK THE CODE
understanding natural speech

- In order for speech to flow quickly and naturally, we often slightly change the sound at the end of a word to make it closer to the sound at the beginning of the next word.

- When the sounds /t/, /d/ and /n/ are at the end of a word and the next word begins with /p/, /b/ or /m/, the first set of sounds can often change to one of the second set.

  ten boys sounds like *te**m** boys* /tem'bɔɪz/
  *tha**t** man* sounds like *tha**p** man* /ðæp'mæn/
  *groun**d** plan* sounds like *grou**m** plan* /graʊm'plæn/

- In the same way, /d/ can change to /g/.

  *goo**d** girl* sounds like *goo**g** girl* /gʊg'gɜːl/

- /s/ and /z/ change to /ʃ/ when the next word begins with a /ʃ/.

  *thi**s** shop* sounds like *thi**sh**-op* /ðɪʃ'ɒp/
  *the**se** shops* sounds like *the**esh**-ops* /ðiːʃ'ɒps/

- It is not important to be able to produce these changes yourself, you will still be understood. However, recognizing them will help you to understand spoken English.

5a **10.9**))) Listen and write down the two words you hear each time.

1 _____ _____
2 _____ _____
3 _____ _____
4 _____ _____
5 _____ _____
6 _____ _____
7 _____ _____

b With a partner, check your answers and then circle the sounds that might change.

6 **10.7**))) Listen to the extract in exercise **3** again and try to complete the sentences with two words.

1 For thousands of years, ever since the _____ philosopher Plato identified them …

2 … the flavour was also found in tomatoes, cheese, such as hard _____, and meat.

3 … though not so much in very _____, or raw meat.

4 … in many Asian foods, such as soya, _____, _____ and green tea …

5 … foods which combine meat, cheese and tomato, such as _____ or a cheeseburger …

7a Which kinds of food (sweet, salty, bitter, sour, umami) do you think are generally better or worse for your health? Why?

b **10.10**))) Listen to another extract from the podcast in exercise **3** and answer the questions.

1 According to Professor Spence, what drink are many people more likely to choose while on an aeroplane?

2 Why do they tend to choose this drink?

3 What effect can music made by brass instruments have on the taste of food?

4 When diners listen to piano music, what could chefs do to make food healthier?

5 Apart from music, what other kind of sound might affect the taste of the food?

6 What difference could choosing a white or a black plate make?

8 **10.11**))) Listen to two pieces of music. What taste do you associate with each of them? Do you think it is possible this music could affect your taste? Discuss with your partner.

Vocabulary   easily confused sense verbs

9 Read the information in the Vocabulary focus box about easily confused sense verbs.

> **VOCABULARY FOCUS** easily confused sense verbs
>
> **see/look/watch**
> - We *see* automatically, if we have our eyes open.
> - We decide to *look at* and *watch* someone or something.
> - We *look at* something to observe it in detail.
> - We *watch* people or things to observe their movement or change.
>
> **hear/listen**
> - We *hear* automatically.
> - *Listening* requires a decision.
>
> **touch/feel**
> - If you put your hand on something, you *touch* it, but this may be accidental.
> - If you *feel* something, you make the decision to touch it in order to know more about what it is like.
>
> *Don't touch that, it's hot!*
> *He felt the material to test its quality.*
>
> *Feel* can also mean *have an emotion*, e.g. *I feel happy today.*

10 Choose the best options to complete the sentences.

1 It's hard to *look / see* very far in this fog.
2 I like *hearing / listening to* the radio while I work.
3 Shhh! I'm trying to *look at / watch* the football match.
4 She *touched / felt* me gently on the hand.
5 *Look at / Watch* that beautiful house! I'd love to live there.
6 *Feel / Touch* how soft my hair is after that treatment at the hairdresser's.
7 Can you speak a bit louder? I can't *listen to / hear* you.

11a **TASK** Imagine that you are going to eat a favourite type of fruit. Make notes about the following.

- What it looks like: what colour is it? Is it all one colour? Is it shiny? Does it have seeds or leaves?
- What it feels like: is it smooth, prickly, rough?
- What it smells like: is the smell sharp, sour, sweet?
- What it tastes like: is it crunchy or soft?

b Now tell your partner about your fruit. Can they guess what the fruit is?

10.4 Speaking and writing

Speaking & Listening checking and clarifying

1 Work with a partner. Look at the two photos and find at least three similarities and three differences between them. Which photo looks most like a café in your country? Why?

2 Student A, turn to page 131. Student B, turn to page 134. You each have a photo of a market. Describe the photos to each other, without looking at your partner's photo, and find three similarities and three differences.

3a **10.12**))) Listen to two people talking about the same photos.

b What similarities and differences do they find? Discuss the questions with a partner.

1 Are either of the photos similar to markets in your countries?

2 How are they different?

4 Read the Language for speaking box and add the following three headings.

• Ways of checking you understand
• Ways of checking the other person understands
• Ways of asking the person to repeat

LANGUAGE FOR SPEAKING checking understanding and clarifying

1 _____
Are you still with me?
Do you see/know what I mean?
a _____

2 _____
Do you mean …?
So, are you saying …?
Am I right in thinking (that) …?
So, if I understand you correctly …
b _____

3 _____
I'm sorry, I didn't quite catch that last bit.
I'm sorry, what did you say about …?
c _____

5 **10.13**))) Listen to three extracts from the listening in exercise **3** and add them to the correct section of the Language for speaking box (a–c).

6 **TASK** Student A, turn to page 131. Student B, turn to page 134. Find three similarities and three differences, and describe the photos to each other. Use the language from the Language for speaking box when you need to check understanding or clarify.

Writing & Reading describing a scene in detail

7 Read the two descriptions of the café in the first photo in exercise **1**. What is missing in the first text?

> It's an old café in Porto, called the Majestic. It was first opened in 1921, and it has not changed since then. As you walk in from the street, it takes a while for your eyes to get used to it, because the only windows are next to the glass door at the front. The walls are covered in large mirrors, making the café feel much larger, and reflecting the lamps in the ceiling.
>
> The smell of the coffee and food makes you want to buy something, so you sit down at one of the tables.
>
> The waiters are wearing old-fashioned jackets, but nowadays they are more likely to be serving tourists wearing shorts and sunglasses than smartly dressed ladies and gentlemen.

> It's a very famous old café in Porto, called the Majestic. It was first opened in 1921, and sitting in there can still can still make you feel like you're in the 1920s. As you walk in from the dazzlingly sunny street, it takes a while for your eyes to get used to the dark within, as the only windows are next to the big stained-glass door at the front. However, the walls are covered in large decorative golden mirrors, making the café appear much larger, and reflecting the twinkling lamps in the ceiling.
>
> The bitter aroma of coffee mixing with the sweet smell of the Majestic's famous almond tarts starts to make you feel hungry as you sit comfortably in the solid wooden chairs. On the table is a stiff white tablecloth, just waiting for you to cover it with delicious food and drink. You might order a *pastel de nata*, a feast of crisp pastry and a smooth, rich yellow cream filling.
>
> The waiters, in their striking white jackets, also have an old-fashioned feel, though these days they are more likely to be serving tourists in their shorts and sunglasses than smartly dressed ladies and gentlemen. If the café is busy, it can be quite noisy as the clatter of cups and saucers and cutlery bounces off the high ceilings; but even the tourists tend to murmur quietly, as if in a sacred place.

8 Read the second description in exercise **7** again. Which words can you find related to the senses? Add them to the Language for writing box.

LANGUAGE FOR WRITING
describing a scene in detail

Sound words
whisper, crunch, _____

Taste/smell words
fresh, savoury, bitter, _____

Touch words
sticky, rough, prickly, _____

Sight words
striped, bright, _____

9 **TASK** Choose a café, park, market or other public place that you know well and write a short description. Try to describe what all your senses experience, not just what you can see.

10.5 Video

Why we see colour

1a Work with a partner. Match sentences 1–3 to photos a–c.

1 In China, red is a very lucky colour and symbolizes good fortune and happiness.

2 Red is considered a spiritual colour in India, signifying purity and commitment.

3 In the West, red is often used as a warning, to alert people to possible dangers.

b What significance does red have in your culture(s)? What about other colours? Do you know any other colours which signify different things in different cultures? Discuss with your partner.

2 ▶ Watch the video. Match the interviewer's questions (1–6) to Beau Lotto's answers (a–f).

1 What first got you interested in colour?

2 How do we see or make sense of what we are seeing?

3 What is colour for?

4 Is it true that we only see in four colours?

5 What is your research discovering about our perceptions of colour?

6 What is a practical outcome of your research?

a Seeing colour helps us to distinguish different surfaces.

b Seeing colour is a key function of the brain.

c If people realize that we all see colour differently, this could help them see other aspects of life differently, too.

d Colour doesn't really exist outside of our brain.

e No one knows exactly how the brain helps us to see.

f We can make lots of subtle distinctions, but everything is basically red, green, blue and yellow.

3a You are going to talk about your favourite colour. Make notes using the following questions.

- In what contexts do you like this colour (e.g. clothes, home furnishings, etc.)?
- What does the colour remind you of?
- Does the colour have any symbolic meaning, and is this important to you?

b Now talk to your partner for 1–2 minutes about this colour.

Review

1   **10.14**))) Listen to six sentences and match the words in the box to the sentences.

> gaze   glance   glare   observe   stare   spot

2   Put the adjectives in brackets in the right order.
1   I bought a/an (silver / old / rare) teapot.
2   He was wearing a (white / red / and / woollen) scarf.
3   In the window was a (red / green / large / and) flag.
4   He looked like a (film / handsome / young) star.
5   She was (tall / and / young / beautiful).
6   A/An (Indian / large / grey) elephant trod on his toe.

3a   Complete the text with conjunctions from the box. Sometimes more than one conjunction is possible.

> as soon as   if   in case   unless   until   when

| HOME   NEWS   BLOG | 🔍 SEARCH   LOG IN |

How shops use your senses to get you to spend more

¹_____ you walk into almost any shop you're immediately overwhelmed with sights, sounds, smells and things to touch.

Supermarkets know what their most popular items are. So they don't put them at the front of the shop ²_____ you just come in and buy a carton of milk. They put them at the back so that you have walk through and see everything else. ³_____ you keep your eyes down, you will probably buy things that you hadn't planned to get. Some shops are even designed so you have to walk around ⁴_____ you have seen everything.

People are more likely to buy something ⁵_____ it's on the centre shelf. So shops put the most expensive items there.

They also try to stimulate your other senses with the smell of fresh baking, or by getting you to touch things because they know that ⁶_____ you touch something, you are more likely to buy it.

---

b   When you go shopping, do you buy things on impulse, or do you stick to your shopping list? Tell your partner.

4a   **10.15**))) Listen to the definitions and choose which word is being defined.
1   comical / ridiculous
2   tedious / irritating
3   pointless / predictable
4   thought-provoking / witty
5   annoying / childish
6   hilarious / distasteful

b   Work with a partner. Describe a film or TV programme using some of these adjectives.

5a   Choose the correct options to complete the statements.
1   The average American child *looks at / watches* around six hours of TV a day.
2   A newborn baby starts to learn his first language before he is born by *hearing / listening carefully to* his mother's voice.
3   Research shows that being able to *touch / feel* an interactive screen while reading makes boys more interested in reading.
4   Babies cannot *look at / see* faces when they are first born.
5   *Listening to / Hearing* Mozart's music will make a young child more intelligent.
6   Around 45% of US companies *look at / watch* the social networking profiles of job applicants.

b   Discuss the statements in exercise **5a** with a partner. Do you think they are true (T) or false (F)?

c   **10.16**))) Listen and check your answers.

6a   **10.17**))) Listen to six phrases. For each one, write down whether the phrase is ...
a   a way of checking you understand.
b   a way of checking the other person understands.
c   a way of asking the other person to repeat what they said.

b   **TASK**   Work with a partner. Explain to your partner how to do something practical (e.g. knitting, making a cake, putting up a shelf). Make sure your partner understands.

Media

11.1 Extreme streaming

GOALS ■ Talk about television viewing habits ■ Use reported speech

Game of Thrones

Vocabulary & Reading television viewing habits

1a Work with a partner. Match programme types 1–6 to things you might see or hear on the programme, a–f.

1	home improvement programme	a	match highlights
2	cookery programme	b	amusing dialogue
3	sitcom	c	celebrity chef
4	current affairs programme	d	DIY tips
5	drama series	e	in-depth news analysis
6	sports programme	f	a gripping plot

b With a partner, think of more programme types. Which type do you watch most/least often? Why?

2 Read the article and make notes under these headings:

1 what binge-watching is
2 why people binge-watch
3 attitudes to binge-watching
4 how we watch TV series nowadays

3 Work with a partner. Look at the highlighted words in the article and guess what they mean. Then use them in the correct form to complete the sentences.

1 The internet has _____ our way of viewing TV.
2 I like dramas with _____ characters, not two-dimensional ones.
3 We watched three movies _____ on Saturday afternoon.
4 The figures _____ that fewer people watch live TV than before.
5 The company did a _____ to find out what customers wanted.
6 Most DVRs have a feature which _____ you to skip the _____.

4 Discuss with a partner. Have your viewing habits changed in the last few years? How and why?

Binge-watching:
how the hungry habit is transforming TV

Have you ever wasted a sunny day indoors with curtains closed, watching your favourite drama series for hours on end? Or gone to bed way too late because you *had* to watch 'just one more' episode? If so, you're not alone. 'Binge-watching' – watching several episodes of a show at a time – is on the rise. According to a recent survey, in which over 15,000 people were asked about their TV viewing habits, 91% said they frequently binge-watched and 40% said that they had binge-watched a show the previous week.

When asked why they binge-watched, respondents said it was because they felt social pressure to be up to date with the story. Some said watching several episodes back to back makes it easier to follow the sometimes very complex storylines. Dramas were the most binge-watched shows, followed by sitcoms, reality shows and news programmes.

'The couch potato has woken up.'

Modern Family

Grammar & Speaking   reported speech

5   Read the rules about reported speech in the Grammar focus box. Then look back at the article and underline examples of rules 1–6.

GRAMMAR FOCUS reported speech

1   If we report what someone said in the past, we usually change the verb by moving it back one tense into the past.
   'The programme's just finished.' He said the programme *had just finished.*

2   If what the person says is still true, tense change is optional.
   She said she rarely has/had time to watch TV.

3   If the reporting verb is in the present, we don't change the tense.
   He says he'll watch it later.

4   We often need to change time references.
   yesterday – the day before, the previous day
   tomorrow – the next day, the following day

Reported questions
In reported questions, the subject goes before the verb. We don't use auxiliary verbs or question marks.

5   To report questions we usually use *ask/want to know/ wonder* with a question word.
   I asked where he was.

6   We use *if* or *whether* to report *yes/no* questions.

→ Grammar Reference   page 156

6   Work with a partner. Change the conversation between Elena (E) and Lucas (L) to reported speech.

E   You look tired. Are you OK?
L   I didn't get much sleep last night.
E   Did you go out?
L   No. I was watching *Sherlock*. I ended up watching all the episodes back to back.
E   Can I borrow it some time?
L   Sure. I'll bring it in for you tomorrow.

Elena told Lucas he looked tired and asked ...

Sherlock Holmes

7a   **TASK** Prepare a questionnaire to find out about TV viewing habits. Use the ideas below and your own ideas.
   • How/watch?
   • Binge-watch?
   • Alone or with others?
   • Favourite programmes?

b   Work with a partner and take it in turns to ask your questions. Make a note of the answers.

8a   Work with a different partner. Tell your partner about your first partner's TV-viewing habits and ask the same questions to your new partner.
   A   I asked Kenji if he had ever binge-watched a drama series. He said that he had once stayed up all night watching *Homeland*. What about you, have you ever done that?
   B   Yes, I have. Once I ...

b   How similar are your new partner's TV viewing habits to your first partner's viewing habits?

▶ VOX POPS VIDEO 11

New technologies, such as DVR (digital video recorders) and streaming, have transformed our viewing habits, enabling us to watch what we want, when and where we want, all of this without the annoying distraction of commercial breaks. Cost is also a factor, with a monthly subscription to Netflix costing just a fraction of a DVD box set.

The survey also indicates an interesting shift in opinion towards binge-watching. When respondents were asked whether they thought binge-viewing was a negative thing, only one-third said it was, whereas when asked the same question a year ago, the majority of people (two-thirds) considered it a bad thing.

This more positive attitude towards TV viewing may be because of the improved quality of the dramas. In the past, TV dramas were seen as culturally inferior to, say, the novel. This is no longer true. Social anthropologist Grant McCracken, who was involved in the research, says we watch TV differently now. In the past, binge viewers were known, disapprovingly, as 'couch potatoes' who spent hours and hours watching TV very passively. Now, however, since people are actively choosing what they watch, they watch with more purpose. He says that younger viewers, especially, watch more critically, frequently commenting on the quality of the acting, the casting, the camera angles. He believes the couch potato has woken up.

■ **binge** to do too much of something you enjoy, especially eating; *binge-watch* first entered the Oxford Dictionary in 2014
■ **couch** another word for *sofa*.

11.2 Positive news

Vocabulary & Speaking talking about news

1a Work with a partner. Think of five stories that are currently in the news.

b How many are 'bad news' stories? How many are 'good news' stories? Do you agree with the saying that 'good news doesn't sell newspapers'? Why might this be true?

2a Do you know any positive news sites?

b Read the article and note down the theories about why bad news sells. Do you agree with them?

NEWS ⟩ SOCIETY

And now for some good news…

It's a sad fact, but bad news attracts more readers than good news. Look at any major online news site or newspaper and you will find the majority of items are about conflict, violence, the economic crisis or someone's unfortunate death. Why is this so? Some might argue that reading about other people's suffering can make you feel better about your own life. Others suggest that it is a matter of conditioning and that people are used to a diet of bad news and want to be fed more and more. However, there are also plenty of us who are tired of reading disturbing and depressing stories. To meet this demand for something more inspiring, encouraging and uplifting, a number of positive news sites have been launched in recent years. These sites report on positive developments from around the world – medical breakthroughs, peace agreements and environmental campaigns – and take a solution-focused view on the challenges facing society.

3a Complete the table with the underlined words in the article.

Adjectives for positive news	Positive news topics
Adjectives for negative news	**Negative news topics**

b Work with a partner. Check the meaning of the bold words in the headlines. Decide whether the news is positive or negative, or positive for some, negative for others.

1 new **cure** for blindness

2 $50,000 stolen in **armed** robbery

3 **victory** for Bayern Munich

4 climber's **survival** of 300-metre fall

5 innocent man **wounded** in police shooting

c Add the bold words to the table in exercise **3a**.

4 **TASK** Write six more news headlines, three positive and three negative, using words from the table in exercise **3a**. Compare with a partner.

Grammar & Listening reporting verbs

5a You are going to listen to three true positive news stories. Before you listen, look at the photos. With a partner, can you guess what each story might be about?

b **11.1** 》 Listen and take notes on each story. How good were your predictions in exercise **5a**? In what sense is each a positive news story?

6 **11.1**))) Listen again and complete the sentences with 1–5 words in each gap.

Story 1

1 … many supermarket buyers **refuse** to buy _____ and vegetables from farmers.

2 Customers were **invited** to blind-taste both the _____ fruit and they **admitted** that **they** _____.

Story 2

3 The local people **assured** the conservationists that the monkeys would _____ locate …

4 … conservationists have **warned** that these monkeys were already on the _____ list.

Story 3

5 The teenagers immediately called the police to **inform** _____ the money.

6 Police have **praised** the teenagers for _____ but the teens **denied** _____ heroically …

7 Match the reporting verbs in bold in exercise **6** to direct speech phrases a–h.

a 'We won't do it …'
b 'It's true that … '
c 'You should be aware …'
d 'Would you like to …'
e 'We didn't do that …'
f 'Well done for doing that …'
g 'You can be sure that …'
h 'We want to give you some information …'

8 Add the reporting verbs in bold in exercise **6** to the correct group in the Grammar focus box.

GRAMMAR FOCUS reporting verbs

- Instead of *say*, we often use specific reporting verbs to report speech.
- Reporting verbs are followed by different structures. Some verbs can be followed by more than one structure.

Reporting verb	Structure
1 _____, _____, *argue, add*	+ (*that*) + clause
2 *remind,* _____, _____	+ person + (*that*) + clause
3 *agree, promise, offer,* _____	+ *to* infinitive
4 *tell, persuade, encourage,* _____, *warn*	+ person + *to* + infinitive
5 _____, *suggest, admit*	+ *-ing*
6 *blame* (sb.) *for,* _____	+ person + prep + *-ing*

- With *deny, promise, report, tell* sb., we can also use *that* + clause.

   They denied doing it. (verb + *-ing*) OR *They denied (that) he had done it.* (verb + (*that*) + clause)

→ Grammar Reference page 157

9a **11.2**))) The following reporting verbs are used in the news stories. Listen and write sentences containing the verbs.

> announce   claim   point out   report

b Add the verbs in exercise **9a** to the correct group in the Grammar focus box.

10a How would these sentences be reported? Match sentences 1–5 to reporting verbs a–e.

1 'You acted very responsibly. Well done.'
2 'I promise you that this fruit juice tastes delicious despite its odd colour.'
3 'Look, someone's left their bag on the seat.'
4 'I never read that paper. It's full of rubbish.'
5 'Yes, we will give you a loan.'

a She refuses _____.
b He pointed out _____.
c She assured me _____.
d The bank agreed _____.
e He praised me _____.

b Complete sentences a–e in exercise **10a** using reported speech.

a *She refuses to read that paper because it's full of rubbish.*

PRONUNCIATION weak syllables /ɪ/ and /ə/ in reporting verbs

11a **11.3**))) Listen and mark the stressed syllables in the reporting verbs.

ad**mit**   announce   assure   confirm   deny   inform invite   persuade   refuse   remind   report

b **11.3**))) Listen again. Is the unstressed syllable pronounced /ɪ/ or /ə/? Mark the sound above the syllable. Practise saying the verbs.

/ə/
admit

c **11.4**))) With a partner, listen to the sentences and say the correct reporting verb from exercise **11a**.

You hear: *'Don't forget to email him.'*
You say: *remind*

d **11.4**))) Listen again and make sentences with the reporting verbs.

She reminded me to email him.

12 TASK You are going to read two more positive news stories. Student A, turn to page 131. Student B, turn to page 135.

11.3 Vocabulary and skills development

Reading & Grammar understanding complex sentences

1 Work with a partner. Look at the photos and discuss the questions.

1 Are you familiar with websites like these?

2 Would you click on these lists? Why/Why not?

2 Read the information in the Unlock the code box about understanding complex sentences.

🔓 **UNLOCK THE CODE**
understanding complex sentences

• To understand a sentence you need to be able to quickly identify the subject, verb and object. Certain features of long sentences can make this difficult.

a **Present or past participle clauses**

| subject | verb | object |

First founded in the US in 2006, *BuzzFeed* now has branches *in several countries*, including France, Germany and Brazil.

b **Relative clauses**

| subject | verb | object |

The site, which used to publish only entertaining lists, *now publishes* serious news, *too*.

c **Subjects or objects consisting of several words**

| subject | verb | object |

BuzzFeed provides a fun, easy-to-read alternative to more serious news items.

3a Look at underlined phrases 1–5 in article A about BuzzFeed. Match them to features a–c mentioned in the Unlock the code box.

A

How BuzzFeed and 'listicles' changed the way we consume news

In 2013, the media industry watched [1] the extraordinary rise of the news and entertainment site BuzzFeed, [2] which, in 2014, just a year after its global launch, was attracting 130 million unique users worldwide, making it one of the biggest sites on the internet. The secret for its success? Listicles – a combination of the words 'list' and 'article'. These present news and entertainment in the form of lists, sometimes accompanied by photos and animated images. Typical listicles are '20 things you never knew about …' or '16 ways to …' or '11 reasons why you should never …' [3] Loved by some for their entertainment value and simplicity but [4] criticized by others for lowering the quality of journalism, the listicle now appears in a number of news websites, [5] including some of the more high-quality ones.

Share:  Tags: comment, news, journalism

b Circle the subject, verb and object(s) in the sentence that each underlined phrase appears in.

4 Read the complete article and answer the questions.

1 What is the evidence of BuzzFeed's popularity?

2 Why are some people critical of listicles?

5 Now read the listicle in article B and answer the questions.

1 Why do readers want scannable content?

2 How are listicles more pleasing than a standard article?

3 Why do listicles make commercial sense?

6 Now look at underlined sections 1–4 of the listicle and match them to the features a–c in the Unlock the code box. Then circle the subject, verb and object in the sentence each underlined phrase appears in.

7 What about you? Do you enjoy listicles or do you think they are a lazy form of journalism?

B

News Entertainment Fun Music TV Gossip

4 reasons
why listicles are
here to stay

1 **Order from chaos.** In a world
where we face a constant stream
of information and news, many of us
welcome somebody else's efforts to
select the important information and
organize it for us.

2 **News snacking.** A recent survey
of news reading habits ¹conducted
by news company Mobiles Republic
found that news reading has been
replaced by 'news snacking'. In other
words, ²people, especially those in their
twenties and below, check news
frequently, but in short, sharp bursts of
attention. As a result, they want
scannable content, the sort of thing you
can read quickly on your phone while in
the bus queue. Listicles offer the ideal
format for mobile phone viewing.

3 **Clear signposts.** Psychologically,
the listicle is attractive because it
simplifies any subject into a manageable
number of individual facts. When you
start reading an ordinary article, you
have ³no way of knowing how many
things it will tell you. It could be fifteen,
or it could be two, which can be quite
frustrating. With a listicle, you know
what you are getting.

4 **Shareable content.** Listicles,
⁴which are specifically designed to
go viral, are frequently shared via social
media. In 2014, BuzzFeed items were the
most shared on Facebook and Twitter.
Advertisers tend to be more interested in
the number of hits an article gets than
the quality of the content. Listicles
therefore make commercial sense for
news companies.

Vocabulary & Listening adjective suffixes

8 Read the information in the Vocabulary focus box about adjective suffixes.

VOCABULARY FOCUS adjective suffixes -al, -able, -ive and -ant
We can make adjectives by adding suffixes.
- -al is the most common adjective suffix; -al adjectives are mainly formed from nouns: *accident – accidental, virus – viral*
- -able, -ive and -ant are mainly added to or formed from verbs: *drink – drinkable, select – selective, dominate – dominant*
  -able is known as 'a living suffix'. This means we can fix it to any existing verb. It is useful for inventing new words, e.g. *to google – googleable*

9 Complete the table with adjectives from the articles in exercises **3a** and **5**.

-al	-able	-ive	-ant

10 **11.5** 》) Listen to two people, Luke and Rosie, being interviewed about how they get their news. Complete the table.

	Luke	Rosie
1 How do they get their news in the morning?		
2 How often do they read the news online during the day?		
3 Do they ever read print newspapers?		
4 What kind of news/news sites do they like to read?		

11a Match adjectives 1–8 from the listening to meanings a–h in this context.

1 addictive — a real
2 objective — b too big or difficult to deal with
3 actual — c that you can trust
4 unmanageable — d important and useful
5 reliable — e considering only facts, not personal opinion
6 informative — f difficult to stop doing
7 mental — g giving useful knowledge
8 relevant — h of the mind

b Add adjectives 1–8 in exercise **11a** to the table in exercise **9**.

12a **TASK** Work in groups and interview each other about the role of online news in your lives. Use the questions in exercise **10** and add two more of your own.

b Who in your group has the most similar news reading habits and preferences to yours?

11.4 Speaking and writing

Speaking retelling a (news) story

40 55 73 127

59 1940s 6 5 million

1 Look at the photos. What do you think the stories are about? What might the numbers refer to?

2 **11.6**))) Listen to two people each telling a news story to a friend and check your answers to exercise **1**.

3a Complete the sentences with words from the box.

> about according apparently around is (x2) other
> something supposedly thing what's

1 … she's the oldest person who has ever lived, _____ …
2 … _____ to the article, she claims she was born in 1887 …
3 … she's got _____ like seventy-three great-grandchildren …
4 The sad _____ _____ that several of them have already died before her.
5 This suit was incredibly heavy, _____ fifty-nine kilos or something.
6 It took him six days, _____.
7 His name's Lloyd something or _____.
8 _____ amazing _____ him is that he was diagnosed with leukaemia several years ago.

b **11.6**))) Listen again and check. Then practise saying the sentences.

4a Match the sentences in exercise **3a** to their functions, a–c.

a quoting from another source (e.g. person/news article)
b giving your own view
c being vague or inexact

b Check your answers in the Language for speaking box.

5 Add the following phrases to the correct category a–c in the Language for speaking box.

1 … or so they say.
2 Somewhere in the region of …
3 They reckon …
4 Personally, I find it …
5 …, something like that

LANGUAGE FOR SPEAKING retelling a (news) story

a Quoting from other sources
Apparently, …
…, supposedly.
According to (the newspaper/magazine/article I read, etc.), …
From what I understand/read, …
_____ _____

b Giving your own view
The sad/strange thing about it is/was …
What's sad/weird/impressive about it is/was that …
_____

c Being vague
Something like … (fifty people)
I can't remember exactly/precisely …
Around (thirty) …
(Ivan) something or other
_____ _____

6 **TASK** Think of a recent news story or use a news story at the back of the book. Student A, turn to page 131. Student B, turn to page 135. Make notes about which phrases in the Language for speaking box you can use to tell the story.

7 Work with a partner. Take it in turns to retell your story. Remember to comment on your own story and to use vague language.

Writing an opinion essay in a formal style

8 Read the essay. Then, with a partner, answer the questions.

1 Does the writer agree or disagree with the statement?
2 Do you agree with this point of view?
3 What is the function of each of the five paragraphs?
4 Find three things that tell you this essay is written in a formal style.

The internet has improved the quality of journalism. Discuss.

There is no question that the internet has transformed the news industry in recent decades, and that its impact has been both positive and negative.

Online news is frequently criticized for being unreliable and based on very little evidence. In addition, commercial pressures in this increasingly competitive market encourage journalists to concentrate on what is popular and what will attract interest on social media, rather than on what is important.

However, it is also true that the internet has brought several benefits to news consumers. We have a more varied choice of news sources than ever before; we are no longer limited to the newspapers and radio and television news services in our particular part of the world. Americans can watch Al Jazeera online, while Australians can read *The New York Times*.

Furthermore, the internet has made it possible for new media companies to join the industry. For example, *The Huffington Post*, now one of the popular and respected news sources worldwide, wouldn't exist without the internet. An additional benefit of online news reporting is that smartphones now enable journalists (both professional and 'citizen journalists') to publish text, photos or video wherever they are, which means that the chances of something important being captured by somebody at the scene are much higher.

On balance, I would argue that the benefits of internet news outweigh the downsides. It should also be remembered that the internet does not replace traditional journalism, whether delivered via the internet or print media: it adds to it.

9 Work with a partner. Decide which of the following are typical features of formal writing. Write *F* or *I* next to each feature.

- passive sentences ___
- contractions (*it's*) ___
- colloquial language (*OK*) ___
- simple linking words (*so, plus, but*) ___
- longer linkers (*however, in addition*) ___
- complex sentences (participles clauses and relative clauses) ___
- abbreviations (*etc., e.g, i.e.*) ___
- impersonal sentences (*it is argued*) ___
- semi-colons (;) ___
- dashes (–, —) ___

10 Match the highlighted examples in the essay in exercise **8** to points a–f in the Language for writing box.

LANGUAGE FOR WRITING achieving a formal style

Academic essays should be written in a formal style. Features of a formal style include:

a full forms, not contractions. _____
b formal vocabulary. NB Latin-based words are often more formal than non-Latin-based synonyms, e.g. *the majority of people* is more formal than *most people*, *improve* is more formal than *get better*, *extremely* is more formal than *very*. _____
c formal, rather than informal, linking words (e.g. *moreover*). _____
d complex sentences, including relative clauses and participles clauses. _____
e passive verbs to report thoughts and speech: *It is thought that, It is believed that …* _____
f certain punctuation, e.g. semi-colons (;) rather than dashes (–). _____

11 Make these sentences more formal.

1 The papers are really pricey these days.
2 Lots of people reckon newspapers won't be around for much longer.
3 You can't trust lots of the stuff you read on the internet.

12 You are going to write an essay about one of the following topics.

- Printed newspapers have no future.
- The press has a right to publish photos and information about celebrities' private lives.

13a **TASK** Work with a partner and choose a title from exercise **12**. Brainstorm some ideas and organize them into paragraphs. Use the model in exercise **8** to help you.

b Write your essay in about 250 words. Include as many of the features from the Language for writing box as you can.

11.5 Video

Going viral

1 Match the words in the box to the definitions.

> circulation   exaggerated   ornate   social media site
> tabloid

1 a newspaper with short articles and lots of images, often considered less serious than other newspapers
2 with a lot of decoration
3 the number of copies of newspapers sold
4 making news seem much bigger, better or worse than it really is
5 websites for social networking, e.g. Facebook, Twitter

2 Which of the things in exercise **1** can you see in the photos? What do you think the video is going to be about?

3 ▶ Watch the video. Choose the correct options to complete the sentences.

1 Fleet Street *is* / *used to be* the centre of the British news industry.
2 The newspaper *The Sun* has a circulation of *over four million* / *under two million*.
3 64% of adults in the USA *get their news online* / *use Facebook*.
4 In 2013, a news story broke about a ship with *rats* / *ghosts* on board.
5 The story was reported in *The Sun* / *The Daily Mirror*.

4a ▶ Watch again. Decide how true sentences 1–6 are:
a) definitely true, b) probably true, c) possibly true
d) probably false, e) definitely false.

1 The UK's first daily newspaper was published in 1702.
2 *The Daily Mirror* sells more copies than *The Sun*.
3 In 2013, a ship got lost in the Atlantic Ocean.
4 The ship had a Twitter account.
5 The ship sank in the Atlantic Ocean.

b Compare your answers with a partner.

5a TASK Work in groups. Prepare 4–5 questions for a survey to find out about people's news-sharing habits. Use the ideas below and your own ideas.
- What/share (e.g. stories, photos, videos)?
- How/share (e.g. via email, social media sites)?
- Who/share/with?

b Ask and answer the questions in your group. Whose news-sharing habits are most similar to your own?

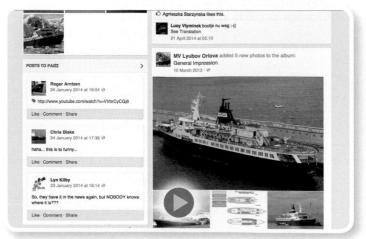

Review

1a Write a question to ask your partner about each of the topics in the box.

> family   likes/dislikes   plans for this evening
> what you did last weekend

b Work with your partner. Ask your questions and make a note of the answers.

c Work with a different partner. Say what you learnt about your first partner, for example:

A *What are you doing this evening?*
B *Meeting some friends.*
A *I asked Ivor what he was doing this evening. He said he was meeting some friends.*

2a Put the sentences into reported speech using a reporting verb from the box.

> admit   deny   point out   promise   remind

1 'Your shoelaces are undone.' She ...
2 'It's true. I did cheat in the exam.' He ...
3 'I won't tell anyone.' She ...
4 'Don't forget to take your pills.' He ...
5 'I didn't read your diary.' She ...

b Work with a partner. Talk about a time when you ...

- refused to do something you were asked to do.
- agreed to do something you later regretted.
- denied doing something you really did.

3a Add vowels to make phrases to describe things you can watch on TV.

1 c__rr__nt __ff__ __rs
2 n__ws __n__lys__s
3 h__m__ __mpr__v__m__nt pr__gr__mm__
4 m__tch h__ghl__ghts
5 dr__m__ s__r__ __s
6 c__l__br__ty ch__f
7 TV c__mm__rc__ __l

b Describe your current favourite TV programme and explain why you like it.

4a **11.7** 》 Listen to the definitions and circle the words being defined.

1 a crisis / a conflict   4 depressing / disturbing
2 suffer / survive   5 encouraging / uplifting
3 armed / wounded   6 a breakthrough / a cure

b Work with a partner. Write definitions for the words which were not defined in exercise **4a**.

5a Complete the sentences with the correct form of the words in brackets.

1 Reading a newspaper in English is perfectly _____ (manage) for me.
2 I find the news quite _____ (addict).
3 I enjoy watching amusing videos that have gone _____ (virus) and often share them on social media.
4 I think very few online news sites provide _____ (rely) and _____ (object) news.

b Tick the sentences in exercise **5a** you agree with. Compare with a partner.

6a Choose the correct options to complete the phrases.

1 *From / In* what I understand ...
2 According *to / with* an article I read ...
3 *That's / What's* strange about it is ...
4 Something *as / like* ten people ...
5 His name is Pavel something *or other / else* ...

b Work with a partner. Think of a news story or an interesting story that someone has told you recently. Take it in turns to retell the story.

12 Life stages

12.1 Nearest and dearest

GOALS ■ Talk about family and relationships ■ Talk about unreal situations

Vocabulary & Listening family and relationships

1a Work with a partner. Decide if the words in the box refer to a relative from an older generation, a younger generation or the same generation as you.

> aunt godparent niece second cousin sister-in-law
> sibling stepfather twin

b Are you any of these? Tell your partner.

c Check you understand the words in bold in the sentences. Find the four sentences that cannot logically be true, and rewrite them so they might be true.

1 He is very **spoilt** by his parents.
2 He **looks up to** his younger brother.
3 I'm very **close to** my stepsister.
4 She's totally **devoted to** her grandfather.
5 She **cares for** her elderly parents.
6 The baby has brought a lot of **joy** to the family.
7 My mother **takes after** my sister.
8 I often **turn to** my older sister for advice.
9 I **brought up** my mother and grandmother.
10 She **gets on** her brother's **nerves**.
11 My little brother doesn't like being **left out**.
12 Her mother **tells** her **off** when she's well behaved.

2a Write the name of the following.
- the person you most take after in your family
- the person you most often turn to for advice
- the relative you are closest to
- a person you look up to
- someone whose behaviour gets on your nerves sometimes

b With a partner, take it in turns to describe each person, giving details.

3a Work with a partner. Look at the photos. What do you think it would be like to belong to a family like the one in each photo?

b Write down five factors that people need to consider when deciding how many children to have, if any. Put them in order of importance.

4a **12.1**))) Listen to three people talking about what they believe is the ideal family size. Write the number of children that each person thinks is ideal.
Speaker 1: _____ Speaker 2: _____ Speaker 3: _____

b **12.2**))) Listen to three more people and do the same.
Speaker 4: _____ Speaker 5: _____ Speaker 6: _____

5 **12.3**))) Listen again to all six speakers in exercises **4a** and **4b**. Which speaker mentions that ...?
a having siblings can help you cope with life's difficulties _____
b they would have been a worse parent if they'd had more children _____
c the pleasures of parenthood outweigh the challenges _____
d they hope to be looked after by their children one day _____
e we should limit the number of children we have, for environmental reasons _____
f having children can affect where you choose to go on holiday _____

6 Which of the opinions that you heard in exercise **5** do you most agree with? Which do you least agree with? Discuss with a partner.

Grammar & Speaking   unreal situations

7 Work with a partner. Look at the *if* sentences from the listening and answer the questions that follow.

1 'If I'd had more children, I'd have been less happy.'

2 'If every couple in a rich country had one less child, they would save tonnes of carbon dioxide.'

3 'If I'd had children ... my travels would be limited to school vacations and child-friendly destinations.'

a Do the sentences describe real or imaginary situations?

b Does each sentence describe a possible situation in the past, the present/future or both?

8 Read the rules about conditional sentences in the Grammar focus box and match sentences 1–3 in exercise **7** to rules a–c.

> ### GRAMMAR FOCUS conditional sentences to talk about unreal situations
>
> **Unreal conditional (or 'second conditional')**
> - We use *if* + past, + *would/might/could* + infinitive to talk about an unreal or improbable situation in the present or future, and how things could be different.
>
>   *If our flat was bigger, the children would have a room each.*
>   a _____
>
> **Unreal past conditional (or 'third conditional')**
> - We use *if* + past perfect, + *would/might/could have* + participle to talk about an unreal situation in the past, to say how it could have been different.
>
>   *If we hadn't worked together, we might not have met.*
>   b _____
>
> **Mixed conditionals**
> - We can mix the second and third conditionals in two ways: to talk about an unreal situation in the past which has a present result, we use:
>
>   *if* + past perfect, + *would*
>   *If you'd listened properly, you'd know what to do.*
>   c _____
>
> - to talk about the possible past result of an unreal situation in the present, we use:
>
>   *if* + past, + *would have*
>   *If he was more confident, he'd have asked her out.*

→ **Grammar Reference** page 158

9a **12.4**))) Listen to four clauses from conditional sentences and answer the questions.

1 What do you notice about the stress on *would/might* and *couldn't/wouldn't* in each sentence?

2 How is *have* pronounced?

b **12.4**))) Listen again and repeat the sentences.

10 Complete the second sentence in each pair so that it has the same meaning as the first.

1 My brother emigrated to New Zealand, so our kids don't see each other much.
   If my brother _____ closer now.

2 I had no idea how physically exhausting bringing up kids was, and I had them late.
   If I _____ had them earlier.

3 I didn't have children because I really value my independence.
   If _____ have children.

4 We need a big house because we're such a large family.
   If we _____ big house.

5 Maybe having no siblings has made me an independent person.
   If I'd _____ independent as I am.

11a **TASK** You are going to ask your partner the questions. Complete the questions with the correct form of the verbs in brackets.

1 How _____ your life _____ (be) different if you _____ (have) ... [add number] siblings?

2 If you _____ (be) brought up in ... [add country] how _____ your life _____ (be) different when you were a child, and how _____ it _____ (be) different now?

3 What _____ (do) in your free time if you _____ (live) in ... [add century]?

4 If you _____ (be) a member of the opposite sex, _____ people _____ (treat) you differently as a child? _____ you _____ (have) a different job/goals now?

b Replace the square brackets in the questions with your own ideas.

How would your life be different if you had five siblings?

c Now work with a partner and ask each other the questions.

▶ **VOX POPS VIDEO 12**

117

12.2 If I could turn back time, …

Vocabulary & Reading life events and choices

1a Work with a partner. Think of two things you have done (or not done) recently and regretted, for example:

- something you bought/didn't buy
- something you said/didn't say
- something you threw away
- an event you attended/didn't attend

b Share your stories and find out more.

c Do you tend to hold on to regrets for a long time or can you forget about them quickly? Give examples.

2 You are going to read an article about regrets. First, discuss the questions with a partner.

1 What do you think are the three most common things people regret?
2 Do you think men and women regret different things?
3 Which regrets stay with us for longer – things we didn't do or things we did?
4 In what sense can regret be a positive emotion?

3 Read the article. How does it answer the questions in exercise **2**?

Our greatest regrets of all

By the time most people reach middle age, they can probably name a list of things they regret from their past: the job opening they ignored, the relationship that failed, the investment they did or didn't make.

But the most frequent regrets involve romance, according to a new study in which 370 American adults, ranging in age from 19 to 103 and from a variety of socio-economic backgrounds, were asked to describe a memorable regret. Nearly one in five described a missed romantic opportunity. The second most common regret involved family issues (16%). Other top regrets involved education (13%), work (12%), money (10%), parenting mistakes (9%) and health (6%).

The findings showed that gender, age and educational level all influence the types of regrets people feel. Women were far more likely to have romantic regrets, with 44% fretting about a lost love, while just 19% of men had relationship regrets.

Another key finding was that regrets about missed opportunities – things we wish we had done, but didn't – last for much longer than regrets about things we did that we wish we could undo.

Dr Neale Roese, the psychologist behind the research, notes that regret can harm mental health when we fixate for too long on a missed opportunity. However, regret, although painful, can help us to move on and use the experience to improve decision-making in the future.

4a Match the common regrets, a–m, to the categories mentioned in the article in exercise **3**.

TOP REGRETS

a not having the **courage** to ask someone on a **date**
   romance

b not **making up** after a family **row** _____

c **settling down** with a partner too soon _____

d **missing out on** an **investment** opportunity _____

e having been **mean** to a sibling as a child _____

f choosing the wrong **career path** _____

g not giving **quality time** to your children _____

h buying a **property** which has decreased in value

   _____

i taking up smoking _____

j **turning down** a job offer _____

k not taking studies seriously _____

l not paying into a private **pension** plan early enough

   _____

m not **standing up to** bullies at work _____

b Match seven of the phrases in bold in exercise **4a** to their meanings in the box.

building   defending yourself against   disagreement
having a quieter life, living in one place   rejecting
romantic meeting   unkind

c Which of these regrets might be felt by someone in their twenties? Which by someone in their sixties?

Grammar & Listening   using *wish* and *if only*

5 **12.5**))) Listen to Greg, Jade, Bill and Michelle talking about major regrets. Which person wishes they had …?

a said more _____

b said less _____

c followed someone's advice _____

d ignored someone's request _____

6 **12.6**))) Listen again and complete the extracts from the listening.

1 If only I _____ _____ to my dad.

2 If only I _____ _____ my big mouth!

3 I wish I _____ _____ a bit less honest
   sometimes …

4 I wish you _____ _____ those records.

5 I just wish I _____ _____ the courage to
   challenge her at the time.

7 Answer the questions about the sentences in exercise **6**.

1 Which sentences describe a regret about the past?

2 Which describe a wish for the present/future?

3 Which describes a desire for somebody else to change their behaviour?

4 What are the full forms of the contraction *'d* in sentences 1, 4 and 5?

8 Read the Grammar focus box and add examples from exercise **6**.

> **GRAMMAR FOCUS** *wish* and *if only*
>
> 1 We use *wish* + past simple or continuous to talk about wishes for unlikely or impossible things in the present.
>   *I wish we lived by the sea.*
>   a _____
>
> 2 We use *wish* + past perfect to express regrets about the past.
>   *I wish I hadn't sold my car.*
>   b _____
>
> 3 We use *wish* + person/thing + *would* to talk about things we want other people to do or not do. It often expresses annoyance or dissatisfaction.
>   *I wish she would stop shouting.*
>   c _____
>
> 4 We can use *If only* instead of *wish* in all these situations. It is more emphatic than *wish*.
>   *If only I could turn back time!*
>   d _____
>   e _____

→ Grammar Reference page 159

9a **TASK** Rewrite the sentences using *I wish* or *if only*.

1 I didn't work hard enough at school.

2 I regret not having more siblings.

3 I'd like to live in the city centre.

4 It irritates me when people park on the pavement.

5 I'd like to be more patient.

6 It annoys me when people spell my name incorrectly.

7 I worry too much about what people think of me.

b Which sentences are true for you? Change the others so they are true for you.

c Compare your sentences with a partner and find out more. Do you share any wishes or regrets?

12.3 Vocabulary and skills development

Listening recognizing vague language

1 Work with a partner and answer the questions.

1 Which of the following words and phrases have a similar meaning to 'fashionable'?
- cool
- trendy
- out
- dated
- in
- the 'in' thing
- hip

2 How important is it to you to be fashionable?

3 Describe the appearance of the man in the photo. What do you think of his 'look'?

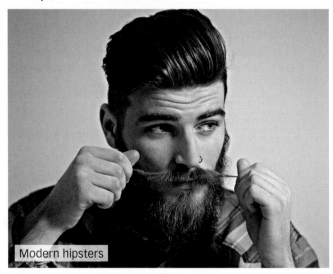
Modern hipsters

2 **12.7**))) Listen to the first part of a radio programme about modern-day hipsters. Correct two facts in the summary below.

> There are hipsters in many countries. They are usually in their teens or twenties. They dislike popular culture, preferring alternative music and fashion. They are mostly students, studying for a career in creative fields such as media or publishing.

3a **12.8**))) Listen and complete these extracts from the listening in exercise **2**.

1 They're _____ _____ anti anything that's popular.

2 That includes _____, music, clothes and _____ _____.

3 Many _____ them work in _____ fields like media or publishing, that _____ _____ thing.

b Underline the examples of vague language in exercise **3a**.

4 **12.9**))) Read and listen to the information in the Unlock the code box about recognizing vague language in fast speech.

> ## 🔓 UNLOCK THE CODE
> recognizing vague language
>
> It is very common in spoken English to use vague expressions. We use them:
>
> 1 when we can't think of a precise word to describe something.
>
> *kind of*   *sort of*
>
> For example: *It's kind of reddish.*
>
> 2 to say there are more examples in a list or category.
>
> *and so on*   *and that kind/sort/type of thing*
> *or whatever*   *and things/stuff/places like that*
>
> For example: *The shop sells vintage clothes, records and that kind of thing.*
>
> Because the phrases are so common, we say them very quickly and often don't pronounce parts of the words. For example:
> *kind of* sounds like /kaɪnə/
> *sort of* sounds like /sədə/ or /sɔː(r)tə/
> *like that* sounds like /laɪðæ/
> *… and so on* sounds like /nsəʊwɒn/

5a **12.10**))) Listen to five sentences and write the number of words you hear. Contractions count as two words (e.g. *it's = it is*).

1 ___   2 ___   3 ___   4 ___   5 ___

b **12.11**))) Listen and complete the sentences.

1 Hipsters reject mainstream culture: music, clothes, _____.

2 Some hipsters are vegan so they don't eat eggs _____.

3 It's a shop that sells old books _____.

4 He's into 1930s music, like jazz, blues _____.

5 She likes _____ you'd buy from a vintage clothes shop.

6 The area is full of hipster barber shops, cafés _____.

6a **12.12**))) Listen to the rest of the radio programme about modern-day hipsters and tick the topics that are mentioned.

- hipster clothing
- objects owned by hipsters
- hipster neighbourhoods
- taste in music
- attitudes to the environment
- hipster transport
- hipster drinks
- hipster hobbies

b **12.12**))) Listen again and check.

7 **12.12**))) Listen again and answer the questions.
1 Where do hipsters often buy their clothes?
2 Why do hipsters dislike being called hipsters?
3 Why are hipsters unpopular?
4 What do we learn about the hipster diet?
5 What is special about the bikes that hipsters ride?
6 What is the most stereotypical hipster hobby?

8 Work with a partner. Discuss the questions.
1 Do you have hipsters in your country? Are they similar to the ones described in the radio programme?
2 Which other youth cultures or subcultures exist in your country? What are they like?

Vocabulary compound adjectives

9a The compound adjectives below all appeared in the radio programme. Use as many of them as you can to describe the photos.

a fixed-wheel bicycle

1	clean-shaven	8	old-fashioned
2	eco-friendly	9	second-hand
3	fixed-wheel	10	little-known
4	floral-patterned	11	run-down
5	home-made	12	thick-rimmed
6	low-tech	13	tight-fitting
7	turned-up		

b With a partner, match some of the compound adjectives in exercise **9a** to their antonyms below.

a plain _4_
b thin-rimmed ___
c famous ___
d baggy ___
e shop-bought/industrially produced ___
f brand new ___
g high-tech ___
h bearded ___
i smart ___
j harmful to the environment ___

10 Read the information in the Vocabulary focus box about compound adjectives.

> **VOCABULARY FOCUS** compound adjectives
>
> - Compound adjectives are made of two words. They are usually written with a hyphen, but occasionally they are written as a single word. Here are some of the common forms they take.
>   1 ending in a past participle: *high-heeled, handmade*
>   2 ending in a present participle: *good-looking, tight-fitting*
>   3 ending in a noun: *last-minute, full-time*
>   4 ending in an adjective: *sugar-free, brand new*
>   5 ending in a preposition: *worn-out, rolled-up*
> - NB Some compound adjectives have a hyphen before a noun, but not after a verb (e.g. *a well-known band* BUT *the band is well known*).

11a Use suitable compound adjectives from exercise **9a** to complete the questionnaire.

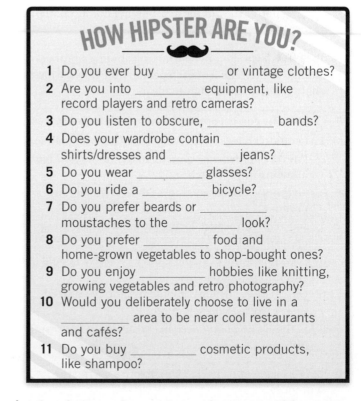

HOW HIPSTER ARE YOU?

1 Do you ever buy _____ or vintage clothes?
2 Are you into _____ equipment, like record players and retro cameras?
3 Do you listen to obscure, _____ bands?
4 Does your wardrobe contain _____ shirts/dresses and _____ jeans?
5 Do you wear _____ glasses?
6 Do you ride a _____ bicycle?
7 Do you prefer beards or _____ moustaches to the _____ look?
8 Do you prefer _____ food and home-grown vegetables to shop-bought ones?
9 Do you enjoy _____ hobbies like knitting, growing vegetables and retro photography?
10 Would you deliberately choose to live in a _____ area to be near cool restaurants and cafés?
11 Do you buy _____ cosmetic products, like shampoo?

b Ask and answer the questions with a partner. If the answer is yes, ask follow-up questions to find out more.

12.4 Speaking and writing

Speaking reflecting on life events and choices

1 Work with a partner and list the three most significant turning points in your life (e.g. moving home, changing career, getting married).

2 **12.13** 》 Listen to four people talking about a significant change in their life. For each person note down what the change was and why they made it.

3a Choose the correct options to complete the sentences.
1 I couldn't have *wished for / desired* a better course.
2 I'm very *appreciate / grateful* to the tutors *for / with* allowing me to switch.
3 So *thank / thanks* goodness I didn't listen to my parents …
4 *In / With* retrospect, losing my job was a blessing *of / in* disguise.
5 … when I think of all the money I wasted, I could really *kick / hit* myself.
6 *On / With* hindsight, I should never have started …
7 *That's / What's* done is done.
8 … there's no *point / need* in crying *about / over* spilt milk …

b **12.14** 》 Listen and check. Then practise saying the sentences.

4 **TASK** Think back over some of the significant life decisions that you've made. Choose four or five topics in the box or your own ideas, and follow the instructions. Use the language in the Language for speaking box and past conditional sentences.

> family   give up a habit   hobby/sport   important purchases
> relationships   school/college/university subjects
> skills learnt   studying English   travel   work   your home

- Tell your partner what you did and why.
- Say what you are pleased about and what you regret.
- Say how your life would be different now if you hadn't made those decisions.

LANGUAGE FOR SPEAKING
reflecting on life events and choices

Looking back
In retrospect, …
With hindsight, …

Things that have gone well
I'm so pleased/glad I …	*I'm so/very/'ll be forever grateful*
Thank goodness I …	*to (person) … for … (+ -ing).*
It's so lucky I …	*It was a blessing in disguise.*
I feel very fortunate	*… was a good call.*
to have …	
I couldn't have wished for	
a better …	

Things you regret
I kick myself about it now.
What was I thinking?

Expressing resignation
What's done is done.
There's no point in crying over spilt milk.

Writing a biography

5   Discuss the questions with a partner.

   1   Do you have a favourite sportsperson? Why do you like them?

   2   Look at the photo in the biography. Do you know this athlete? What makes a sportsperson qualify as 'a legend'?

6   Complete the biography of Emil Zátopek with suitable prepositions.

7   Work with a partner. Without looking back at the biography, can you remember …?

   1   his main achievement

   2   his training style

   3   why he was popular with other athletes

   4   what he had in common with his wife

8   Match the highlighted words and phrases in the biography to their meanings, 1–5.

   1   never been done before

   2   a person who is the first to develop an idea

   3   a ceremony that takes place when someone dies

   4   a very famous name

   5   not known

9   Read about language that is used in a biography in the Language for writing box. Which of the phrases are in the biography of Emil Zátopek?

LANGUAGE FOR WRITING writing a biography

Describing achievements
He was one of the greatest … of all time
He was renowned/best known/famed for …

Biographical details
He was born and brought up in …
He spent his childhood …
He was one of six children …
At the age of …, he …
His life took an unexpected turn for the better/worse when …
His life was turned upside down when …
Life changed dramatically for X when Y happened …
His funeral was attended by …

10   Write a biography about someone, either a famous person who interests you or someone you know, who has led an inspiring life. Follow the structure of the model biography of Emil Zátopek.

EMIL ZÁTOPEK:

AN OLYMPIC LEGEND

Emil Zátopek (1922–2000) was a Czech long-distance runner, considered one of the greatest athletes **1**_____ all time. He is best known **2**_____ winning three gold medals at the 1952 Helsinki Olympics, when he won the 5,000 metres, 10,000 metres and the marathon in just over a week, earning himself the nickname 'The Czech Locomotive'.

Zátopek was born and brought **3**_____ in the north-east Czech town of Kopřivnice, and **4**_____ the age of sixteen he left school to work in a factory. His life took an unexpected turn when he was selected by the factory sports coach to take part **5**_____ a race. Despite protesting that he was too unfit to take part, he ended up coming second out of 100. This sparked off his interest in running.

In 1948, he became a household name after he won an unprecedented thirty-eight 10,000-metre races in a row and set eighteen world records over various distances.

Zátopek was renowned **6**_____ his hard training routines. He was a pioneer of 'interval training' – making short, intense efforts, sometimes running 400 metres eighty times in succession. This method was unheard of at the time but later became standard for athletes across many sports.

He was also famed for his cheerful and sociable personality. He gained the respect of other athletes because he made an effort to communicate with them after learning a variety of languages.

Zátopek got married **7**_____ Zana Ingrova, who, **8**_____ coincidence, was born on the same day as him, in the same year. Zana was a great athlete in her own right, winning a gold in the javelin in 1952.

When Zátopek died in 2000, aged seventy-eight, leading figures from the world of sport travelled from round the globe to attend his funeral.

12.5 Video

Dynasty – the Churchills

1 Complete the table with the words and phrases in the box.

> ancestor battle Chancellor descendant distant relative
> dynasty general House of Commons House of Lords
> Member of Parliament (MP) orator paternal grandfather
> prime minister soldier speech

Family	Politics	War

2 Work with a partner and discuss the questions.

1 What do you know about Winston Churchill?
2 Look at the photos of Blenheim Palace, where he was born and brought up. How did being brought up here shape his future, do you think?

3 You are going to watch a video about Churchill's life. Which of the words in the box do you expect to hear?

> duke Glastonbury Festival illness MP Nobel Prize
> Princess Diana school Second World War wealthiest

4 ▶ Watch the video. Check your answers to exercise **3**.

5 ▶ Watch again and complete the sentences.

1 Blenheim Palace was built for Winston Churchill's ancestor John Churchill as a reward for …
2 Winston's father, Randolph Churchill, held a number of political positions, including Leader of …
3 Winston's mother, Jennie, came from …
4 Winston didn't have a close relationship with …
5 Winston Churchill was prime minister during …
6 Winston Churchill is particularly famous for making …
7 Winston Churchill won a Nobel prize for …

6a **TASK** You are going to write a short biography of Winston Churchill's life based on the video you just saw. Make some notes. Include only the key pieces of information.

b Write your biography in 100–120 words. Try not to use exactly the same words as those in exercise **5**.

c Read your summary to a partner. Did you include the same information?

Review

1a Complete the sentences with the correct form of the verbs in brackets.

1   If my friends hadn't encouraged me, I _____ (not set up) my own online shop.

2   If I hadn't taken up cycling, I _____ (be) very unfit now.

3   If I had a chance to live in a different country, I _____ (go) somewhere with a better climate.

4   If I _____ (not have) a university degree, I wouldn't have such a good job now.

5   If I didn't have such a supportive boss, I _____ (leave) this company years ago.

b Work with a partner. Think of three people or situations that have had a big influence on your life. Explain how they have affected your life, using conditional sentences.

2a Write an example of each of the following.
- a skill you would like to have
- something you would like to own
- something you did that you now regret
- an opportunity you missed
- something that other people do that annoys you

b Make sentences about the things in exercise **2a** with *I wish* and *if only*.
I wish he would reply to his texts.

c Work with a partner and compare your sentences.

3a Complete the sentences with the missing words. The first letter is given.

1   My mother t_____ me off more than my father when I misbehaved as a child.

2   I was b_____ up by my mother and stepfather.

3   I generally t_____ to friends rather than family for advice about relationships.

4   I don't t_____ after my mother at all.

5   I think I was slightly s_____ as a child. My parents gave me everything I wanted.

b Change the sentences in exercise **3a** so that they are true for you. Compare with a partner.

4 Match verbs 1–8 to phrases a–h.

1	miss	a	into a pension
2	make	b	out on all the fun
3	ask	c	up after a row with someone
4	stand	d	down with a life partner
5	choose	e	a career path
6	turn	f	someone out on a date
7	pay	g	up to a bully
8	settle	h	down an invitation or offer

5a **12.15**))) Listen and write seven words. Match them to the words in the box to form compound adjectives.

clean- tight- little- eco- home- high- run-

b Choose four of the compound adjectives in exercise **5a** and make sentences.

c Work with a partner. Read out your sentences, without saying the compound adjective. Your partner tries to guess the compound adjective.

6a Put the words in the right order to make sentences.

1   is / what's / done / done .

2   thank / her / advice / ignored / goodness / I .

3   kick / I / about / it / now / could / myself .

4   I / better / teacher / couldn't / for / a / have / wished .

5   no / spilt / there's / milk / point / over / in / crying .

b Work with a partner. Decide which of the sentences in exercise **6a** describe a) regret, b) relief or gratitude and c) an attitude of acceptance towards something bad that has happened.

Communication

In a, the man is pointing or wagging his finger, which in some cultures might be considered very rude as it can seem like an accusation.

In b, the man finds the question 'How much do you earn?' too personal.

In c, Carlos is sitting very close to the other man, who comes from a culture where it is not usual to sit so close to another person.

Student A
1.1 Exercise 11

a Read the sentences. Write questions, beginning with the question word provided, to find out what words fit in the gaps. Student B has the answers.

1 About _____ people in the world speak English, 359 million of whom speak it as a native language. *How ...?*

2 Approximately 6,000 languages exist in the world today. Every year about _____ of these disappear. *How ...?*

3 The @ sign has different names in different countries. In Dutch it is sometimes known as _____. In Danish it is known as a *snabel-a*, which means 'elephant's trunk'. *What ...?*

4 The number four brings bad luck in some Asian countries because it sounds similar to _____. *What ...?*

5 There are a number of phobias connected to language. For example, a person with sesquipedalophobia is afraid of long words, and a person with xenoglossophobia has a fear of _____! *What does a person ...?*

b Take it in turns to ask questions and complete the information. You begin.

c Which fact did you find most surprising?

All students
1.2 Exercise 9

a Imagine you are a famous person – either from the past or the present day – for example, an actor, an artist, a politician or sportsperson. Write a short letter to a friend describing things you have done, and things you have been doing recently. Use the topics listed below or your own ideas.

- entertainment
- places you have visited
- social life
- work

b Work in small groups and read out your letters. Can the others guess who you are?

Student A
1.4 Exercise 5

2 You work at the same company as Student B, but in different offices. It's 5 p.m. and you've finished your work, but can't leave till 5.30. Call Student B to arrange to meet for a drink some time. You're bored and in the mood for a chat. You have some interesting gossip (decide what) that you want to share.

3 You have arranged to meet your friend, Student B, for dinner tonight, but haven't decided on a place or time. Call Student B to finalize arrangements. The line is very bad and you can't hear him/her very well.

2.1 Student A
Exercise 11

a Read about Marianne North and think about (don't write) the answer to these questions.

1 Who was she?
2 Why and where did she travel?
3 What difficulties did she face?
4 What did she achieve?

In 1860, Marianne North, who was a keen gardener and painter, travelled from her home in England to North America, Jamaica and Brazil in search of new flowers to paint. As there were no planes and cars in those days, North rode donkeys, climbed steep cliffs and crossed muddy swamps to reach the plants she wanted. She did all of this wearing the typical clothing for women of her time: a floor-length dress. Over the next fourteen years she went to six continents. While she was travelling, she produced over 1,000 oil paintings. As photography had not yet become popular, North's paintings provided botanists back in Europe with the first images of some of the world's most unusual plants.

b Use the questions to help you tell Student B about Marianne North.

c Listen to Student B telling you about Nellie Bly.

d Which of the two travellers do you think made the most important contribution to society? Why?

3.1 All students
Exercise 12

a Complete the sentences about your plans using different future tenses. Think about qualifications and experiences you might gain and contacts you might make.
1 This week …
2 This month …
3 Next year …

b Talk to other class members and find someone with at least one plan which is similar to one of yours.

3.2 Student A
Exercise 4a

3 Create 'buffer' time ⊙ ⊕ ⊗

Apparently people who are always late are actually people who are more optimistic and hopeful about life – they expect things to take less time than they actually will.

It's nice to be optimistic, but it's also quite stressful being late all the time, and you may also upset the people who have to wait for you.

So make a point of building in an extra 5–10 minutes 'buffer' time throughout the day. Your friends and colleagues will thank you for it.

4 Make your life easier ⊙ ⊕ ⊗

Although it may take a little bit of effort, there are a lot of things you can do to make your life run more smoothly. For example, think how many hours you have spent in your life sorting out light and dark laundry – why not put them into two separate bags in the first place?

And always try to get ready the things that you will need the night before.

Invest some time in getting better organized and by the end of the year you'll have saved hours of running around in a panic.

3.3 Student A
Exercise 9

assist   construct   excellent   pronounce   scene

4.1 Student A
Exercise 9

Oltu, Spain.
Powered by excess heat behind fridge.
Stores fruit and vegetables.
More space.
Fruit and vegetables fresher – four sections: cold dry, cold wet, fresh wet, dry warm, to make the perfect storage conditions for different types of fruit and vegetables.

5.1 Student A
Exercise 11

a   Choose four of the following. Write the answer in one word.
   - someone you'll never forget meeting
   - a programme you remember enjoying when you were a child
   - something you must remember to do soon
   - something you regret buying
   - something your parents made you do when you were a child

b   Look at the words your partner has written and find out what they refer to. Ask for more information.

   A *Why did you write 'motorbike'?*
   B *My wife didn't want me to get a motorbike but I got one.*
   A *What kind of motorbike is it? How often do you ride it?*

5.4 All students
Exercise 5a

A

> You all live in the same street. You are having problems with the antisocial behaviour of the occupants of one of the houses. They are constantly arguing in the street, playing loud music and having parties. There is a lot of rubbish outside their house, which is attracting rats. You are going to have a residents' meeting to try to solve the problems.

B

> You all work as part of a small team. One team member wastes a lot of work time playing games, making personal phone calls, taking long cigarette breaks and takes a lot of time off sick. As a result, the rest of the team has to work extra hours in order to meet the team's targets. He also happens to be the CEO's nephew. You're going to have a meeting to discuss a plan of action.

5.2 Student A
Exercise 10b

a   Complete the article with the infinitive or *-ing* form of the verbs in the box.

check	express	find	learn	look	observe	point
put	suffer	tell				

Do animals get bored?

It's very easy ¹_____ at caged animals and assume that, like people, they must get bored. While nobody likes the idea of animals ²_____ from boredom, it's hard ³_____ how they feel because animals have no way of verbally ⁴_____ their feelings.

Recently, however, researchers in Ontario undertook a study in the hope of ⁵_____ out whether animals do experience boredom. In the study, a group of minks were divided into two cages: one had plenty for the minks to do; the other was bare. Both groups were given the same amount of food and were offered objects to investigate. Some of the objects were appealing to the animals; others were objects such as leather gloves, that are normally frightening to minks.

You probably won't be surprised ⁶_____ that the minks in the bare cage were much more interested in ⁷_____ out the objects – including the frightening objects – in search of excitement. They also ate more food and slept for longer periods, just like bored humans do.

Researchers were keen ⁸_____ out that although the experiments don't prove that animals feel truly bored, it is interesting ⁹_____ that when animals have little to do, they are willing ¹⁰_____ themselves in risky situations in order to find excitement.

b   Read the article again and underline the key points. Try to remember the information.

c   Work with Student B and exchange the information that you learnt. What were the most surprising facts?

6.1 Student A
Exercise 8

Complete the text with *a/an, the* or – (no article). Then tell your partner about what you read.

Little Havana is a Cuban ethnic neighbourhood in ¹_____ Miami, in ²_____ United States. Its annual *Calle Ocho* street festival (part of the overall Carnaval Miami celebration), is one of ³_____ largest in ⁴_____ world, with over one million visitors. Although it is held in a Cuban area, ⁵_____ festival is really ⁶_____ celebration of all Latin American cultures. People eat food from countries such as ⁷_____ Cuba, Colombia, Nicaragua, and dance and listen to ⁸_____ music.

7.1 All students
Exercise 9

a Discuss the situations.

1 While you are revising online, you accidentally find the answers to the test you are taking tomorrow. What would you do? What do you think your partner would do? Discuss the situation with your partner. Did you guess their reply correctly?

2 While you are in your boss's office waiting for her, you see a report on her desk with your name on it. It is marked 'strictly confidential'. What would you do? What do you think your partner would do? Discuss the situation with your partner. Did you guess their reply correctly?

b Compare your ideas with another pair.

7.2 All students
Exercise 12b

No make-up, no job

A sales assistant at a top London store claims she has been forced out of her job after refusing to wear make-up to work. The shop's dress code insists on 'full make-up at all times'. When she refused, she was told that she would look better with make-up. 'I was appalled, it was insulting,' she said.

The sales assistant had been given an award for excellent customer service and met every other requirement of the dress code, but decided to resign rather than start wearing make-up.

A spokesperson from the store said, 'All our staff are subject to a dress code which they sign up to on joining the company.'

8.1 Student A
Exercise 12

a Work with another Student A. Look at the internet-connected things, which currently exist, and decide how they might be useful and who they might be useful for. Use relative clauses where you can.

This is a device that ...
It's useful for people who ...

Smart key ring

Smart rubbish bin

Smart animal tag

b Work with a Student B. Tell each other about your objects. Rank the six objects in order of 1) usefulness and 2) potential risk.

c Compare your rankings with another pair.

d In A/B pairs, think of two more things which would be useful if connected to the internet, and share your ideas with the class.

9.4 All students
Exercise 6

You are a student aged 19–20. You usually stay up late and the noise doesn't bother you. You think the new food quarter is a good idea because:
- you can go out to eat, rather than having to cook.
- it will be great to have your social life nearby.

You are a parent of two small children. You are opposed to the new food quarter because:
- the noise will keep your children awake.
- you need to get up early for work.

You are planning to open a new restaurant in the new food quarter. You are very much in favour of the plan because:
- it will bring new customers to the town.
- people who want to eat out will naturally go to the restaurant quarter and you should get more business.

You are a local councillor for the Eco Party. You are against the new food quarter because:
- it will create a lot of noise pollution, and probably more litter as well.
- lights will be left on in the street all night, wasting energy and stopping people from sleeping.
- the restaurants are mostly big chain companies, and small independent restaurants in the town may be put out of business.

You are a local councillor and the food quarter was your idea. You think it is a great idea because:
- quite a few shop units are empty because people are shopping more online. Opening restaurants in them will bring the town alive again.
- it will bring more jobs to the area.
- people will have to pay for parking, which will bring money to the council.

10.1 Student A
Exercise 6

10.1 Student A
Exercise 11

Describe your photo to Student B, then listen to the description of their photo. Find two ways in which the photos are similar and two ways in which they are different.

10.1 All students
Exercise 1a

10.2 Student A
Exercise 1b

Why is a tractor magic?
Because it can go down a road and turn into a field.

10.4 Student A
Exercise 2

10.4 Student A
Exercise 6

11.4 Student A
Exercise 6

> **Twins meet after 78 years apart**
> Twin sisters born in the UK, 1936. Separated at birth. Reunited 78 years later.
> Ann Hunt remained in Hampshire, UK. Elizabeth Hamel based in Oregon, USA.
> Ann had no idea she had a twin. Daughter made discovery while researching family history.
> Both had married man called Jim. Similar sense of humour.
> Now in *The Guinness Book of Records* – longest separated twins.
> Agreed to take part in research into lives of reunited twins.

11.2 Student A
Exercise 12

a Complete the good news story with words from the box.

> added   admitted   announced   breakthrough   claim
> explained   wounds

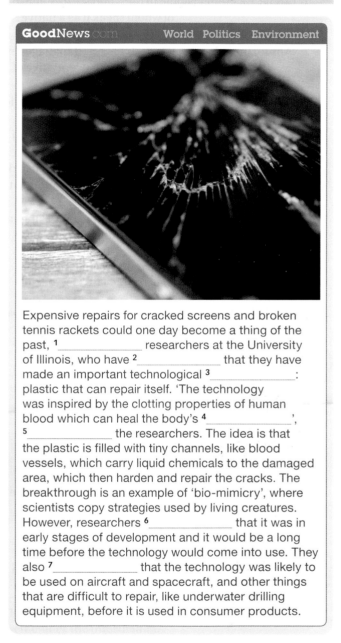

GoodNews.com   World Politics Environment

Expensive repairs for cracked screens and broken tennis rackets could one day become a thing of the past, ¹_____ researchers at the University of Illinois, who have ²_____ that they have made an important technological ³_____: plastic that can repair itself. 'The technology was inspired by the clotting properties of human blood which can heal the body's ⁴_____', ⁵_____ the researchers. The idea is that the plastic is filled with tiny channels, like blood vessels, which carry liquid chemicals to the damaged area, which then harden and repair the cracks. The breakthrough is an example of 'bio-mimicry', where scientists copy strategies used by living creatures. However, researchers ⁶_____ that it was in early stages of development and it would be a long time before the technology would come into use. They also ⁷_____ that the technology was likely to be used on aircraft and spacecraft, and other things that are difficult to repair, like underwater drilling equipment, before it is used in consumer products.

b Underline the key points of the story. Then try to remember as much as you can about the story.

c Work with Student B. Take it in turns to tell your story. Use reporting verbs where possible.

d Which do you think is the most the most inspiring/exciting/positive piece of news?

6.1 Student B
Exercise 8

Complete the text with *a/an*, *the* or – (no article). Then tell your partner about what you read.

For more than 125 years, Canadians of Icelandic ancestry have been holding an annual Icelandic Festival in ¹_____ Gimli, Manitoba. ²_____ town was founded by ³_____ Icelandic settlers in 1875 and it is home to ⁴_____ largest concentration of people of Icelandic descent outside ⁵_____ Iceland itself.

Many people dress up in ⁶_____ Viking costumes and there are Viking boats and games on ⁷_____ Lake Manitoba. Approximately 50,000 people attend ⁸_____ festival.

8.1 Student B
Exercise 12

a Work with another Student B. Look at the internet-connected things, which currently exist, and decide how they might be useful and who they might be useful for. Use relative clauses where you can.

This is a device that ...   *It's useful for people who ...*

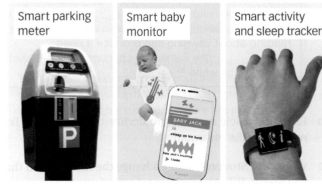

| Smart parking meter | Smart baby monitor | Smart activity and sleep tracker |

b Work with a Student A. Tell each other about your objects. Rank the six objects in order of 1) usefulness and 2) potential risk.

c Compare your rankings with another pair.

d In A/B pairs, think of two more things which would be useful if connected to the internet, and share your ideas with the class.

9.1 Student B
Exercise 5a

1 It sounds really _____ ... but actually, ...
2 ... it's much more _____ here in Norway.
3 ... the first winter is really a _____ time of year ...
4 ... indoors, nice and _____ ...
5 ... even if it's under _____ light.
6 The nights are as _____ as the days, ...

10.2 Student B
Exercise 1b

Bob has recently bought a new car and is driving back home down the freeway. Suddenly, he hears a news broadcast on the radio: 'This is breaking news! There is one car going the wrong way down the freeway. Drivers, please be aware.'

Bob looks around and says, 'One? There are hundreds!'

10.4 Student B
Exercise 2

10.4 Student B
Exercise 6

11.2 Student B
Exercise 12

a Complete the good news story with words from the box.

added   admitted   confirmed   discovery   economic
promised

GoodNews.com   World   Politics   Environment

A visitor centre has opened in Leicester, England,
which tells the extraordinary story of the
¹_____ of the skeleton of King Richard III, the
famous tyrannical subject of a play by Shakespeare
who died in battle in 1485. Last year, archaeologists
²_____ that a skeleton they had found under
a car park in the city was indeed that of the king.
Richard Buckley, the director of the project, said it had
been an honour to work on a project that has such
phenomenal global interest and ³_____ that
'the remains came close to being destroyed forever in
the 19th century, when a toilet was built directly above
the site. The foundations missed the skeleton by a few
centimetres'. Dr Buckley ⁴_____ that he had
been extremely doubtful that the skeleton would be
found and that he had ⁵_____ to 'eat his hat'
if the king was discovered. One of the photographs
on display at the exhibition shows Buckley eating
a hat-shaped cake that one of his colleagues had
baked for him. The centre is expected to attract
visitors from around the world and give the city an
⁶_____ boost.

b Underline the key points of the story. Then try to
remember as much as you can about the story.

c Work with Student A. Take turns to tell your story.
Use reporting verbs where possible.

d Which do you think is the most inspiring/exciting/positive
piece of news?

10.1 Student B
Exercise 11

Listen to Student A's
description of their
photo, then describe
your photo to Student
A. Find two ways in
which the photos
are similar and two
ways in which they
are different.

11.4 Student B
Exercise 6

Restaurant in China staffed by robots.
Restaurant in Jiangsu Province. Fifteen robots.
They cook food, carry it to the table and make conversation
(can use forty phrases).
Robots cost 50,000 Yuan ($8,100) each but don't need salary.
Can work for up to eight years.
Increasing number of hotels and restaurants in China using
robots to perform tasks.

4.1 Student C
Exercise 9a

Revolights, UK
LED bike lights.
It is important that
drivers see cyclists
at night.
Ordinary lights not very
powerful. Sometimes
people steal them.
Attach revolights
to wheels.

Grammar reference

1.1 Different question types

We form most questions by putting an auxiliary verb before the subject. For the present and past simple, we use the auxiliary *do/does/did*.

Does Sam speak French?   Where **did they** go?
Have you been to Italy?   When **are you** leaving?

Subject questions

When we are asking about the subject of a sentence, the word order is the same as in a statement and the question word replaces the subject. We do not use the auxiliary verbs *do/does/did*.

Which countries **border** Russia?
(NOT ~~Which countries do border Russia?~~)
What **happened**? (NOT ~~What did happen?~~)

- However, we use *don't/doesn't/didn't* in subject questions to ask about negative ideas.

  Who **didn't receive** the email?

Indirect questions

If we begin a question with a phrase like *Do you think* …, *Do you know* … and *Have you any idea* …, we do not put the auxiliary verb before the subject and we do not use the auxiliary verbs *do/does/did*. The word order is the same as in a statement.

Do you know where **Dariusz works**?
(NOT ~~Do you know where does Dariusz work?~~)
Have you any idea where **Alex is**?
(NOT ~~Have you any idea where is Alex?~~)

Questions with prepositions

When we are asking about the object of a preposition, the preposition usually goes at the end of the question.

What are you looking **at**?
How long did you wait **for**?

We can, however, sometimes put the preposition at the beginning of the question, but this generally sounds very formal, or rather old-fashioned.
For how long did you wait?

In this formal style we can use *whom* as an object in a question.
For **whom** did she work?

---

1 Read the text and then write the questions for the answers.

It's estimated that there are up to 7,000 different languages in the world. Languages are grouped into families that share a common ancestry. For example, English is related to German and Dutch, and they are all part of the Indo-European family of languages. Another group of Indo-European languages is the Romance languages, such as French, Spanish and Italian, which come from Latin. Nearly every language shares a broadly similar grammatical structure, even though they may not be linked in vocabulary or origin. In many parts of the world where communities were historically isolated from each other, multiple languages may have developed. Papua New Guinea, for example, where many tribes were isolated by mountain ranges, has around 830 different languages. The world's five most spoken languages, according to figures from UNESCO, are Mandarin Chinese, English, Spanish, Hindi and Arabic. Mandarin Chinese has around a billion speakers and most come from north and south-central China. The United Nations uses six official languages to conduct business: English, French, Spanish, Chinese, Russian and Arabic.

1 *IN WHAT LANGUAGES GROUPED?*
   Families that share a common ancestry. *ITALIAN*
2 *FROM WHICH LANGUAGE ARE FRANTAL SPAN*
   From Latin.
3 *WHAT EVERY LANGUAGE SHARES?*
   A similar grammatical structure.
4 *WITCH COMMUNITIE DEVELOPED 830DIY. Lang*
   Papua New Guinea.
5 *HOW MANY SPEAKERS HAS MANDRIN CHINA*
   A billion.
6 *WHERE M.L IS IN MOST USED*
   From north and south-central China.
7 *WITCH LANGUAGES ARE OFFICIAL IN USE*
   English, French, Spanish, Chinese, Russian and Arabic.

2 Rewrite the questions as indirect questions. Use the word in brackets.
1 What time will you be arriving? (know)
   DO YOU KNOW WHAT TIME…
2 Is it going to rain? (think)
   DO YOU THINK IS going to rain
3 How many languages do they speak in India? (idea)
   DO YOU HAVE ANY IDEA How many
4 What time does the museum close? (idea)
   DO YOU HAVE ANY IDEA WHAT TIME IB M

1.2 Present perfect simple and continuous

> **GR1.2)))**
>
> 1 Do you know if Peter **has called**?
> 2 My manager won't be pleased because I **haven't finished** the report yet.
> 3 **Haven't** you **sent** that email yet?
> 4 She **has been living** here for six months.
> 5 We're exhausted. We've **been driving** all night.
> 6 How long **have** you **been waiting**?

Form

- The present perfect simple is *have* + past participle.
  *I've never **been** to Africa.*
- The present perfect continuous is *have* + *been* + *-ing*.
  *It's **been raining** since 10 o'clock this morning.*

Use

We use the present perfect to connect the past and the present.

- We can often use either the present perfect simple or the present perfect continuous with *since* or *for* when something started in the past and continues now, or is repeated up to now.

  We've lived/'ve been living here for about a year now.
  I've listened/been listening to the new album a lot since I got it.

> However, if we want to put a focus on activity or on the 'doing' and to emphasize 'how long', we tend to use the present perfect continuous. And to say 'how many times' something has happened, we use the present perfect simple.
>
> *I've **been working** hard since the start of term.*
> *I've **written** three assignments since the start of term.*
>
> Also, to emphasize that something is short-term and perhaps temporary, we tend to use the present perfect continuous.
>
> *He's only **been working** here for a few weeks.*
>
> We usually use the present perfect simple and not the present perfect continuous to talk about states rather than actions with verbs like *be*, *have*, *know*, *seem*.
>
> *We've **known** each other since university.*
> *She's **had** that laptop for over ten years!*

- We usually use the present perfect continuous for actions continuing or repeated for a short time up to the present, e.g. with phrases like *all day* and *recently*.

  *I've **been sending** emails all morning.*
  *What **have** you **been doing** recently?*

- We use the present perfect simple to talk about something that happened at an unspecified time in the past, when there is present relevance or an impact on the present. We often use it to announce news.

  *I've **finished** the assignment at last!*
  ***Have** you **heard**? Tom's **lost** his job.*

1 Choose the correct options to complete the sentences.

1 A Are you ready for your exam tomorrow?
  B I hope so. I*'ve revised / 've been revising* for it all week.
2 A Do you want some lunch?
  B I*'ve eaten / 've been eating* already.
3 A *Have you waited / Have you been waiting* long?
  B No, not long. Just a few minutes.
4 A Good news! Alex*'s fixed / 's been fixing* the computer.
  B Great! I*'ve had / 've been having* enough of using my phone to send emails.
5 A How long *have you learnt / have you been learning* English?
  B For about five years.
  A And *have you been / have you been going* to the UK?
  B Yes, I*'ve been / 've been going* there a couple of times.
6 A You're late! What *have you done / have you been doing* for the last hour?
  B Sorry. We*'ve tried / 've been trying* to find my wallet. I*'ve lost / 've been losing* it.

2 Complete the text with the present perfect simple or present perfect continuous form of the verbs in brackets.

> Research ¹_____ (predict) that about half of the languages spoken on Earth today will be extinct by the end of the century. Globalization and online communication, both of which ²_____ (increase) at an unprecedented rate in recent years, are usually blamed. However, these aspects of the modern world may also help to save many of these endangered languages. For example, linguists ³_____ (develop) a smartphone app to teach Tuvan, an indigenous language spoken in Siberia and Mongolia, which is in danger of disappearing. In fact, for some time now a number of endangered languages ⁴_____ (use) social media and other online technologies to keep themselves alive. And while globalization ⁵_____ (be) responsible for a lot of negative pressures on small cultures to change, a positive effect of globalization is that through digital technology, some languages ⁶_____ (bring back) from extinction.

2.1 Past events – narrative forms

GR2.1))

1 Mary Kingsley **decided** to travel to Africa, a place she **had** always **dreamt** of visiting.

2 She **had** two missions to complete while she **was travelling** the continent.

3 Her father's friends **had warned her** of the dangers, but she **ignored** them.

4 She **encountered** animals and sights she **hadn't seen** before.

A narrative is a description of a past event. The main tenses we generally use in a narrative are the past simple, the past continuous and the past perfect.

- We use the past simple to describe the main events of the story.

  I **looked** out of the window and **saw** the Taj Mahal for the first time.

- We use the past continuous to talk about a) background actions or situations that were in progress at the time of the main events or b) two actions in progress at the same time.

  I **was waiting** for them to arrive when I heard the news.
  We **were drinking** coffee and Haruki **was doing** some shopping.

- We use the past perfect to show that a past action or situation took place a) before one of the main events or b) before the story began.

  We'**d been driving** all day and were totally exhausted.
  The hotel was not as nice as we **had expected**.

Note that we often use time words such as *when, while, before, after, as soon as* and *by the time* to connect events using the different narrative tenses.
They were both working in Paris **when** they first met.
By the time we arrived, we had got lost several times.

1 Complete the sentences with the correct past simple, past continuous or past perfect form of the verbs in brackets.

1 As Eva _was walking_ (walk) through the square, she _saw_ (see) an old friend who she _hadn't seen_ (not see) for years.

2 We _had been_ (be) at the airport for over two hours before they _told_ (tell) us that the flight was cancelled.

3 I _fell_ (fall) asleep while I _was watching_ (watch) TV last night. We _had been watching_ (watch) a really boring film.

4 Dr Brown _was walking_ (walk) out of the station when he _realized_ (realize) that he _had left_ (leave) one of his bags on the train.

5 Laurent _had lived_ (live) in three different countries by the time he _____ (be) five years old.

6 The accident _happened_ (happen) because the driver _was looking_ (look) at his mobile when the car in front of him suddenly _stopped_ (stop) and he _wasn't able_ (not be able) to brake in time.

2 Complete the text with the correct past simple, past continuous or past perfect form or the verbs in brackets.

In 2010, a British adventurer [1]_____ (become) the first person to walk the entire length of the Amazon after a 6,000-mile trek. When he finally [2]_____ (reach) the finish, he [3]_____ (walk) for nearly two-and-a-half years.

Ex-army officer Ed Stafford, 34, [4]_____ (arrive) at the finishing point, the mouth of the river in Brazil, 859 days after he [5]_____ (set off) from its source in Peru. He [6]_____ (begin) the epic journey with walking partner Luke Collyer, 37, an outdoor activities instructor. But three months after they [7]_____ (set off) on their journey, the pair [8]_____ (fall out) after an argument and Collyer [9]_____ (return) to the UK.

Along the way Stafford [10]_____ (encounter) poisonous snakes, scorpions, electric eels and piranhas. But Stafford's scariest moment was at the hands of local tribesmen. One day, Stafford [11]_____ (approach) a small village when five or six locals suddenly [12]_____ (start) running towards him with machetes, guns, and bows and arrows. The tribesmen [13]_____ (capture) Stafford, but they [14]_____ (allow) him to leave soon after. By the end of the trip, Stafford [15]_____ (endure) hundreds of wasp stings and [16]_____ (suffer) an estimated 50,000 mosquito bites.

2.2 Past perfect forms

GR2.2)))

1 I **hadn't set** the alarm, so I got to work late.
2 By the time Nicola called, Anna **had left** for the station.
3 Sara **hadn't been working** there long when she was **promoted**.
4 They**'d been painting** the room for nearly an hour when they realized **they'd been using** the wrong colour.

Form

We form the past perfect simple with *had* + past participle.

*The play **had started** when he got to the theatre.*
*They **hadn't met** before.*

We form the past perfect continuous with *had + been + -ing*.

*It **had been raining** for hours.*
*I **hadn't been feeling** well for a few days.*

> In speaking and in informal writing, we often contract had to *'d*, especially after subject pronouns.
> *We**'d** met a few times before.*
> *It**'d** been raining for days.*

Use

We use the past perfect to show that something happened before something else in the past.

- We use the past perfect simple to talk about actions that were completed before the moment we are talking about.

  *Francis **had left** when we arrived.*
  ***Had** the meeting **started** by the time you got there?*

- We use the past perfect continuous to talk about actions that continued for a period of time or were repeated over a period of time. This action may or may not have continued up to the moment we are talking about it.

  *I**'d been living** in Italy for three years when we first met.*
  *When I woke up, I saw that it **had been raining**.*

- We usually use the past perfect simple and not the past perfect continuous when we are talking about states rather than actions, with verbs like *be, have, know*.

  *We**'d known** each other for about five years before we became friends.*

> Note that we usually use the past simple to refer to the more recent action.
> *By the time we **got** to the station, the train had already left.*
> Also, we often use *already* with the past perfect to emphasize that the action happened earlier. We also often use *just* to show that the action happened a very short time before.
> *The bank had **already** closed by the time we got there.*
> *Samir had **just** left when we arrived.*

---

1 Complete the sentences using the past perfect simple form of the verbs in the box.

already/eat   not/see   sell

1 A Did you get a ticket for the concert?
  B No, they _had sold_ out by the time I tried to get one.
2 A You and Adrian talked a lot last night.
  B Yes, we _hadn't seen_ each other for months. We had a lot to talk about.
3 A Why didn't you join us for lunch?
  B Because I _had already eaten_.

2 Complete the sentences using the past perfect continuous form of the verbs in the box.

look   not wait   travel

1 A Where was this photo taken? You look exhausted.
  B I was. I _had been travelling_ for days. I'd just arrived in Nepal from the south of India, by bus.
2 A I saw you yesterday coming out of that new clothes shop.
  B That's right. I _had been looking_ at suits. I need a new one.
3 A Sorry I was so late last night.
  B Oh, don't worry about it. We _hadn't been waiting_ very long – only about ten minutes.

3 Complete the story of the Bermuda Triangle with the past perfect simple or past perfect continuous form of the verbs in brackets.

> In December 1945, five military planes were on a training flight after they **1** _had taken off_ (take off) from an airbase in Florida in the USA. The planes **2** _had been flying_ (fly) for about an hour and they **3** _had flown_ (fly) about 300 miles when without warning, the navigational instruments on all the planes, which **4** _had been working_ (work) perfectly up to that point, suddenly stopped working. Radio contact was then lost. None of the planes or crew was ever seen again. The official explanation is that before they vanished, the planes **5** _had flown_ (fly) into an area of unusual magnetic activity. It is believed that this **6** _had caused_ (cause) their compasses and other equipment to malfunction. The planes were flying over the Atlantic Ocean near Bermuda and the story of the Bermuda Triangle was born. By the mid-1970s, sixteen more planes **7** _had mysteriously disappeared_ (mysteriously/disappear) in the same area. And it appears that in almost all cases, the navigational equipment **8** _had stopped_ (stop) working just before the planes disappeared.

4.1 Passive forms

GR4.1 🔊

1 I'll have to go in by train, as my car **is being serviced** at the moment.

2 Machu Picchu **was built** sometime in the fifteenth century.

3 I couldn't get my money back because the name on the ticket **can't be changed**.

4 The machine **had been designed** to use as little energy as possible.

Form

We form the passive with *be* + past participle. Passive verbs can be in the same tenses as active verbs.

*Billions of text messages **are sent** every day.*
*Our office **is being decorated** at the moment.*
*The computer mouse **was invented** in the late 1960s.*
*I **wasn't sent** the email.*
*Our rooms **were** still **being cleaned** when we arrived.*
*Why **has** the conference **been postponed**?*
*The design **had been altered** a number of times.*

- We use the passive infinitive (*be done, be opened*, etc.) after modal verbs, *be going to* and verbs followed by *to* (*need to, have to, want to*, etc.).

  *Bags **must not be left** unattended. Bags left unattended **will be removed** and **destroyed**.*
  *The film **is going to be released** next year.*
  *The software **needs to be updated**.*

Use

We use the passive to say what happens to someone or something. We most often use the passive because we do not say who or what does the action. This is usually because this person or thing is not known, or is obvious or unimportant.

The mixture is heated to over 100°C.
Tickets can be booked in advance.
The film was nominated for six Oscars.

- If we want to say who or what does the action, we use *by*. This is usually when we are adding this information to an existing topic.

  *The modern computer mouse was invented **by** Douglas Engelbart.*

- When a verb has two objects, there are two possible passive structures.

  ***The wrong person** was sent **the email**.*
  ***The email** was sent to **the wrong person**.*

A common idiomatic use of the passive is *was/were born*.
*I **was born** in Milan.*
*Where **were** you **born**?* NOT ~~I born in Milan. Where you born?~~

---

1 Complete the extracts about some great inventors and pioneers by putting the verbs in brackets into the correct passive tense.

> James Dyson is a British industrial designer, inventor and businessman and 1 _____ (best/know) as the inventor of the Dyson vacuum cleaner. He initiated the James Dyson Award, which 2 _____ (give) each year to an upcoming young design engineer.
>
> An astronomical telescope for observing the planets 3 _____ (first/use) by the astronomer, mathematician and physicist Galileo Galilei. Later in life, Galileo 4 _____ (criticize) by the church in Italy for supporting the theory that the Earth revolved around the sun.
>
> Pablo Picasso 5 _____ (consider) by many to be the most influential painter of the twentieth century. A number of his paintings 6 _____ (recently/sell) for over $100 million.
>
> Football legend Pelé played 1,362 professional matches and 7 _____ (select) to play for his country in four World Cups. He 8 _____ (consider) by many to be the greatest footballer of all time and, in 1999, he 9 _____ (name) athlete of the century by the IOC.
>
> J. K. Rowling is a British novelist, best known as the author of the Harry Potter series. The first Harry Potter book 10 _____ (publish) in 1997 and since then around half a billion books 11 _____ (sell) worldwide. They 12 _____ (translate) into over thirty languages. It 13 _____ (think) that J. K. Rowling has done more to encourage children to read than any other author.

2 Complete the sentences about designer Sir Jonathan Ive using the correct passive form of the verbs in the box.

design	describe	develop	identify	widely/consider

1 Sir Jonathan Ive is an English designer at Apple Inc. Many of Apple's products, including the MacBook, iPod and iPad 1 _____ by Ive.

2 Ive _____ by Apple boss Steve Jobs as his 'spiritual partner at Apple.'

3 Ive's designs for Apple _____ to have a great influence on the world of design more broadly.

4 Ive believes that his best work is yet to emerge and that today he prefers to _____ as a maker of products, rather than a designer.

5 In a recent interview, he said that 'we are at the beginning of a remarkable time' and that, in the future, 'a remarkable number of products _____.'

4.2 Causative *have* and *get*

GR4.2 》

1 We**'re having the roof repaired** in the summer.
2 At this hotel, you **can get your dry-cleaning done** for free.
3 He had to **have his head shaved** when he joined the army.
4 We **had the doctor check** her blood pressure.
5 I'm getting Alex to pick my parents up** from the airport.

have/get something done

We use *have/get something done* to say that someone does something for us, usually when we have arranged it. We do not say who does the action. We generally use *get* for more informal situations.

- The structure is *have/get* + object + past participle:

  I **had my apartment valued** last week.
  We**'re having our office decorated** at the moment.
  Where **do** you **get your hair cut**?
  I**'m getting my car serviced** tomorrow.

- We also use this structure to say that something unwelcome or negative happens to us. We do not use *get* in this way.

  I**'ve had my car broken** into.
  Sarah**'s had her bike stolen**.

have someone do something/get someone to do something

We use *have/get someone (to) do something* when we arrange for somebody to do something for us. With this structure we say who does the action.

- The structures with *have* and *get* are slightly different:
  have + someone + infinitive (without *to*)

  I **had someone clean** the carpets.
  We**'re going to have some of the students teach** one of the lessons.

  get + someone + infinitive (with *to*)
  I **got someone to clean** the carpets.
  We**'re going to get some of the students to teach** one of the lessons.

1 Put the words in italics into the right order to complete the sentences.

1 I've lost my house key. *cut / need / I / to / a new one / get* as soon as I can.
   I need to get a new one cut as soon as I can.

2 How often *cut / your hair / you / do / get* ?
   Do you get your hair cut.

3 We do our weekly shopping online and *it / delivered / have / we* to the house.
   We have it delivered.

4 I can't give you a lift tomorrow I'm afraid. *'m having / I / serviced / my car* .
   I'm having serviced my car.

5 The windows are dirty. *cleaned / need / get / we / to / them* .
   We need to get cleaned them.

6 *the house / we / someone / have / clean* once a week.
   We have someone clean the house.

7 There's a problem with my computer. *'m going / look at it / I / to / someone / get / to* .
   I'm going to get someone to look at it.

2 Complete the text, using the words in the brackets in an appropriate causative structure.

Productivity in the workplace

Research has shown a moderate noise level is good for productivity and creativity in the workplace. High noise levels, especially when it's stop-start, make it difficult to process information efficiently. Anyone who has tried to work at home while their neighbours are playing loud music, speaking loudly on the phone or, even worse, [1] *their have apart* (their apartment/renovate), will have experienced this.

Research about temperatures in the workplace has shown that productivity decreases significantly and up to 40% more mistakes are made when the temperature is below 20°C. So, if you're feeling cold, [2] *have boss* (your boss/turn up) the heating, but not too much, as too high temperatures cause an even greater decrease in creativity.

When it comes to lighting, too little light and too much light can both reduce productivity. Natural light is generally preferable as long there is enough of it. So, if your workplace is too dim, you should consider [3] *have* (skylights or large windows/install).

Finally, research has shown that an untidy workspace is better for creative thinking than a tidy one. So if you are a naturally tidy person, it may be worth [4] *the coll* (a colleague/mess up) your desk from time to time.

1. having their apartment renovated
2. get your boss turn up
3. having sky ... intaled
4. having a colleagu to mess up.

5.1 Using verbs with -ing and infinitive

GR5.1))

1 I'm not sure I want the job because it **involves working** with children and animals.
2 I **don't mind not having** dessert; I'm watching my weight.
3 The staff **agreed to work** overtime, provided they were paid overtime.
4 Roger **chose not to buy** the sports car.
5 The bank **has authorized me to pay** the full amount.

When one verb follows another verb, the second verb is either the -ing form or the infinitive, with or without to.

- Verbs which are followed by the –ing form include:
  adore, hate, love, like, can't help, can't imagine, can't stand, enjoy, fancy, feel like, involve, (don't) mind, miss.
  *I don't feel like **going** out tonight.*

- Verbs which are followed by the infinitive with to include:
  agree, aim, appear, arrange, expect, hope, learn (how), offer, plan, refuse, tend, want, wish.
  *We've arranged **to meet** on the 25th.*

- Verbs which are followed by object + infinitive with to include:
  advise, allow, ask, authorize, encourage, expect, forbid, need, remind, teach (how), tell, want.
  *They encouraged **me to do it**.*
  *I'm teaching **my cousin to play** the drums.*

- *make* and *let* are followed by object + infinitive without *to*:
  *My boss never lets **me leave** work early. He always makes **us stay** until 5.30 p.m.*

- *help* is followed by object + infinitive with or without *to*:
  *Can you help **me cook** / **help me to cook** dinner?*

Some verbs are followed by -ing or the infinitive (with *to*) with a change of meaning. These include:

remember/forget

- We use *remember/forget* + -ing to talk about memories.
  *He'll never forget **meeting** Alice for the first time.*

- We use *remember/forget* + infinitive with *to* to say we do or don't do something.
  *I forgot **to post** your letter. Sorry.*

regret

- We use *regret* + -ing to express regret about something in the past.
  *I really regret **not speaking** to her when I had the chance.*

- We use *regret* + infinitive with *to* to express regret about something we are just about to do. Used in formal contexts.
  *We regret **to inform** you that the train has been cancelled.*

stop

- We use *stop* + -ing when we stop an action.
  *I stopped **playing** computer games when I was about 30.*

- We use *stop* + infinitive with *to* to give the reason why we stop another action.
  *Sorry we're late. We stopped **to get** some petrol.*

1 Choose the correct options to complete the sentences about adolescence. One item has two correct answers.

> My parents generally allowed me [1] *go / to go / going* to bed whenever I wanted as a teenager.
> They were constantly asking me [2] *turn / to turn / turning* my music down.
> They only let me [3] *stay / to stay / staying* out late at the weekend.
> They always made me [4] *help / to help / helping* them [5] *do / to do / doing* the housework once a week. I didn't mind [6] *do / to do / doing* most of it, but I hated [7] *wash up / to wash up / washing up*.
> Two things my parents taught me were [8] *be / to be / being* positive about life and [9] *take / to take / taking* every opportunity that came my way.

2 Put the verbs in brackets into the correct -ing form or the infinitive with or without *to*.
1 Oliver's offered _helping_ to help (help) me with my assignment. We've arranged _meet_ (meet) in the library after school.
2 Elisa's hoping _to study_ (study) history at university, but her family want her _to sing_ (study) law.
3 I don't remember _thing_ (take) this photo! But I can't imagine anyone else _taking_ (take) it with my phone.
4 I really don't want _to go_ (go) on the work training day. I can't stand _doing_ (do) all those team-building exercises and so on. I've tried _to find_ (find) an excuse not to go, but they say everyone has to go.
5 James has decided _not to_ apply (not apply) for a promotion. He's intending _to look_ (look) for a new job with a new company instead.

3 Complete the second sentence so the meaning is similar to the first sentence.
1 The plan is to leave at around six in the morning.
   We're aiming _to leave at around six in the morning._
2 Hua watched TV for two hours last night.
   Hua spent two hours _watching TV_
3 She won't say who broke the window.
   She's refusing _to say who broke the window_
4 We should arrive in about ten minutes.
   We expect _arriving in about ten minutes_
5 I wish I could see my friends back home.
   I really miss _seeing my friends back home_
6 Henrik wishes he hadn't said all those things last night.
   Henrik really regrets _saying all those_
7 I'm having programming lessons from Peter.
   Peter is teaching me how _programming lessons fr. P_
8 Opening the window may help if you're too hot.
   Try _to open window may help if you too hot_

6.2 Determiners and quantifiers

GR6.2 🔊

1 **Far too many people** drive to work every day. It causes terrible pollution in our cities.

2 Are you sure there are **enough chairs** for everyone?

3 **Few people** learn Latin at school these days. It's such a pity.

4 **All students** must register before Tuesday.

5 Although they trained in Glasgow, **both doctors** now have practices in Edinburgh.

Determiners are words that come before a noun or noun phrase.

much, many, some, any, a few, etc.

- We use *(too) many, (a) few, several, a number of* and *hundreds/thousands of* with countable nouns.

  There are **several multiple-occupancy houses** on my road.

- We use *(too) much, (a) little, a great deal of* and *a large quantity of* with uncountable nouns.

  Did you do **much sightseeing** in Paris?
  A little, but it was mainly work.

- We can use *a lot of, lots of, some, any* and *enough* with countable and uncountable nouns.

  There are **a lot of cafés** in the area.

Note that *few* and *little* (without *a*) emphasize less than expected or hoped for (**Few** *people passed the exam*). *A few* and *a little* are more neutral (**A few** *people passed the exam*).

All, each and every

We use *all, every,* and *each* to talk about more than two things. We can, however, sometimes use *each* to talk about just two things (e.g. **Each** *side of the coin is different*).

- *All* is used with plural nouns. You can use *all the/all (of) the* …

  All visitors must report to reception.
  All (of) the apartments have been sold.

- *Every* and *each* are used with singular nouns. You cannot use *each/every the* …

  Every apartment has been sold.

Both, either and neither

We use *both, either* and *neither* to talk about two people or things (e.g. **Both David and Andrew** speak French).

- *Both* is used with plural nouns. Before a determiner (e.g. *the, my, these*) we can use *both* or *both of*. When we use a pronoun (e.g. *them, us, you*), we must use *both of*.

  Both of them speak French. NOT ~~Both them speak French~~.

- *Either* and *neither* are used with a singular noun. We use *either … or* and *neither … nor* when there are two nouns. When we use a plural pronoun or a plural noun with a determiner such as *the, my,* or *these*, we use *either/neither of*.

  I don't like **either house**.
  Neither David nor Andrew *speaks German*.
  I don't like **either of** *the houses*. NOT ~~I don't like either the houses~~.

1 Choose the correct options to complete the sentences.

1 A I think *all / every / each* cars should be banned in city centres.

  B I agree. In fact, cars should be banned in *all / every / many* part of the city, not just the centre.

2 A You should print on *every / each / both* side of the paper – think of the environment.

  B True, but I can't be bothered to put the paper back in the printer *every / both / all* time.

3 A Have you done *all / many / much* your homework?

  B Almost, but I haven't quite finished *all / much / many* of it.

4 A Would you like a drink? Tea? Coffee?

  B *Either / Both / Any* tea *and / or / nor* coffee. I don't mind.

5 A Are you from the USA or Canada?

  B I'm from *either / neither / any*. I'm British, actually. But *either / all / both* my parents are American, so I've got their accent.

6 A I hear it was 2–2 in the game last night.

  B Yes, it was a good game. *Both / either / all* teams played really well. There were lots of chances and *both / either / any* team could have won.

7 A Would you like *some / a few / several* coffee?

  B Yes, thanks. With just *a few / a little / some* milk if you have some.

8 A Did you know *either / much / many* people at the party on Saturday?

  B Just *a little / a few / either* people from work.

2 Complete the brochure extracts with the words in the box.

all (x2) both each (x2) either a few

Offering a sense of community yet affording you total privacy, the new Riverside apartments are truly luxurious and set in peaceful and private surroundings. ¹ _all_ the apartments are finished to the same high standard and include state-of-the-art appliances. At the same time, ² _each_ apartment has its own unique colour scheme and style of furnishings. You can choose an apartment with a river view or a view of the parkland behind. ³ _both_ of the apartments have ⁴ _both_ these views. You can choose ⁵ _either_ a one-bedroom or two-bedroom option and, whichever you choose, ⁶ _all_ bedrooms have en-suite bathrooms. ⁷ _a few_ apartment also has a dedicated parking spot.

7.1 Present modal verbs

GR7.1 🔊

1 I **might leave** early this afternoon, as the meeting has been cancelled.
2 You **needn't buy** any sugar – I've given it up.
3 Children no longer **have to wear** uniforms in school, thank goodness. I hated wearing mine.
4 They **shouldn't behave** like that in class. The teacher **ought to be** much stricter with them.
5 You **can't smoke** inside the building. You **have to go** to the smoking area.
6 Do you think that young man **could be** Angela's brother? He looks very like her.

We use modal verbs (e.g. *must, can, could, might, should*) in a number of ways. We also use some non-modal verbs (e.g. *have to, need (to), ought to*) in a similar way. These uses include:

Obligation and necessity

• We use *must, mustn't* and *have to* to talk about what we are obliged to do (or obliged not to do) or what is necessary (or not necessary).

*You **must be** at work by 9 a.m.*
*We **mustn't be** late for the meeting.*

Lack of obligation and necessity

• We use *don't have to*, to talk about what we are not obliged to do. We do not use *mustn't* in this way.

*We **don't have to wear** a tie at work. It's our choice.*

• We use *don't need to* to talk about what isn't necessary. We can also use *needn't*, but this is less common.

*We **don't need to leave/needn't leave** until this afternoon.*

Advice and recommendation

• We use *should, shouldn't* and *ought to* to give advice, recommendations and suggestions. We generally do not use *ought to* in direct questions and negatives.

*Do you think I **should say** something?*
*You **ought to talk** to your boss.*

Permission and prohibition

• We use *can* to talk about what is permitted or allowed. We also use *may*, but this is less common and more formal.

*Employees **can use** the gym for free.*

• We use *can't* to talk about what is not permitted or not allowed. To give more emphasis, we can use *mustn't*.

*You **can't smoke** in public buildings.*

Possibility and probability

• We use *could, might* and *may* to talk about what is possible.

*The meeting **might be** quite interesting.*

---

1 Choose the correct options to complete the email.

> Dear Mr Bertrand,
>
> This email is to confirm that you have been entered for the ITE exam at 9.30 a.m. on 24th April.
>
> If you are unable to attend the exam on this date, you **1** *should / can* let us know as soon as possible so that we **2** *must / may* offer the place to another candidate. If you are able to attend the exam, you **3** *do not need to / shouldn't* contact us. However, if due to unforeseen circumstances you fail to attend the exam on the day, you **4** *must / might* contact us within 24 hours so that we **5** *can / must* enter you for the exam on another date at no extra cost.
>
> You **6** *must / can* bring some form of photo ID to the exam. This **7** *must / might* be an original document and not a photocopy. If you do not provide photo ID, you **8** *will not have to / will not be able to* take the exam. You also **9** *could / need to* bring your own pen and pencil. You **10** *have to / can* also take one bottle of water into the examination room.
>
> Directions for how to find the examination centre are in the attachment.
>
> Best wishes,
>
> The Examinations Office

2 Complete the conversations with appropriate modal verbs or *(don't) have to/(don't) need to/ought to*.

A Are you going to the meeting tomorrow?
B I **1**_____ go, but I'm not sure.

A You **2**_____ tell Suzy about my new job. I don't want her to know just yet.
B OK, don't worry. I won't say anything to her.

A **3**_____ (you) smoke in public buildings in England?
B No, you **4**_____. It was banned in 2007.

A Do you think I **5**_____ look for a new job? What's your advice?
B Well, you've been saying for ages you're fed up with your job. So, maybe yes, you **6**_____.

A **7**_____ (you) wear jeans at your work?
B Yes, we **8**_____ if we want to. But they **9**_____ be dark blue and smart.

A **10**_____ (you) wear a suit at your work?
B No, we **11**_____. But of course we **12**_____ if we want to. Some people do and some don't.

7.2 Past modals of deduction

GR7.2)))

1 It's awfully quiet up there. I think the children **must have fallen** asleep.

2 Do you think he **could have heard** us? He doesn't look very pleased.

3 Go back and look for it. You **might have dropped** it in the car.

We can use *may/must/can't/might/could* + *have* + past participle to make deductions about something in the past.

- We use *must have* + past participle when we feel we are certain something happened or is true.

  *James isn't in his office. He **must have** just **left**.*
  *I didn't know Olivia lived in Berlin. She **must've moved** there quite recently.*

  In speaking and informal writing we generally use *'ve* instead of the full form *have*.
  *He must**'ve** been mistaken.*
  *They might**'ve** got lost.*

- We use *can't/couldn't have* + past participle when we feel we are certain something didn't happen or wasn't true.

  *Jim wasn't at the meeting this morning, which isn't like him. He **can't have known** about it.*
  *You **couldn't have seen** Alice earlier. She's in Dubai at the moment.*

  We can sometimes use *must not have* in the same way. However, we do not usually use the contracted form ~~mustn't have~~.
  *They **must not have** read the notice.*

- We use *might/could/may have* + past participle when we think something possibly happened or was possibly true. We do not use *can have*.

  *She's late. She **might've missed** the bus.*
  *I've looked everywhere for my phone. I suppose I **could've left** it in the taxi.*
  *They don't know what to do. They **may not have understood** the instructions correctly.*

1 Complete the sentences with words from each box.

A | can't have   could have   might have   must have (x2)

B | been   finished   had   handed in   met

1 You _____ already! You only started a few minutes ago.

2 The new accounts manager Silvia looks familiar. I think we _____ before. But I'm not sure.

3 I saw Carlos driving a new sports car. He _____ a pay rise!

4 Someone _____ your keys at reception. Let's go and ask.

5 You were still in the office when the burglars broke in? You _____ terrified!

2 Complete the conversations using an appropriate modal verb of deduction and the verb in brackets.

1 A Where on earth are Olga and Bogdan? They should've been here half an hour ago.
  B Well, they _____ (get) lost. They've never been here before, I don't think.

2 A The bill is £75!
  B That can't be right. I think they _____ (overcharge) us.

3 A Erica hasn't been in touch yet.
  B Well, she _____ (not/get) your message asking her to call you.

4 A I had a drink with Andrew Horton last night.
  B That _____ (be) fun! He just seems to talk about work all the time, doesn't he?

5 A I didn't see you at the reception last night.
  B Oh, we _____ (just/miss) each other. I left quite early – at about 7.30 a.m.

3 Complete the second sentence using an appropriate modal verb of deduction so the meaning is the same.

1 Maybe she missed the bus.
  She might've missed the bus.

2 I'm sure there was some mistake.
  There _____

3 Perhaps he didn't understand.
  He _____

4 I'm sure they didn't realize.
  They _____

5 It's possible Karen went home early.
  Karen _____

8.1 Relative clauses

1 Steve Jobs, **who co-founded Apple**, was widely recognized as one of the most creative people in the computer industry.

2 He came up with ideas **that revolutionized** how we use computers.

3 The bicycle **you told me about** was on offer. I got it for €100 less than the recommended price.

4 That's the girl **whose** brother has just moved in next door to you.

There are two types of relative clause.

- An identifying relative clause identifies, classifies or defines a noun.

  *Do you know anyone **who designs websites**?*
  *Have you seen the DVD **I bought yesterday**?*

- A non-identifying relative clause gives us extra information about something already identified.

  *James Reed, **who is a Harvard professor**, will be the main speaker at the conference.*
  *He was born in Sheffield, **which is one of the UK's biggest cities**.*

- A relative clause begins with a relative pronoun. We use *who* for people and *which* for things. In an identifying relative clause, we can also often use *that* for both people and things.

  *There are many people **who/that** have never used a computer.*
  *I need some software **which/that** can edit songs.*

We can use *whom* for a person who is the object of a relative clause. However, this is often considered formal and in everyday English, we can generally use *who*.
*This is the person **whom/who** I told you about.*
We do however always use *whom* after a preposition.
*To **whom** it may concern, …*

- We use *whose* to talk about possession.

  *Is that the person **whose** party we went to last week?*

- In an identifying relative clause, we can leave out the relative pronoun when it is the object of the relative clause.

  This is the book I was telling you about. OR
  *This is the book **which** I was telling you about.*

  Is this the laptop you got for your birthday? OR
  *Is this the laptop **that** you got for your birthday?*

- In a non-identifying relative clause, we use commas to separate the clause from the rest of a sentence.

  *Steve Jobs, **who died in 2011**, was one of the founders of Apple.*

- We can generally put a preposition at the end of a relative clause or before the relative pronouns *whom* or *which*. When we put a preposition before *whom* or *which*, it can sound rather formal or old-fashioned. Note that we cannot put a preposition before *that*.

  I know the man you were waiting for.
  *I know the man **for whom** you were waiting.*

1 Choose the correct options to complete these quotations about computers and the internet.

1 'We're entering a new world in *that / which* data may be more important than software.' (Tim O'Reilly)

2 'The future lies in designing and selling computers *who / that* people don't realize are computers at all.' (Adam Osborne)

3 'Your computer needn't be the first thing – / *who* you see in the morning and the last thing you see at night.' (Simon Mainwaring)

4 'Right now, computers, *which / that* are supposed to be our servants, are oppressing us.' (Jef Raskin)

5 'The internet is not just one thing, it's a collection of things – of numerous communications networks *that / who* all speak the same digital language.' (Jim Clark)

2 Complete the text using appropriate relative pronouns.

Skype is a telecommunications application software **1**_____ specializes in providing video chat and voice calls from computers, tablets and mobile devices via the internet to other devices **2**_____ have the Skype software. Users, **3**_____ can sign up for free and **4**_____ can contact one another for free, can also send instant messages, exchange files, send video messages and create conference calls.

Skype, **5**_____ was first released in August 2003 and **6**_____ headquarters are in Luxembourg, was created by a European team of programmers and entrepreneurs, **7**_____ also helped to develop the music-sharing application Kazaa.

In September 2005, Skype was acquired for $2.6 billion by eBay, **8**_____ then sold it to Microsoft in May 2011 for $8.5 billion.

3 Rephrase the sentences as one sentence that includes a relative clause.

1 I installed that new software. It's really good.
   That new software which I installed is really good.

2 Have you seen the DVD? Danny lent it to us.
   Have you seen _____

3 We went to a restaurant last night. It was awful.
   The restaurant _____

4 I met someone the other day. He says he knows you.
   I met _____

5 Did you get the email? I sent it this morning.
   Did _____

6 There's that hotel. We stayed in it last year.
   There's the _____

7 There was a photo on your desk. Where is it?
   Where's _____

4 In which sentences in exercise **3** can we remove the relative pronoun? Cross out the relative pronoun in these sentences.

8.2 Participle clauses

> **GR8.2**))
>
> 1 **Hearing** a noise downstairs, Jason got up to investigate.
> 2 **Not speaking** any German, we missed the announcement and got on the wrong bus.
> 3 Often **referred to** as baby boomers, this generation is now coming up to retirement age.
> 4 **Having lived** abroad since she was a child, Catherine has never really felt English.

A participle clause begins with a **present participle** (e.g. *leaving, taking*) or a **past participle** (e.g. *left, taken*).

- A participle clause replaces a clause that includes a subject + verb and allows us to include information more concisely in a sentence. We generally use participles in this way in more formal contexts.

  Being from the area, Jose knew his way around.
  Because he was from the area, Jose knew his way around.

  Not knowing the area, we got lost.
  Because we didn't know the area, we got lost.

  Born in the 1960s, he is part of the baby boomer generation.
  As he was born in the 1960s, he is part of the baby boomer generation.

- We use *having* + past participle to talk about the past.
  Having missed the bus, he was again late for work.

  Having been born in 1998, she is quite likely to live in three different centuries.

- We can sometimes use a participle clause in place of a relative clause. The past participle has passive meaning and the present participle has active meaning.

  *People **born** between the early 1960s and the early 1980s are known as Generation X. (= who were born)*

  *Who's the man **standing** next to the window? (= who is standing)*

  *We stayed in a room **overlooking** the town square. (= which overlooked)*

1 Complete the text with the correct participle form of the verbs in brackets.

> 1 _____ (already/increase) significantly over the last century, average life expectancy is now increasing at a faster rate than ever. And according to scientists, some children born at the beginning of the 21st century could live until the age of 130. A recent study 2 _____ (look) at the effects of an ageing population on society predicts that life expectancy in the developed world, 3 _____ (currently/increase) at over one year per decade, will start to increase at a much quicker rate. This means that the average age at which the oldest few per cent of people die, 4 _____ (know) as the average maximum age, will soon be 120. And it is very likely that some people 5 _____ (live) today will live longer than this and reach 130.

2 Complete the second sentence so the meaning is similar to the first using a participle clause.

1 A bag which contained over a million dollars was found during the raid on the house.
_____ was found during the raid on the house.

2 We arrived late, so we were not allowed into the theatre.
_____, we were not allowed into the theatre.

3 Hamburg played really well and they won 4–1.
Hamburg played really well, _____.

4 Because I'm not American, I really don't understand American football.
_____, I really don't understand American football.

5 Joey Jones, who is called Jo-Jo by the fans, made his 500th appearance for the club on Saturday.
_____, made his 500th appearance for the club on Saturday.

6 They were woken by a noise, so they ran outside to see what had happened.
_____, they ran outside to see what had happened.

7 There were several people who were waiting for us.
There were _____.

8 Jake hadn't stayed in the hotel before, so he didn't know what to expect.
_____, Jake didn't know what to expect.

9.1 Adjectives and adverbs

Adjectives

We use adjectives to add descriptive detail to people or things. Adjectives can be used:

- before a noun.

  *We had a **fantastic** time.*

- after a noun or pronoun in questions with *to be*.

  *Was the hotel **expensive**?*

- after a verb such as *be, seem, look, feel, sound, become, get*.

  *Did the new guy seem **nice**?*
  *Hurry up – it's getting **late**!*

Not all adjectives can be used in all positions.

Adverbs

We use adverbs in a number of ways:

- We use adverbs of manner to say **how** something happens. They most commonly go after the verb and its object, but those ending in *-ly* can sometimes go before the verb.

  *The roads were icy, so we drove very **carefully**.*
  *He was driving **at over 150 kmh**.*

- We use adverbs of frequency to say **how often** something is done. They generally go before the verb, but they go after *to be*.

  *It **sometimes** rains here.*
  *The meetings are **usually** in Room 10.*

- We use adverbs of time to say *when* something happens.

  *I've **just** emailed you those photos.*

- We use adverbs of place to say *where* something happens.

  *I saw Jenny **in town** yesterday.*

> When you are mentioning both time and place, the position of the adverbs can depend on the verb. For verbs that have a strong connection with place (e.g. *go, come, arrive, leave, stay, live*) we generally put the place before the time.
> *We went **to London at the weekend**.*

- We use adverbs of degree to express the **degree or extent** of something. We use adverbs of degree with adjectives, adverbs and verbs. It goes directly before the word it is modifying.

  *It's **really** sunny today.*
  *I'm **absolutely** freezing!*

- We use some adverbs to *express an attitude* towards something.

  *I disagree with you, **actually**.*

1 Choose the correct options to complete the sentences.

1 *Amazing / Amazingly*, it didn't rain once when we were *last year in the UK / in the UK last year.*

2 It's *great really / really great* now that the days *are longer getting / are getting longer.*

3 He's been working really *hard / hardly* for his exams. In fact, he's always a *hard / hardly* worker.

4 We *usually go / go usually* to the gym *at 7 a.m. / at 7 a.m. to the gym.*

5 I *often am / am often* the *last / lastly* person to leave *work these days / these days work.*

2 Complete each extract with the correct words and phrases in the box.

1

| between the North and South Pole imaginary |
| on its axis ~~steadily~~ |

We have day and night because the Earth
1 _steadily_ rotates 2 _On its axis_
The Earth's axis is a/an 3 _imaginary_ line passing
through the centre of the Earth 4 _between the North and South Pole_

2

| ~~at other times~~ ~~other~~ sometimes visible |

At any time, half of the Earth faces the sun, giving it
daylight, and the 5 _other_ half faces away
from the sun, giving it night-time. This explains why the sun
is 6 _sometimes_ 7 _visible_ and
why we can't see it 8 _at other times_

3

| across the sky during the day ~~from east to west~~ |
| highest however ~~12 noon~~ |

9 _during the day_, the sun seems to move
10 _from east to west_ 11 _across the sky_
reaching its 12 _highest_ position at
13 _12 noon_. 14 _however_,
the sun does not move. It is the movement of the Earth
that gives this impression.

4

| ~~all the time~~ constant smoothly |

The Earth rotates 15 _all the time_, but
we don't feel any movement because it turns
16 _smoothly_ and at a/an
17 _constant_ speed.

5

| away from the sun longer different (x2) towards the sun |

The angle of the Earth means that days and nights are
18 _different_ lengths at 19 _different_
times of year. Days are 20 _longer_ where
the Earth is angled 21 _towards the sun_ and shorter in
those places which are angled 22 _away from the sun_

9.2 Past and present habits

GR9.2))

1 I never **used to** like classical music, but now I find listening to it very relaxing.

2 My grandfather **would always check** the farm animals were content before he went to bed.

3 I'**m not used to making** phone calls in Spanish. I find them a bit stressful.

4 I don't think I'**ll ever get used to taking** my tea without sugar.

Past habits

- We use *used to* + infinitive to talk about past habits, typical behaviour, states and situations that no longer exist.

  I **used to go** to bed around midnight when I was a teenager.
  We **used to live** in Manchester for a few years.

  Note that there is no final -d in negatives and questions.
  I didn't **use to** read much as a child.
  Did you **use to** do any sports?

- We also use *would* + infinitive to talk about past habits and typical behaviour. However, we do not use *would* to talk about past states.

  I **would go** to bed around midnight when I was a teenager.
  NOT ~~We would live in Manchester for a few years~~.

Present habits

- To talk about present habits, we can use the present simple tense, often with an adverb of frequency, such as *usually, often, always*, etc.

  I **usually** watch TV for an hour or so in the evening.

- We use *be used to* + -ing to say that we are, or aren't, familiar with or accustomed to something.

  I'**m used to getting** up early these days.
  I'**m not used to driving** on the left.

- We use *get used to* + -ing to say that we are becoming, or have become, familiar with or accustomed to something.

  We'**re getting used to living** here.
  I **got used to driving** on the right pretty quickly when I lived in Italy.

  We can also use *be/get used to* + noun
  I'm not used to **the weather** here.
  I'm getting used to **the food**.

1 Complete the sentences using the correct form of *used to* and the verb in brackets. In which sentences can we use *would* in place of *used to*?

1 Alaska _used to_ ~belong~ (belong) to Russia. The United States bought it from Russia in 1867.

2 There _used to be_ (be) nine planets in the solar system, but now there are only eight. Pluto was declassified as a planet in 2006.

3 **A** How did people communicate before writing was invented?

B They _used to use_ (use) images and symbols called pictograms. These developed into writing.

2 Complete the extracts using the correct form of *be/get used to* and the verbs in brackets.

1 In Sweden, on 3 September, 1967, at exactly 4.50 a.m. all cars changed from driving on the left side of the road to the right. It took some time for people to _____ (drive) on the 'wrong' side and there were quite a few accidents at first.

2 In today's globalized world, most people in cities _____ (hear) a number of different languages as they walk along the street. For example, over 250 languages are spoken in London, making it the most linguistically diverse city in the world.

3 Today, thanks to the internet, we _____ (get) a lot of the information we need almost instantly. While this is certainly a positive thing, this also means that we are _____ (not wait) for things, and are perhaps becoming more and more impatient.

3 Complete the text with the correct form of the verbs in the box.

get/used/go   ~~used/be~~   used/go   used/sleep
would/begin   would/be/follow

Sleep patterns today are not the same as they ¹ _used to be_. Today, we ² _____ to bed and sleeping for up to eight hours. However, recent research suggests that the eight-hour unbroken sleep may be unnatural. There is a great deal of historical evidence that humans ³ _____ in two distinct phases. The first phase of sleep ⁴ _____ about two hours after dusk, and this ⁵ _____ a few hours later by a waking period of one or two hours.

The change towards an unbroken night's sleep started in the late 17th century. Due to improvements in street lighting and domestic lighting, people were now able to do much more after nightfall. As a result, people soon ⁶ _____ to bed later and sleeping all night. It wasn't until the 1920s that the idea of a first and second sleep had completely disappeared.

10.1 Order of adjectives

1 It was a **lovely bright sunny day** when we arrived at the beach, but it wasn't long till the **nasty black clouds** appeared.

2 The model was wearing **shiny black leather high heels** and a **beautiful, elegant black suit**.

3 He bought an **exquisite 18th-century silver teapot** at the auction.

4 I've just thrown out my mother's **old black-and-white TV**. She had put it in the attic.

5 She was **young, charming and fearless**.

When we use more than one adjective before a noun, the adjectives are usually put in the following particular order:

opinion/value → size → age → shape → colour → origin/nationality → purpose/function/definition → material

*They live in a **beautiful old** cottage near a river.* (opinion → age)
*They're building a **big car** factory.* (size → purpose)
*We watched a **brilliant old French** film.* (opinion → age → origin/nationality)
*The library is the **big red-and-grey** building behind the car park.* (size → colour)

- To express purpose/function/definition, we often use a noun instead of an adjective (e.g. *car door*).
- We always use *and* between two colours (e.g. *red-and-grey*, *black-and-white*).
- Before nouns, we usually use commas between adjectives which give similar information, for example in descriptions: *a cheap, ill-fitting leather coat*
  – If the adjectives are short and common, we can drop the commas: *a big red fluffy teddy*

When adjectives come after a verb, rather than before a noun, the order of adjectives is more flexible and we often put an opinion adjective last. Also, we generally put *and* before the final adjective.

*I thought the film was **boring and totally predictable**.*
*The room was **small, dark and damp-smelling**.*

1 Choose the correct options to complete the sentences.

1 We had *lovely sunny / sunny lovely* weather for the whole week.

2 Mine are the *leather black / black leather* boots by the door.

3 My in-laws live in a *little lovely / lovely little* village just outside Durham.

4 I've just sold a *silver 19th-century / 19th-century silver* plate for £500.

5 The guy with *short dark / dark short* hair is Jim, and the one wearing the *football red and white / red and white football* shirt is Luke.

6 We watched a/an *old black-and-white French / black-and-white French old / French old black-and-white* film last night.

2 Rewrite the sentences to include the adjective or adjectives in brackets in the correct position. Add *and* if needed.

1 We had fantastic weather on holiday. (*sunny*)
We had fantastic sunny weather on

2 We saw lots of amazing architecture. (*16th-century*)
We saw lots of amazing 16th-century a

3 We had some homemade cake. (*chocolate / delicious*)
We had some homemade delicious choco cake

4 Jenny was wearing a dress. (*silk / long / beautiful / red-and-gold*)
Jenny was wearing a beautiful long red-and-silk dress.

3 Put the words in brackets in the right order to complete the text.

truly incredible structural achievem

The Taj Mahal is a **1**_____ (achievement / structural / truly incredible) and the most famous example of **2** 17th ce arch _____ (17th-century / architecture / Indo-Islamic) anywhere. Its **3** s_____ (beauty / visual / stunning) has a combination of arches and domes and light and shadow. The beauty of the building is enhanced by its **4**_____ (green / sub-tropical / surroundings) and the **5**_____ (sky / blue / clear) above it. The **6**_____ (white / ornate / walls), which are embedded with thousands of **7**_____ (stones / wonderful / semi-precious), constantly change colour during the day as the sun changes its position in the sky. The **8**_____ (large / chamber / domed), which houses the **9**_____ (resting / final / places) of the Emperor Shah Jahan and his wife Mumtaz Mahal, is at the centre of the building. There are four **10**_____ (round / imposing / minarets / tall) at each corner of the main chamber. The view as you walk through the **11**_____ (gate / majestic / main) which stands in the centre of the southern wall is one that a visitor will never forget.

10.2 Conditional and conjunction clauses

GR10.2 》 *[handwritten: Present simple ALWAYS TRUE]*

1 You **get** a medal **if** you **finish** in the top three. *[handwritten: O grammlik]*
2 If anyone **asks**, you **can say** you're with me.
3 If I **get** the job, I'm **going to move** to San Francisco. *[handwritten: Present tense / FUTURE]*
4 We'**ll decide** what to do **when** we **get** there.
5 Give me your number **in case** I **need** to call you.
6 I won't call you **unless** I'm **running** late.
7 I know Sam will open his present **as soon as** he **gets** it.

We can use conditional sentences to express something real or possible.

if + present tense + present tense. *[handwritten: Zero conditional]*

- To talk about something which automatically happens as a result of something else we usually use *if* + **present tense** + **present tense**. This structure is sometimes called a 'zero conditional'.

  *If the battery **is** low, the red light **flashes**.*
  *If the red light **is flashing**, it **means** that the ink is low.*
  *If you'**ve finished** the exam, you **can** leave.*

- Note that we can use any present tense, including the present continuous, present perfect and modal verbs in either clause.

if + present + future. *[handwritten: First conditional]*

- To talk about something which is possible in the future, we usually use *if* + **present** + **future**. The structure is sometimes called a 'first conditional'.

  *If you **don't listen**, you **won't know** what to do, will you?*
  *We'**re going to be** late if we **don't leave** now.*
  *If I **can**, I'**ll call** you later tonight.*
  *If it **gets** any colder, it **might** snow.*

- As above, note that we can use any present tense in the *if*-clause and any future form (*going to, will,* future continuous, future perfect) or a modal verb in the main clause.

> We can put the *if*-clause and the main clause in either order. When the *if*-clause is first, it is followed by a comma. When it is at the end, there is no comma.
> *If you're late, you'll get into trouble.*
> *You'll get into trouble if you're late.*

- Conjunctions such as *unless, in case* and *as long as* and time conjunctions such as *when, as soon as, while, before,* etc. are followed by a present tense.

  *You should take your umbrella **in case** it **rains**.*
  ***Unless** I **call** you, I'll meet you at 6.30 p.m.*
  *I'll let you know **as soon as** I'**ve heard** any news.*
  *I'll be waiting for you **when** you **arrive**.*

[handwritten: Conjection woird]

1 Choose the correct options to complete the sentences.

1 If they *don't sell / won't sell* many tickets, the show *is cancelled / will be cancelled*.
2 It's an open-air show, but if *it's raining / will be raining*, they *have / 'll have* it inside the hall.
3 In football, if you *win / will win* a game, you *get / 'll get* three points and if you draw, you *get / will get* one point.
4 I think the band *does / will do* an encore if people *cheer / will cheer* loudly enough.
5 I *get / 'll get* you a ticket for the concert if you *want / 'll want* me to.
6 *Is there / Will there be* a charge if I *pay / will pay* by credit card?
7 I *come / might come* to the concert with you if that*'s / will be* OK.
8 If I*'m running / run* late, I *call / 'll call* to let you know.

2 Complete the sentences with the words in the box. For each set there is one extra option.

1 | as soon as   in case   while

A I'm afraid Mr James is running a little late. He'll be with you ___as soon as___ his meeting finishes.
B That's OK. I'll do a bit of work ___while___ I'm waiting.

2 | as long as   as soon as   in case   once

A Hurry up! They won't let us in the theatre ___once___ the play has started. And it starts in twenty minutes.
B OK. I'll be ready to leave ___as soon as___ I've sent these emails.
A OK, ___in case___ it doesn't take too long. *[handwritten: long as]*

3 | as long as   in case   unless   when

A I'll take the satnav ___in case___ there's a problem with the traffic and I have to take a different route.
B Good idea. I think you'll be fine ___unless___ there's an accident or something. Anyway, let me know ___when___ you arrive.

4 | as long as   as soon as   unless

A I'll lend you the money ___as long as___ you can pay me back before next week.
B No problem. I'll pay you back ___as soon as___ I can get to a cash machine.

11.1 Reported speech

GR11.1 》)

1 'I arrived at 6.00 p.m.'
   He told me **he'd arrived** at 6.00 p.m.

2 'Have you always lived in Edinburgh?'
   He **asked** me if **I'd always lived** in Edinburgh.

3 'When did you learn to drive?'
   She wanted to know when I'd **learnt** to drive.

We can report what someone says using the verbs *say* and *tell*. We use an indirect object, e.g. *me, them,* after *tell* and we do not use an indirect object after *say.*

He **said** he never watched TV. He **told me** he never watched TV.

- We can use *that* after the reporting verbs.

  He said he was hungry. or *He said that he was hungry.*

- When we are reporting, we generally use the past tense of the reporting verb, e.g. *said/told,* and we usually change the verb by moving it back one tense into the past. For example:
  present tense ➔ past tense
  past tense/present perfect ➔ past perfect
  will/can/must ➔ *would/could/had to*

  We've been shopping. ➔ *He said they'd been shopping.*
  I'll be there at 6.30 p.m. ➔ *He told us he'd be there at 6.30 p.m.*

- However, if what the person says is still true, relevant or important, we often do not change the tense.

  I don't like action films. ➔ *She said she doesn't like action films.*

- We can also use the reporting verb in the present. When the reporting verb is present, we don't change the tense.

  I'm going to be a bit late. ➔ *Sarah says that she's going to be a bit late.*

- We sometimes need to change time references
  (e.g. *yesterday* ➔ *the day before/the previous day, tomorrow* ➔ *the next day/the following day, next week* ➔ *the week after*).

  I spoke to Alex yesterday. ➔ *He said he'd spoken to Alex the previous day.*

Reported questions

We can report questions using verbs such as *ask, want to know* and *wonder.* We generally use an indirect object after *ask.*

They wanted to know how old I was.
Paula was wondering why you left the party so early.

Note that the word order is different from direct questions; the subject comes before the verb and we do not use the auxiliary verb *do.*

- The rules described above for changing or not changing the tense of the reporting verb and the words being reported are generally the same for reporting questions.

  I asked Oliver why he hadn't replied to my email.
  Eva asked me what time the film starts.
  Sam wants to know what's for dinner.

- We use *if* or *whether* to report yes/no questions.

  Michelle asked us if she could come with us to the cinema.

1 Report the comments and questions. Add an indirect object where necessary and use an appropriate tense for the words you report.

   1 'I'm from Washington.'
      She said _____

   2 'There are too many commercial breaks on TV.'
      He says _____

   3 'I'm going to Moscow next week.'
      Harold told _____

   4 'My plane has been delayed.'
      Jasmina says _____

   5 'I'll call you later.'
      Vera says _____

   6 'I'm going to be late for work tomorrow.'
      Karen said _____

   7 'What time does the film start?'
      Charles wants _____

   8 'Will you help me later?'
      Milos asked _____

   9 'How long have you worked here?'
      She wanted _____

   10 'What are you going to say to him?'
      Renata is asking _____

2 Report these questions and answers from an interview with actor James Jones. Add an indirect object and change the tense of the words you report.

1 Where are you from?
She asked _____
I'm originally from Texas.
He said _____
2 Have you always wanted to be an actor?
She asked _____
Yes. For as long as I can remember.
He said _____
3 Is acting your only job?
She wanted _____
I've been a full-time actor for about five years now.
He told _____
4 What kind of roles do you prefer?
She wondered _____
I'm happy to play all different kinds of roles.
He said _____
5 Where do you see yourself in five years' time?
She wondered _____
In five years' time, I'll be a household name.
He said _____

11.2 Reporting verbs

GR11.2)))

1 'I ate the last biscuit.'
  He **admitted that** he'd eaten the last biscuit.

2 'The course is full.'
  She **informed us that** the course was full.

3 'Don't touch it – it's hot!'
  He **warned me not to touch** it.

4 'I won't tidy my room.'
  She **refused to tidy** her room.

5 'I didn't lose the key.'
  He **denied losing** the key.

6 I'm sorry I broke the glass.'
  She **apologized for breaking** the glass.

7 'The accident was Molly's fault.'
  He **blamed Molly for causing** the accident.

We can use reporting verbs to report the nature or attitude of what was said, e.g. *He promised …, She offered …, He suggested …* Reporting verbs are followed by a number of different structures.

• verb + (*that*) + clause: *add, admit, argue, claim, complain, deny, explain, mention, predict, promise, suggest, tell, think, warn*
  Helen promised (that) she wouldn't be late.

• verb + person + (*that*) + clause: *assure, convince, inform, promise, reassure, remind, warn*
  She reassured me that everything was OK.

When we use a reporting verb followed by a (*that*) clause, we usually change the verb by moving it back one tense.
The room is too small. → *He complained that the room **was** too small.*
*I think they'**ll win** 2–0.* → *He predicted they'**d win** 2–0.*

• verb + *to* + infinitive: *agree, ask, demand, offer, promise, refuse, threaten*
  *Jana **agreed to** come with us.*

• verb + person + *to* + infinitive: *advise, convince, encourage, invite, order, persuade, remind, tell, warn*
  *Xavier **advised me** to talk to my boss.*

• verb + (preposition) + *-ing*: *admit, apologize for, deny, insist on, suggest*
  *He **didn't apologize for** be**ing** late.*

• verb + person + preposition + *-ing*: *accuse … of, blame … for, congratulate … on/for, praise … for, thank … for, warn … against*
  *Did **you** thank Claire **for helping you**?*

• Note that some verbs can be followed by more than one structure.
  He admitted that he had broken the window. OR
  He admitted breaking the window.

  Erica promised she would be on time. OR
  Erica promised to be on time.

1 Complete the news extracts using the past tense of the reporting verbs in the box.

persuade   reassure   remind   suggest

1 The prime minister's advisors _____ holding the election in May.
2 Gareth's parents _____ him to hand himself in to the police.
3 The hospital _____ Miss Williams that she would make a full recovery.
4 The judge _____ the witness that lying in court was an offence.

admit   insist   predict   warn

5 The court was told that Harry Palmer _____ on paying for everything.
6 Susan Evans _____ stealing the coat and was fined £500.
7 Ashley _____ that Rotherham United would win 2–0.
8 The minister _____ Mr Jones against saying too much.

2 Report the comments, beginning with the words given.
  1 'Don't forget to watch the news this evening.'
    She reminded _____
  2 'I'll pay you back tomorrow. I promise.'
    He promised _____
  3 'I'm really sorry I missed the meeting.'
    Maya apologized _____
  4 'I'm not going to do it!'
    Magda refused _____
  5 'I can have a look at your computer if you like.'
    Diana has offered _____
  6 'Your tickets will arrive in time. Don't worry.'
    She assured _____
  7 'You should do it. You won't regret it.'
    Dina tried to convince _____
  8 'I didn't tell anyone about it.'
    Yvette completely denies _____

3 Report these famous quotations. Change the tense of the verbs.
  1 'I never turn on the news over the weekend.'
    US entertainer Rush Limbaugh claimed _____
  2 'There's no such thing as good news in America.'
    Pop singer Morrissey once suggested _____
  3 'I never think about the future.'
    Albert Einstein once admitted _____

12.1 Conditional sentences to talk about unreal situations

GR12.1)))

1 If we **had** a car, we **would drive** there.
2 You **could apply** for the job **if** you **had** the qualifications.
3 If he'**d left** on time, he **wouldn't have missed** the flight. *lll conditional*
4 They **could have won** the match **if** the referee **hadn't given** the last penalty to the opposition.

We can use conditional sentences to express something unreal, imaginary or hypothetical and to say how things could be or could have been different.

- To talk about an unreal or improbable situation in the present and future we use *if + past tense + would/might/could + infinitive*. This structure is sometimes called a 'second conditional'.

  *If we **had** more time, we'**d stay** a bit longer.*
  *I'**d email** you if the internet **was working**.*

  We can generally use *was* or *were* with *I/he/she/it* in an *if*-clause.
  *If I **was/were** younger, I'd learn to surf.*
  However, we only use *were* in the phrase *If I were you, …*
  *If I **were you**, I'd talk to your parents.* NOT ~~If I was you, I'd …~~

- To talk about an unreal situation in the past, we use *if + past perfect + would have + past participle*. This structure is sometimes called a 'third conditional'.

  *I'm sure if he'**d known** about the meeting, he **would've gone** to it.*
  *I **would've said** hello if I'**d seen** you.*

- We can connect the past and the present by mixing the second and third conditionals. These structures are sometimes called 'mixed conditional'.

- To talk about an unreal situation in the past which has a present result, we use *if + past perfect + would + infinitive*.

  *If you'**d had** some breakfast, you **wouldn't be** so hungry now.*

- To talk about the possible past result of an unreal situation in the present, we use *if + past tense + would have + past participle*.

  *If I had more money, I **would have** bought it.*

- We can use other modal verbs, particularly *could* and *might* in the main clause.

  *If we'd got up earlier, we **might not have missed** the bus.*
  *We **could go** for a walk if it wasn't raining.*
  *If you'd been listening, you **might know** what to do.*

  Note that we often contract *would* and *had* to '*d* and we often contract *have* to '*ve*. Also note that the *if*-clause and the main clause can go in either order.
  *If I had more money, I'**d get** a bigger apartment.*
  *I **would've told** you if I'**d known**.*

  Where the *if*-clause is first, we need a comma. If it is second in the sentence, we do not use a comma.
  If I knew the answers, I would tell you.
  I would tell you if I knew the answer.

1 Put the verbs in brackets into the correct tense or form.

1 **A** If we _didn't have_ (not/have) children, we _would have_ (have) a lot more free time. //
  B You _would have_ (have) a lot more money as well!

2 **A** Where _would you live_ (you/live) if you _could you live_ (can/live) anywhere?
  B I'm not sure, but ideally it _would be_ (be) somewhere by the sea.

3 **A** We called at your house earlier, but you weren't at home.
  B That's a shame. If I _had known_ (know) you were coming, I _would stayed_ (stay) in. //

4 **A** How many children do you think you'll have?
  B Well, if I _could choose_ (can/choose), I _would have_ (have) two girls and a boy.

5 **A** Did you hear that Chris failed his final exams?
  B Well, if he _had spend_ (spend) more time studying instead of partying, I'm sure he _would have passed_ (pass) them. ///

6 **A** A colleague at work is really getting on my nerves. What _would you do_ (you/do) if you _were_ (be) in my position?
  B If I _were_ (be) you, I _would tell_ (talk) to him or her about it.

2 For each situation, write a conditional sentence to say how the situation could be or could have been different.

1 I missed the bus, so I was late for work.
  If I hadn't missed the bus, I wouldn't have been late for work.

2 You're feeling tired now because you went to bed late last night. _IF YOU HADN'T GONE TO BE LATE LAST NIGHT, YOU WOULD'T_

3 Alina isn't here tomorrow, so she can't help us.

4 We can't get in the house because you lost the key!

5 Gabby didn't go to the meeting because she didn't know about it.

6 You weren't listening, so you don't know what to do.

7 I don't have your number, so I couldn't call you last night.

8 The internet isn't working, so I can't send them the photos.

12.2 *wish* and *if only*

GR12.2))

1 I wish I **could run** faster.

2 She wishes she **had** a car; then she wouldn't have to use the bus.

3 I wish I **hadn't said** anything – now you're angry.

4 The students **wish their lecturers would give** them fewer assignments.

5 If only she **hadn't taken** the diamond ring, then she **wouldn't have been arrested**.

We use *wish* to say that we want things to be different from how they are or were.

- To talk about the present, we use *wish* + past tense.

  *She wishes she **was** a bit older.*
  *I wish I **could** play a musical instrument.*
  *I wish it **wasn't raining**.*

- To express regrets about the past, we use *wish* + past perfect.

  *I wish I **hadn't eaten** so much.*
  *I think Jim wishes he'**d studied** a bit more for the exam.*

- We use *wish* + person/thing + *would* to talk about things we want to happen or change in the future. We often use this structure to express annoyance or dissatisfaction.

  *I **wish it would stop** raining.*
  *I think he **wishes his boss would be** a bit more flexible.*

- Note that *would* cannot have the same subject and object. NOT *I wish I would be richer.*

- We can use *if only* instead of *wish* in all these situations. *If only* is generally more emphatic than *wish*.

  ***If only** we had more time.*
  ***If only** I had spoken to him!*

- We can also sometimes include a second clause after *if only*.

  ***If only** it wasn't raining, **we could go for a walk**.*

1 Choose the correct options to complete the wishes and regrets.

1 I imagine they wish they *had / would have* a bigger house.

2 I wish I *had / would have* the courage to ask Rachel out on a date.

3 I wish it *stopped / would stop* raining. I want to go outside.

4 I hate my job. If only I *chose / had chosen* a different career path.

5 I wish my sister *settled down / would settle down* and have kids soon.

6 If only I *didn't turn down / hadn't turned down* that job offer last week.

2 Jane is in a boring lecture at university. Write what she is thinking using *I wish* and the words given.

1 the lecture/be/more interesting

_____

2 I/not be/here

_____

3 I/can/go home

_____

4 the lecturer/involve/the students more

_____

5 I/enjoy/being a student

_____

6 I/not choose/to study this subject

_____

3 Rephrase the sentences so the meaning is similar, using the word(s) in italics.

1 She regrets not speaking to Michael last night. (*wish*)

_____

2 It's a real shame that you can't come with us. (*if only*)

_____

3 It would be great to have a bit more money. (*wish*)

_____

4 I imagine Karl regrets saying all those things. (*wish*)

_____

5 It's a pity we don't know his address. (*if only*)

_____

6 I really want him to call me. (*wish*)

_____

Audioscripts

Unit 1 Communication

1.1))

Communication between people from different cultures involves far more than simply understanding each other's words. For communication to be successful, we need to be aware of others' rules of conversation, like how far apart we should stand, which topics are acceptable to talk about, or whether it's OK to interrupt a person or to be silent. Getting these things wrong can lead to misunderstandings or even cause offence.

So let's look first at the question of personal space. How far apart do you stand during conversation? Well, this varies widely between cultures. In North America, the average distance between two people, who are not close friends, who are engaged in casual conversation, is 45 centimetres. But in Western Europe, this distance is a little less – 36–40 centimetres. In Japan, a respectful distance is considered to be around 90 centimetres, whereas in the Middle East a distance of 20–30 centimetres is the norm. You need to get these distances right. Stand too close and you might make someone feel awkward; too far away and you will give the impression of being distant and unfriendly.

Another important aspect of cross-cultural communication is the number of silences in a conversation. Most Europeans and North Americans avoid long silences. For them, silence suggests something negative – it can mean that you feel uncomfortable, or shy, or angry or that you are not interested in the topic. But in some East Asian countries, for example, silences are perfectly acceptable. In fact, silence is seen as a positive thing. It shows respect ... it shows you are listening.

Voice volume also differs greatly between cultures. People from South America, for example, or southern Europe, tend to speak more loudly than people from northern Europe. It is easy, for example, to think a group of people from Brazil are having an argument when in fact they are just having an enthusiastic discussion. In some parts of East Asia, on the other hand, people speak more softly than either Europeans or Americans.

Another key to successful communication between cultures is knowing which topics are appropriate to discuss. Different cultures have different rules, and it's easy to put your foot in it by asking the wrong questions, particularly when making small talk with people you don't know well. In many countries, like China, for instance, it's very normal to ask somebody how old they are, or how much they earn. But a person from the UK, for example, wouldn't feel at ease with these questions. Questions about somebody's political views are also not appropriate. Safer topics of conversation would include questions about where they are from or about sport. And of course the weather is also a favourite.

And finally, I'd like to talk about gestures – the signs we make with our hands. Although many gestures have the same meaning the world over, there are a few common ones which can offend people in some countries. The 'come here' sign made by curling your finger towards you is extremely rude in many countries, including Slovakia and many parts of South East Asia. In the Philippines, you can actually be arrested for making this gesture! And then there's the 'thumbs up' sign, which in many parts of the world means 'Well done!' or 'I like it'. However, in some countries, like Greece and countries in the Middle East, it can cause great offence.

1.2))

I've been working very hard lately.
Have you been waiting long?
How long have you been here?

1.3))

1   Have you been practising your English much this week?
2   Have you been having a good day?
3   Have you been watching any good TV programmes recently?
4   Have you been spending much time outdoors lately?
5   Have you been going out much in the evenings?

1.4))

How many whistling sounds are you familiar with? There are quite a few in common use, aren't there? We whistle when we want to get someone's attention ...

We whistle to show our appreciation at a concert, for example ...

And then there's this whistle ...

But did you know that on the Spanish island of La Gomera there is an entire whistling language? This language has existed for thousands of years and is still spoken ... I mean, whistled ... today.

Listen to this ...

Extraordinary, isn't it? Have you any idea what the conversation was about? Well, according to the translation I have here, they were discussing a party and one was asking the other to go and get a musical instrument to bring to it ...

The language is called Silbo Gomero – the whistling language of the island of La Gomera.

Last year, I decided to go to La Gomera to find out for myself ...

1.5))

Conversation 1

A   Hello, am I speaking to Mrs Helen Carter?
B   Er yes, speaking.
A   How are you today, Mrs Carter?
B   Fine ... erm ... Who am I speaking to?
A   I'm calling from The Northern Energy Company, and I would like to inform you of a superb electricity deal that we are offering ...
B   Er, no, can you just stop there, please? I'm not interested.

A   You're not interested in saving money on your energy bills, Mrs Carter?
B   No, I'm not interested in buying anything from you. I don't take sales calls. So would you remove my details from your database, please? Thank you. Goodbye.

Conversation 2

A   ... Well, Joe, it's been great talking to you. Thanks a lot for calling.
B   My pleasure. It's been good to hear all your news.
A   Yeah ... No ... Absolutely ... But listen, I'd better get off the phone ... I'm still at the office and I've got a ton of work to do.
B   Yes, yes. I'll let you get on. OK. Listen, before you go ... tell me, do you ever see anything of Clive?
A   Clive? Yes, yes, I see him occasionally. He's fine. Anyway, ...
B   We used to have such a laugh together, me and Clive. Never hear anything from him these days ...
A   No, well, you know, he's pretty busy ... Anyway, listen Joe, I've really got to get off the phone. I'll give you a call soon. We'll get together for a drink or something.
B   Yes, that would be good. We could go to that place down by the river, er ... what's it called?
A   Yeah, yeah, we'll work that out when we speak. OK. Cheers, Joe. I'll be in touch. Bye.

Conversation 3

A   Hello, is that Sarah Fox?
B   Yes, it is.
A   Oh hello, this is Steve from the garage. Just calling to let you know that we've had a look at the car and we estimate that it's going to cost £550 to repair the engine. So if you'd like us to go ahead with it, could you ...
B   Sorry, Steve ... just bear with me a moment ... Rosie, let Thomas play with the balloon, please ... What? Yes, I know it's your special birthday balloon, but I told you you've got to share.
Sorry about that. Yes, 550, did you say? ... Erm ... well, yes, that's more than I'd hoped, but if it needs to be done, then ... Sorry. Oi! Children! Stop that! ... Steve, look, I'm going to have to go and deal with this. I'm afraid you've caught me at a bad time. I'll call you back in a few minutes.
A   That's no problem at all. I'll wait to hear from you.

Conversation 4

Hi Rafa, thanks for getting back to me. Yes, I was just calling to talk through the agenda for the management training day next Tuesday. Yes, that's right. Yes ... Yes ... Yes ... Sorry? ... Sorry, it's just that I can't hear you very well. I'm working from home today, and the coverage isn't too good here ... Yes ... Sorry, Rafa, you're breaking up again. Could you just say that again? ... Yes, yes, I'll contact the managers about that ... Yes ... Rafa, sorry ... I'm losing you again. Could you do me a favour? Could you call me back on my landline? You've got my number, haven't you? Cheers.

1.6))）
1 I don't take sales calls.
2 Would you remove my name from your database?
3 It's been great talking to you.
4 I'd better get off the phone.
5 I'll let you get on.
6 I've got a ton of work to do.
7 I won't take up any more of your time.
8 Just bear with me a moment.
9 I'm afraid you've caught me at a bad time.
10 Could you just hold the line?
11 The coverage isn't too good here.
12 You're breaking up…
13 I'm losing you again.
14 Could you call me back on my landline?

1.7))）
1 If an email is confidential, should it be shared with other people?
2 Do you cross out a word with a rubber?
3 Do stationery shops sell envelopes?
4 Can you cc somebody into a handwritten letter?
5 Does an emoticon show your feelings?
6 Is an instant message the same as a text message?
7 Can you keep an inbox on your desk?
8 Do you put a postage stamp inside an envelope?

Unit 2 Escape

2.1))）
Conversation 1
A You know what I'd love to do one day?
B What's that?
A I'd love to go to Peru and walk the Inca Trail. You know, the path that takes you from the Amazon Rainforest through the Andes Mountains to Machu Picchu, 'the lost city of the Incas'.
B Ah, I'd love to go to Machu Picchu. Apparently, the views are absolutely stunning. Not sure about the trek, though. Sounds like hard work to me – trekking up and down mountains, with all your baggage. You'd have to be really fit.
A That's all part of the challenge …
B Mmm. And then you'd have to camp in tents, with very basic facilities. It's not really my thing … I'm not very good at roughing it. I like life's little luxuries.
A Oh, come on … You need to be more adventurous. Step out of your comfort zone. It's really good for you sometimes, you know.
B Yes, I guess you're right.
Conversation 2
A If you could go anywhere in the world, where would you go?
B Mmm … Antarctica.
A Antarctica?
B Yes … Antarctica … because … well, because it's so different from anywhere else in the world. I'd like to experience being in a completely remote environment with nothing else around … I'd like to see the penguins in their natural habitat. I'd like to see the icebergs in all their different shapes and colours.
A Brrrr!
B What? Wouldn't you like to see an iceberg with your own eyes? It would be a breathtaking sight.

A Yes, of course I would … It's just … the cold weather that doesn't appeal to me that much.
B Don't be silly – you'd be wearing a special thick coat. It wouldn't be that bad. And anyway, it'd be really interesting to experience the extreme conditions the Antarctic explorers had to face.
A Yes, it would. For a minute …

Conversation 3
A A place I'd really like to go to on holiday this year is Istanbul. Have you ever been?
B To Istanbul? No … but it sounds wonderful, with all those magnificent historic buildings, like the Blue Mosque and the royal palaces.
A Yeah, I'd love to see those … and it would be great just to wander around the old streets and soak up the atmosphere …
B Ah … that sounds brilliant. Wasn't Istanbul a European City of Culture a few years ago?
A Yes, it was. So it's become quite a popular destination now. I imagine it gets quite touristy in the summer, so it's probably best to go out of season.
B Yeah, true. So will you learn some Turkish before you go?
A I'm sure I'll learn a few phrases. But actually, I quite like the idea of going somewhere I don't speak the language. It kind of adds to the adventure, if you know what I mean …
B Ha, ha, I do … Well, if you need a travelling companion, let me know!

2.2))）
Henry Box Brown was born a slave in 1816 in Virginia. From the age of fifteen, he worked at a tobacco factory. His owner, a man named William Barret, treated him kindly in comparison to some slave owners. Brown received payment for the work he did and, unlike other slaves, he didn't suffer physical abuse. But his was a different kind of suffering:

In 1836, when Brown was in his early twenties, he fell in love with a young woman, named Nancy, who was owned by a different master. In order to get married, they needed both masters' agreement. Both gave their permission and Nancy's master also agreed that he wouldn't sell her to another owner, as this might lead to the couple's separation.

The two got married and lived in their own house. They had three children together and were expecting another, when one day Nancy's master broke his promise and she and the children were sold to a slave-owner in North Carolina.

Brown asked his master, Barret, to help, but was told 'you can get another wife'. The next morning, Nancy and the children were marched through the streets with 350 other slaves. Brown held his wife's hand for four miles until the slaves were herded into wagons for their journey to North Carolina. They never saw each other again.

This terrible loss made Brown determined to escape slavery, and one day he came up with the idea of mailing himself to freedom in a box. With the assistance of two friends, he contacted the anti-slavery organization in Philadelphia and made arrangements for them to receive the package. He asked another friend, who was a carpenter, to build him a box that was three feet long, two and a half feet deep and two feet in width. On the outside, Brown painted 'right side up with care' and squeezed himself inside.

Brown had water in the box and breathing holes, but the 27-hour journey, during which he travelled on three trains, two boats and three road wagons, was horrendous. At one point, he almost died after he had been sitting in an upside down position for several hours.

Amazingly, he survived the journey; and after he arrived in Philadelphia, he was free. He became a member of the anti-slavery movement. Also, because of the extraordinary courage and determination that he had shown, his story became famous. And the box itself became a symbol of the injustice of slavery.

2.3))）
anxious bitter delighted disorientated down furious hurt miserable petrified puzzled relieved satisfied tense terrified

2.4))）
P Hello, and welcome to the programme. This morning, we're talking about one of the hottest new trends in travel – learning holidays. Ilana Canter is senior editor of the travel magazine *Escape*, and she's here to give us her selection of the most interesting and unusual learning holidays that are on offer today. Welcome, Ilana.
I Thanks for having me.
P So some people, when you say the words 'learning holiday', they're going to think 'boring' … but that's not the case at all, is it?
I Ha, ha, no, not at all. They're not boring at all. Nowadays, there are so many interesting learning vacations that you can go on …

2.6))）
1 castle
2 arm
3 rocket
4 learning
5 matter
6 got
7 falconry

2.7))）
1 No, not at all.
2 You've got a chance to train.
3 What an incredible opportunity!
4 Have you ever wanted to go to space camp?
5 I'm more of a water person.

2.8))）
1 You get a little certificate.
2 One of the hottest new trends in travel.
3 Where did you learn to surf?
4 I read about it on the internet.

2.9))）
I … like, for example, last fall I did a falconry course at Ashford Castle in Ireland. It's so incredible; you're walking through the grounds of this historic castle, which dates all the way back to 1228, with this huge bird perched on your arm.
P Amazing!
I Yeah, it's magical. You feel like you're in a Harry Potter film.
P Yeah … But isn't it a bit dangerous?
I No, not dangerous at all. The falcons are well-trained, so it's super, super safe.
P I love that one. So, what's next on your list of recommendations?
I Well, if you ever wanted to go to space camp as a child but never got the chance, then this one might be for you. The Adult Space Academy at the US Space and Rocket Centre in Alabama, USA, holds three-day courses

that give you a taste of what it's like to train as an astronaut. So you're taught how to launch and land a space shuttle and, using flight simulator machines, you get to experience the conditions of low gravity and you get to have a go at 'moon-walking'.

P Sounds amazing.

I Yeah, it does, right? And the cost of the course includes accommodation in the space centre, where you share small rooms with up to seven people, so you really get the full astronaut experience.

P Sounds wonderful ... So, tell us about the last learning holiday on your list.

I Well, this one is really quite unusual – in Rome, Italy, there's actually a gladiator school.

P Seriously?

I I know, crazy, isn't it? You've got a chance to train and experience what it was like to fight as a gladiator. It's kind of like a martial arts workout. You engage in hand-to-hand combat with your instructors and they give you the full Roman outfit, so you're wearing the tunic, the belt, the sandals ... The instructors are from 'The Historic Group of Rome', and at the end you get a little certificate saying that you've completed your course.

P Thank you so much for coming in, Ilana. These sound like fun and rewarding learning holidays.

2.10))⟩
Conversation 1: Jamie

A Have I ever told you about the camping experience we had in France?

B Don't think so, no.

A No? OK, well this happened about ... ten years ago, when the kids were really young. We'd been camping in the south of France, in our camper van, and we were on our way home. We'd booked into a campsite outside Paris – you know, just for one night, to break up the long journey.

B Uh huh.

A Anyway, we reached the suburbs of Paris at about three in the morning. The kids were fast asleep in the back. I was driving and Liz was reading the map – this was in the days before satnav, of course. But Liz was doing a rubbish job of navigating and we kept on getting lost.

B I'm not surprised. At three in the morning!

A Yeah, well, anyway, I was getting more and more annoyed with her, and in the end she threw the map at me and said 'OK, you find the campsite' ... and then fell asleep!

B Ha, ha, ah!

A So, I carried on driving for a bit, but I was feeling pretty exhausted. So when I saw a big empty car park by the side of the road, I thought: 'Forget the campsite. I'll just park here for the night.' Anyway, next morning, I woke up. Suddenly, I could hear children's voices. Lots of them. Talking, shouting, laughing. I thought: 'What on earth is going on?' So I got up, opened the door and ... you'll never guess what I saw ...

B What?

A Hundreds of children. Staring at me. You know what I'd done? I'd parked in a school playground!

B Oh no! Ha, ha! You must have been so embarrassed!

A I couldn't believe it! So I threw on my clothes, jumped into the driver's seat and made a very quick exit ...

B That is hilarious!

A Yeah, well, it sounds funny now, but it wasn't so funny at the time, I can tell you!

Conversation 2: Sabrina

A Did you hear about my recent travel nightmare?

B No, what happened?

A Well, I was going to Mumbai for a work conference ... This was about a month ago now. I had to get up at four in the morning to get the coach to the airport. Anyway, about half an hour into the coach journey we got stuck in a traffic jam.

B What? At that time of the morning?

A Yeah, well, apparently there'd been an accident on the motorway ahead of us – a lorry had turned over. So we were crawling along and I was beginning to get a bit nervous about missing my flight. Anyway, we ended up getting to the airport about an hour late. So I ran to the check-in desk and got there just as it was closing. Then I dashed to security control and – just my luck – there was a massive queue there. By now, I was getting seriously stressed about missing the flight. And then, to make matters worse, they decided to search my hand luggage. Anyway, I then ran through to the departure lounge and you're not going to believe this ...

B What?!

A The flight had been cancelled!

B No way!

A Yep! Technical problems with the aircraft, apparently. So, to cut a long story short, I had to wait in the airport for nine hours before the next flight to Mumbai – nine hours, just waiting, and with very little information about what was going on.

B Sounds awful!

A It was. But that isn't the end of the story ...

B You're joking! What else could possibly go wrong? Oh, no ... don't tell me – they lost your luggage!?

A Yep, you guessed it!

B You can't be serious!

A Totally serious. They lost my luggage. Just for a day, but still very inconvenient.

B I bet you were furious.

A I was absolutely furious.

B Did you complain?

A I certainly did ...

2.11))⟩
1 I'm not surprised!
2 You must have been so embarrassed!
3 I bet you were furious!
4 You're kidding!
5 That is hilarious!
6 You can't be serious!

2.12))⟩
1 A You're kidding!
  B You're kidding!
2 A That's hilarious!
  B That's hilarious!
3 A I bet you were furious!
  B I bet you were furious!

2.13))⟩
1	vacation	5	truck
2	restroom	6	trunk
3	sidewalk	7	garbage
4	travel trailer	8	gasoline

Unit 3 Invest

3.1))⟩

P Hello, and welcome to *Future Perfect*. With us in the studio today, we have careers consultant John Moody. John, how do you think our working lives and careers will change in the future?

J Well, life is changing pretty fast, and the world of work will naturally change with it. For example, in many countries in the world, populations are ageing. This means there will probably be more jobs in the health care sector, but it also means there will be a smaller workforce overall.

P And what impact will that have?

J Well, for one thing, we are likely to have more and more automation. For example, trains and buses probably won't have drivers and conductors any more. Instead, we'll have self-driving vehicles and a handful of humans acting as auto transport analysts – that means someone who is responsible for managing the automatic transport system, making sure it's running smoothly and efficiently.

P So IT skills will be important?

J Certainly, but I don't think we'll see them as specific skills in the future. Pretty much everyone will have these skills, just like they can read and write nowadays. Another factor that will lead to the creation of new jobs is the environment, both dealing with the effects of climate change and preventing further damage. For example, you might become a garbage designer – someone who designs products using stuff we currently throw away. Or you could be a rewilder – someone who undoes environmental damage to the countryside by replanting, reintroducing native species of animals and so on. There will still be traditional jobs, of course, but there are likely to be a lot of jobs you've never even thought of.

P Well, we've also got two students here today, Ben Cummins and Lucy Carmichael. Ben, you've recently gone back to studying, haven't you? Can you see yourself doing any of these jobs in the future?

B When I was a kid, I always wanted to be a train driver. After hearing that, I think I'll be an auto transport analyst! No, seriously, I'm not sure that any of those jobs would be for me, but I completely agree that IT skills are going to be vital. My IT skills aren't bad, but I'm nearly thirty and I'm very well aware that younger generations are going to be much more proficient. So I'm taking a course in app design at the University of Westminster. It starts next week, and I'm really excited. Lots of people can use social media, but not many people know how to programme.

P That's great. Things are moving so fast these days that it's important to keep your qualifications up to date. What about you, Lucy?

L Actually, I'm studying design, so I might quite fancy being a garbage designer. I'm certainly going to work in design in some way.

J How about being a nostalgist? Another big trend is customization – providing goods and services specifically tailored to what individuals want. Nostalgists will be interior designers who specialize in recreating a particular time in the past. This will be particularly attractive to older people who often like to relive happy memories, and might like their house to be decorated in the style of the 1960s or 1970s, for example.

L That sounds fascinating. I'd love to research the past for people …

P Well, let me know if you do decide to become a nostalgist!

L Yeah, I will do.

3.2)))

B When I was a kid, I always wanted to be a train driver. After hearing that, I think I'll be an auto transport analyst! No, seriously, I'm not sure that any of those jobs would be for me, but I completely agree that IT skills are going to be vital. My IT skills aren't bad, but I'm nearly thirty and I'm very well aware that younger generations are going to be much more proficient. So I'm taking a course in app design at the University of Westminster. It starts next week, and I'm really excited. Lots of people can use social media, but not many people know how to programme.

J That's great. Things are moving so fast these days that it's important to keep your qualifications up to date. What about you, Lucy?

L Actually, I'm studying design, so I might quite fancy being a garbage designer. I'm certainly going to work in design in some way.

J How about being a nostalgist? Another big trend is customization – providing goods and services specifically tailored to what individuals want. Nostalgists will be interior designers who specialize in recreating a particular time in the past. This will be particularly attractive to older people who often like to relive happy memories, and might like their house to be decorated in the style of the 1960s or 1970s for example.

L That sounds fascinating. I'd love to research the past for people …

J Well, let me know if you do decide to become a nostalgist!

L Yeah, I will do.

3.3)))

I'm in my third year at university, which means that I graduate this summer – assuming I pass the course! There's a lot of unemployment at the moment, so it's probably going to be quite hard to get a good job straightaway. I'm going to work in my parents' shop over the summer and get some money together, and then, in September, I'm planning on visiting a friend in Vancouver, Canada. It will be lovely to see her again; and who knows, I might find a job there, too.

3.4)))
light   will

3.5)))
life   slow   lost
final   we'll   help   caller   told   spell

3.6)))
1 Winning a gold medal is quite an achievement.
2 All her gold jewellery was taken in the robbery.
3 The gold necklace was part of her inheritance.
4 The Incas were an ancient civilization.
5 Thank you for your generosity.
6 The whole village received an invitation to the wedding.
7 Having enough money gives you the freedom to do what you want.
8 Gold has a special significance in some countries.
9 I have a preference for silver jewellery, rather than gold.
10 I get a lot of enjoyment from shopping.

3.7)))
1 achievement   6 invitation
2 robbery   7 freedom
3 inheritance   8 significance
4 civilization   9 preference
5 generosity   10 enjoyment

3.8)))
E So, what do you think about the first one?
G I wouldn't be surprised if it happened. After all, we can't all keep flying to places all the time, can we? The planet would get so polluted.
E Well, you may be right about that, but I still doubt people would be satisfied with a virtual holiday. I expect they'll just travel more within their own countries.
G I don't like the sound of a printed meal much, do you? But I think it's bound to happen. In fact, I think they're already developing the technology.
E Really? There's no chance of me eating something like that!
G And what about the last one?
E Oh, that's sure to happen. People will get fed up with being in front of a screen all the time.
G Well, yes, I suppose it might happen …

3.9)))
1 I wouldn't be surprised if it happened.
2 I still doubt people would be satisfied with a virtual holiday.
3 I expect they'll just travel more within their own countries.
4 I think it's bound to happen.
5 There's no chance of me eating something like that!
6 Oh, that's sure to happen.
7 Well, yes, I suppose it might happen …

3.10)))
1 Later today, I'm going to …
2 This time next week, I will be …
3 By the time I'm seventy, I will have …
4 After work next Friday, I …
5 As soon as possible, I …
6 After I've finished this course, I think I'll …

3.11)))
1 The firefighter received an award for her bravery.
2 People usually work better if they are given encouragement.
3 He has a lot of ability in the subject but doesn't work very hard.
4 **A** Thank you for your assistance.

B I was glad to help.
5 I dream of being a pop star, but in reality I know it isn't very likely.
6 Older people have greater wisdom because of their life experience.

Unit 4 Creativity

4.1)))
… So today on *Wired World*, we're looking at some of the entries for this year's James Dyson Award. The British engineer James Dyson created the award in 2007 to inspire university students and graduates around the world to come up with some great new ideas in design and engineering.

So, this year: well, first of all we have a simple but very clever idea by industrial designer Muji Yakamoto. This invention has been designed to take up as little space as possible. It is called 'Stack' because the printer is placed on top of a pile, or stack, of paper. When something is being printed, Stack moves slowly downwards. The paper disappears under the printer and exits on top, where a new pile is created.

The next invention has been given a Japanese name, Mamori, which means 'protect', but the inventor, Mark Dillon, is actually Irish. The name is a good one, however, because that's exactly what this device does. Gaelic football, very popular in Ireland, is quite a dangerous sport. Recent research showed that, on average, two out of every three players on a team had been injured last year. Mamori is worn inside the mouth. It protects the players' teeth, but the players are also monitored for injury, and the information is sent wirelessly to a computer. If a player is moving more slowly than usual, for example, it will be measured and noticed, and the player will be taken out of the game so he can be treated.

The third invention we're looking at today, Xarius, was created by a German team. It can be attached to almost anything and then used to make electricity using wind power. The energy which has been generated is then used to recharge mobile phones and so on.

And finally, Sono, designed by a team from Austria. This is fixed to a window and helps to stop outside noise coming inside. And, not only is noise from outside reduced, but the person inside can actually choose which sounds he or she does or doesn't want to hear! The sounds can be controlled by twisting the middle of the Sono. So you can keep the sound of birds singing while getting rid of the sound of that car alarm. Ha! Amazing.

4.2)))
The problem of drought-affected farmers may have been solved by a recent Dyson Award winner, Edward Linacre. Linacre had been inspired by Australia's worst drought in a century when he invented Airdrop. Using his system, water can be collected from the air. Linacre says the idea was given to him by the Namib Beetle, which survives in the desert by collecting tiny amounts of moisture. Linacre has recently been asked to develop his device by the Chinese government and companies in the Middle East, but, for now, he wants to keep working on it himself. Up until now the system has been developed in his mum's backyard. In the future, it will be taken up to a more industrial level.

4.3))
1   The problem of drought-affected farmers may have been solved by a recent James Dyson Award winner.
2   Linacre had been inspired by Australia's worst drought in a century …
3   The idea was given to him by the Namib beetle.
4   Linacre has recently been asked to develop his device by the Chinese government.
5   The system has been developed in his mum's backyard.
6   In the future, it'll be taken up to a more industrial level.

4.4))
Most people have particular ways of working or studying that they feel work best for them. For example, my partner always has music on while she works, whereas I prefer silence. Is this just a personal preference, or is one actually better than the other? Some of the things that scientists have been finding out about how we can be most creative might surprise you. It turns out that she's right and I'm wrong (not for the first time!). According to Professor Ravi Mehta, a moderate level of noise is better for our creativity than silence. So quiet music is a good idea. Too much noise isn't good, though – especially listening to other people's telephone conversations. This is particularly distracting because our brain is automatically trying to solve the puzzle of what is being said by the person we can't hear.

And what about heating? Surely it's better to be in a cooler room to stop yourself from being sleepy? Well, apparently not. One study from Cornell University showed that when temperatures were lower, at twenty degrees Celsius, employees made 44% more mistakes than when it was twenty-five degrees. If you're feeling cold, you are using a lot of your precious energy to keep warm, so there's less energy for being innovative.

And that's not all. Ever been told 'tidy desk, tidy mind'? Well, apparently, having a messy desk is actually better for being inventive. Think that being tired makes it difficult to come up with good ideas? Think again. When we're tired, our brain is less efficient, but it's also more likely to make new connections, which means we're more likely to come up with something truly creative. Naps can also be good, though, especially at helping you remember things.

It seems that most of what I thought about being creative is wrong!

4.6))
1   It looks a bit weird to me.
2   What does it mean?
3   What does it mean?
4   I'd like to knit something like that.
5   I'd like to knit something like that.
6   It looks amazing!
7   I'd rather see this than graffiti.
8   They shouldn't put it on statues.
9   It doesn't do any harm.

4.7))
Knitting seems to be having a moment. That lamp post that you never noticed before … suddenly, it's multicoloured. Trees, statues, even buses and bridges are finding themselves decorated with a warm, brightly coloured knitted woollen cover. It's called yarn-bombing.

It's believed to have started in the United States, but is now a global phenomenon. In Paris, a yarn-bomber has filled the cracks in the pavement with brightly knitted wool. In Poland, well-known yarn-bomber Agata Oleksiak has covered her grandmother's country house with a loose knitted cover. And in Mexico City, another yarn-bomber, artist Magda Sayeg, has specially designed a perfectly fitting cover for a city bus.

It's a kind of street art, a little bit like graffiti, but considerably less damaging as it can be easily removed. Nonetheless, many local governments don't like yarn-bombing, and therefore it is often done secretly at night. Yarn-bombing is very quiet. The yarn-bombers then take photos of their creations and post them online for others to admire.

It's very much a social thing, with groups of knitters working together to plan and create something. Even the well-known yarn-bombing artists, such as Oleksiak and Sayeg, have teams of people to assist them with the bigger projects.

So, why do they do it? Unlike much graffiti, yarn-bombing is often very much about making an ugly public space or object more beautiful. It's about putting something personal and handmade into an urban, industrial environment. And, of course, it aims to put a smile on people's faces.

4.8))
1   especially   3   loose
2   quite   4   advise

4.9))
1   specially   especially
2   quite   quiet
3   lose   loose
4   advise   advice

4.10))
M   Well, I have to say that, for me, the most important quality of a teacher is being patient. Teachers need to understand that it isn't necessarily that easy to learn something. Oh, and being kind is important, too.
J   Well, you've got a point, but if they're actually going to teach you something, they need to be more than kind and patient. They need to have good ideas, too – to be creative, to be able to come up with something that will really make the lesson interesting and fun.
M   Yes, but on the other hand, sometimes teachers create really fun lessons, but you don't really learn anything. I'm all for having fun, but I do want to get more than that out of the class, don't you?
J   Oh, yes, obviously that's important.
M   But I still want them to be encouraging and supportive.
J   No, but look, it is possible for a teacher to be too nice sometimes, isn't it? Personally, I think a good teacher is quite strict.
M   Really? Isn't that kind of teacher a bit old-fashioned? As I see it, if a teacher is motivating, the students won't want to be silly and waste time.
J   OK, I can agree with motivating, and supportive. What about creative as well?
M   Yes, OK, I guess it is pretty important. And hard-working. It seems to me that teachers have to work pretty hard.

J   They do, and they have to be pretty well organized, too. So that's motivating, supportive, creative, hard-working … what about the fifth one? Well organized?

4.11))
1   Yes, but on the other hand …
2   No, but look …
3   Well, you've got a point, but …

4.12))
1   describing a new way of doing something
2   very noticeable
3   not showing thought or understanding
4   unusual and surprising
5   easy to understand and use
6   always behaving in a traditional or normal way

4.13))
A   Well, I do really enjoy my job, but I also earn quite a good salary, so I guess I'm lucky. But if I had to choose, I have to say that I would choose to enjoy my job over the money. It seems to me that you spend so much of your life at work, that you have to enjoy it, or life is just miserable!
B   Well, you've got a point, but if you don't have enough money you can be pretty miserable, too, can't you?
C   As I see it, you don't need loads of money, but you do need enough, so that has to be the priority. If you don't enjoy your job, you can always do things you enjoy in your free time.
A   Yes, but don't you think you should change jobs if you hate what you're doing? I think …

Unit 5   Mind

5.1))

1   Irene from England

My clearest childhood memory is definitely the day the Second World War ended. It was May 1945, so I must have been four years old. I don't know how it happened so quickly, but my mother and father and I went down to the train station, and hundreds of us went on to the train to London – which was about a hundred miles away, a long way on a steam train – and we went straight to Buckingham Palace.

The royal family and the prime minister, Winston Churchill, were on the balcony of the palace. They waved and waved, and everyone was cheering and cheering and singing. It was unbelievably noisy and happy. That was my main memory of the day. My father let me sit on his shoulders so I could have a better view.

I can also remember that the queen was wearing a pale blue dress, and I clearly remember feeling very disappointed because Princess Elizabeth, now Queen Elizabeth, of course, was wearing an army uniform, which was brown, and she didn't look like a princess at all.

I have absolutely no recollection of how we got home again …

2   Tobias from Germany

I'll never forget going horse riding for the first – and last – time when I was about ten. It was on a school activity holiday. I remember all the other kids were really excited about going horse riding. I pretended to be excited, but actually I was feeling really nervous because I'd never done it before and I was a bit frightened of horses. Anyway, everything was fine while the horse was walking, but when it started to trot … well …

suddenly, I felt completely out of control. I didn't expect the horse to run so fast. I tried to get it to slow down, but it just kept on running, faster and faster. In my panic, I didn't remember to follow the teacher's instructions. And, to make matters worse, my helmet had slipped down and was covering my eyes, so I couldn't see a thing. That's the thing I remember most clearly – not being able to see! Anyway, I didn't dare to take my hands off the reins to push the helmet back up. So instead I decided to do something very silly: I made myself fall off the horse. So I fell on the ground and all the other children had to avoid riding over me. I don't remember whether I was injured or not, but my pride was very hurt!

5.2)))

1 My father let me sit on his shoulders.
2 I remember feeling disappointed because Princess Elizabeth didn't look like a princess.
3 I tried to get the horse to slow down …
4 I made myself fall off the horse.
5 In my panic, I didn't remember to follow the teacher's instructions.

5.3)))

Speaker 1

Listening to my boss. She always gives you far too much information … you know, goes into too much detail about things you don't need to know, and I'm thinking: 'For goodness sake, just get to the point, will you!'

Speaker 2

Watching a slow-moving film at the cinema. So many films nowadays are three hours long. If you ask me, that's a long time to be sitting in one place, even with a good film. I hate that feeling when you can't sit still and you just want to stretch your legs and basically you just can't wait for the film to finish.

Speaker 3

Doing the ironing is, for me, the most boring and repetitive of all household jobs. It just seems to take forever.

Speaker 4

For me, it's long-haul flights – my job involves a lot of overseas travel. I can usually amuse myself with films and music for the first few hours, but towards the end of the flight I'm usually absolutely desperate to get off that plane.

Speaker 5

Rainy days are the worst for me. I get really fed up with being stuck indoors in my flat. I feel a real need to get out and do something active.

Speaker 6

There's nothing that's more likely to send me to sleep than a dull lecture. The ones I hate most usually involve a PowerPoint presentation, where the lecturer just reads what's on the slides and doesn't give us an opportunity to discuss or ask questions. I normally find myself losing concentration after about half an hour, my mind starts to wander, I start yawning … and basically, I find it really hard not to fall asleep.

Speaker 7

For me, the most boring thing in the world is not having enough to keep me occupied at work. You ask your boss and they give you a simple task that you finish in five minutes and then you're back to doing nothing again. You don't want to be

annoying, asking for tasks every five minutes, so you just sit there feeling awkward … It's awful.

5.4)))

In most people, the left side of the brain is dominant for language, especially grammar, writing and spelling. It is dominant for thinking logically, and it is best at hearing the rhythm of music. The left side of the brain controls the right side of your body.

The right side of the brain is best at appreciating the melody of music, at understanding jokes and recognizing objects.

5.5)))

A Mike, what are we going to do about this vandalism problem here at the factory? It's the second time it's happened this month. First it was graffiti, now broken windows.
B I know, it's obviously kids – bored kids – with nothing better to do. I mean, they're clearly not interested in stealing anything. They're just looking for trouble.
A Yeah, well, I've had enough of it now. We need to find a way of dealing with it. One alternative would be to install some security cameras.
B Well, that would be the obvious solution, but we need to take cost into consideration. Security cameras are expensive to set up and difficult to maintain. We're just a small business – we don't have that much money to invest. So I don't think that's an option, I'm afraid.
C Well, would it be worth putting in some of those fake cameras? You know, the ones that look like security cameras but aren't actually real.
B Mmm, I'm not convinced by those, to be honest, and I don't think the vandals are either. I think a better way forward would be to put in some of those lights … those ones that come on only when they sense movement. Vandals are less likely to commit crimes in well-lit areas.
A Yes, I think that would be an effective solution – and not too costly, I don't think. Let's do that. I'll look into it.
B Hmm. Do you think there would be any point in changing the lock on the gate?
C No, the gate lock hasn't been broken. They've obviously climbed over the wall.
B In that case, what if we also paint the walls with anti-climb paint, just as an extra precaution?
C Yes, there's no harm in doing that as well. It shouldn't be too expensive.
A OK, so lights and anti-climb paint, then. That should sort the problem out.

5.6)))

1 One alternative would be to install some security cameras.
2 We need to take cost into consideration.
3 I don't think that's an option.
4 Would it be worth putting in some of those fake cameras?
5 I think a better way forward would be to put in some of those lights.
6 That would be an effective solution.
7 Do you think there would be any point in changing the lock?

8 What if we also paint the walls with anti-climb paint?
9 There's no harm in doing that.

5.7)))

1 One alternative would be to …
2 We need to take cost into consideration …
3 I don't think that's an option …
4 Would it be worth …
5 I think a better way forward would be to …
6 That would be an effective solution …
7 Do you think there would be any point in …
8 What if we …
9 There's no harm in …

5.8)))

1 'Zoning out' is something you do when you're very excited.
2 If you're 'still', it means you don't move.
3 'Yawning' is a gesture you make to show your approval.
4 If something is described as 'dull', it means it isn't interesting.
5 If you're 'fed up', it means you've had enough to eat.
6 If your mind 'wanders', it means you have stopped paying attention.
7 If you are 'trapped', it means you can't escape.

Unit 6 Community

6.1)))

P According to recent research, more and more people around the world are choosing to live alone, but equally, many people are starting to build and live in closer communities, in some ways returning to a kind of village lifestyle. In today's programme, we speak to two people who are living in these very different ways. Emma, who lives completely alone, on a remote Scottish island, and Harry, who last year moved with his young family into the Lilac co-housing project in Yorkshire. Emma, why do you think so many people are choosing to live in one-person households?
E Well, the first thing to say is that it's perfectly possible to live alone and to be part of a close community. I'm sure there are plenty of people living in the Lilac co-housing community who live alone, aren't there, Harry?
H Yes, absolutely. It can be a great way of having your own private space, but not being completely isolated. You know people are there if you need them …
P But that isn't the case for you, is it, Emma? Am I right in saying that you are the only person living on your island?
E Yes, that's right. Not many people choose to live so completely alone, but, I have to say, I love it. Don't get me wrong, I like people, and it's very exciting for me coming here today and meeting so many new people, but I love the peace of being completely on my own.
P Don't you get lonely?
E Er, no, not really. I live on a farm, so there are the animals. And if I really want to talk to someone, I do have a phone. Though I don't really use it very much.
P And what about you, Harry? Presumably, you like being around other people?
H Well, yes, but not all the time. What appealed to me about co-housing was that we would have our own private house, but that there would be other people around whenever

we wanted, so we wouldn't ever feel lonely. And it's a very practical thing as well, co-housing. For example, a lot of people in this country have a spare bedroom for guests. What a waste of space! When my brother and his family come to stay, we just book a guest room in the shared Common Hall. And instead of every family having a tiny private garden (though some still do), we share a huge garden, with a play area for the kids. It makes it easier for them to make friends as well.

P It sounds interesting …

6.2)))
1 Hundreds of people are living this way.
2 Most of us love the footpaths.
3 Plenty of people live alone.
4 A lot of people don't have a car.
5 Neither of us wants to move.

6.4)))
1 How do I make a P2PU course?
2 All the courses are open to anyone.
3 Users can set up their own courses.
4 … so other people can see it.
5 … with over a million members worldwide.
6 Leave it for another person to find.

6.5)))
When we talk about communities, we usually imagine a group of people who live close to each other. However, the fastest-growing types of community these days are online. Online or virtual communities are used to get people with similar interests together, so that they can share their interests or help each other in different ways.

Many of these communities cross international borders. For example, 'BookCrossing', where people leave books for those who enjoy the experience of reading with others, has members in 132 different countries.

Virtual communities can just be for fun, but plenty of them have a serious purpose. For example, many people who have a relatively rare illness can now get support and advice from others with the same condition.

And, of course, education is a major reason for joining a virtual community. MOOCs, or 'massive open online courses', are places where anyone can join in an educational course using the internet. Distance learning is nothing new, but being able to talk and see each other online makes all the difference to the learning experience.

People in an online community may simply communicate with each other online, but they may also meet up face to face in the real world. For example, people interested in cosplay may use online communities to organize conventions where everyone can get dressed up and meet with other cosplayers.

And, finally, some online communities are more about improving the real community that you live in. For example, StreetBank, which is an online community where real life neighbours can offer to lend things like barbecue equipment, or they might offer to help each other out as they do up their houses or gardens. The ultimate aim is to encourage neighbours to be friendlier and to know each other better.

6.6)))
Conversation 1
A I hope you don't mind me asking, but haven't we met somewhere before?
B I'm not sure, you do look familiar …
A Are you a friend of Nicola's?
B Yes, we went to school together.
A Ah! So did I. What class were you in …?

Conversation 2
C Sorry, but I couldn't help overhearing … it's your first day today, isn't it?
D Yes, I'm Peter's new personal assistant.
C Ah. Welcome to the firm. I'm Josie, I work in Sales.
D Good to meet you – I'm Sita.

Conversation 3
E Excuse me, is anyone sitting there?
F No, go ahead.
E Is it always this busy?
F Yes, I'm afraid so. You don't usually take this one, then?
E No, I've just started a new job in the city …

6.7)))
Conversation 1
A I hope you don't mind me asking, but haven't we met somewhere before?
B I'm not sure, you do look familiar …
A Are you a friend of Nicola's?
B Yes, we went to school together.

Conversation 2
C Sorry, but I couldn't help overhearing … it's your first day today, isn't it?
D Yes, I'm Peter's new personal assistant.

Conversation 3
E Excuse me, is anyone sitting there?
F Er, no, go ahead.
E Is it always this busy?
F Yes, I'm afraid so.

6.8)))
1 a person who lives in a place
2 a building, equipment and so on that makes it possible to do something
3 affecting the whole world
4 all the people who live in one house
5 belonging to one particular person or group, not to be shared by others
6 a change in opinion or attitude

Unit 7 Rules

7.1)))
A scrap metal dealer who bought an antique gold egg for $13,000 has made a profit of more than $32 million after discovering that the egg was in fact one of the famous Russian Fabergé eggs, made for the Russian royal family before the revolution. The dealer had planned to sell it for the value of its gold and jewels, but when he researched it online he found a news report about the eight Fabergé eggs still missing and discovered that one of them was the egg he had bought.

A Californian couple out for a walk around their property have accidentally found eight old tin cans … full of gold coins. It is estimated that the coins are worth around $10 million. The couple's claim to ownership is strong, as the coins were found on their property. But they have still had to hand the coins over to an official while a decision is made about who the coins actually belong to.

An Italian car worker has discovered that two paintings hanging in his kitchen are, in fact, by the French painters Gauguin and Bonnard, and worth around 30 million euros. They had been stolen from a house in London in 1970, and the car worker bought them at an auction of lost property left on Italian trains in 1974. The police now suspect that the thieves must have abandoned the valuable paintings on the train, perhaps fearing arrest.

A bag containing $200,000 worth of diamonds found on the street has been returned to its grateful owner, a diamond dealer who had dropped the bag while taking the diamonds to be polished. The dealer didn't expect to ever see the diamonds again, but they were found by a young man who handed them in to the police. He has received a reward from the dealer.

7.2)))
A The first one just sounds ridiculous. Why would they do that? I suppose it must have been a way of making the car park look tidier or something!
B No, actually I think it might have been a safety issue. If all the cars are backed into the car parking spaces then there will be fewer accidents when people are leaving at the end of the day.
A Really? Oh, I suppose it could have been something like that … What about the next one? Surely they can't have stopped them having a lunch break? That's awful.
B Yeah, I agree, but a lot of places don't actually like it if you leave the office. They may have needed people to stay in order to answer the phones.
A The third one seems fair enough to me. It might have been in a hot country where you need to get up early to avoid the heat of the day.
B Yeah, it's fine so long as you also get to go home early or you get a long lunch break.
A And what about the last one?
B Ah, someone must have spilt a drink over a computer!
A Oh, yes, you're probably right.

7.3)))
1 They can't have worked such long hours.
2 They might have had a long lunch break.
3 They must have hated their jobs.
4 He must have been fired.
5 He could have resigned.
6 He may have been made redundant.
7 They can't have been friends.

7.4)))
A Have you heard about these new parking meters they're bringing in? Apparently, the more pollution your car causes, the more you pay. I think it's a great idea, don't you?
B Well, that's not really how I see it. My car is quite old, so I'll have to pay more. I can't afford to buy a new car, so how is it fair to make me pay more for parking as well?
C I'm with you there. Everyone should have to pay the same for the same service, or it isn't fair.
A You can't be serious! Haven't you seen how bad the pollution is these days? We need to encourage people to buy cars which are better for the environment. Or maybe you

should just use your cars less in the first place?

B Come off it! You use your car all the time …

7.5)))
I'm with you there.
I completely agree.
True enough.
Yes, that's spot on.
Absolutely!
I don't think anyone would disagree with that.
That's just what I was thinking.
I couldn't agree more.
That's not really how I see it.
You can't be serious!
Come off it!
I'm not sure I quite agree.
I can't agree with you there.
I beg to differ.
I'm not sure about that.

7.6)))
Yes, that's spot on.
Absolutely!
That's just what I was thinking.
I couldn't agree more.
You can't be serious!
Come off it!

7.7)))
1   When she saw him, she screamed loudly.
2   The man was wearing a very smart suit.
3   There were lots of people at the party.
4   He was crying.
5   It was hot and sunny.

7.8)))
1   with lots of different colours
2   only speaking one language
3   between different states in a country
4   a vehicle with two wheels and no engine
5   a house which is joined to another house
6   believing in your own abilities

Unit 8 Old and new

8.1)))
P Well, you've probably heard the phrase 'The Internet of Things', or 'IoT' for short. It's a phrase we hear a lot nowadays, and experts say this latest revolution in technology will change our lives in a big way. But what is it exactly, and how will it affect us? My guest on today's programme is Duncan Bates, whose award-winning blog covers the latest news in the world of technology. Duncan …

DB Hello. Well, IoT is the technology which allows any physical object – a fridge, say, or smoke alarm or TV – to communicate with other objects or with people.

P Right, but people have been talking about smart fridges and so on for years, haven't they? So what's new about it?

DB Well, in the past, these smart devices were relatively rare. What is new is the fact that internet-connected things are now so commonplace.

P And why now?

DB Because, thanks to advances in technology, tiny computers or 'microchips' can be manufactured very cheaply. These can be connected to objects, which can then be put on the internet via Wi-fi.

8.2)))
P So how many things, roughly, are now online?

DB It's estimated that there are around ten to fifteen billion things that are connected to the internet, compared with only two billion people. And this number is set to rise dramatically in the next ten years or so. And as you can imagine, IoT is an area in which huge amounts of money are being invested, by governments and private companies. Some say this figure will soon reach trillions of dollars.

P Wow … So how will IoT affect our everyday lives?

DB For example, you could have a central heating system that turns itself on when you are a certain distance from home by accessing the GPS in your mobile phone, so you get back to a warm house without wasting energy when you're not there. Or you could have a washing machine, or car, whose inbuilt computer could go online when it develops a fault and could look up local repair companies, then book itself in for a service after checking your diary for suitable dates.

P So these smart devices will help our lives run more smoothly by saving us time and money, and save energy, too?

DB That's right. And it's not just objects that can be connected, but also living things. For example, cows in a field can be fitted with devices which can send a text to a farmer letting them know when a cow gets sick or pregnant. This is already happening on some farms.

P Brilliant. I guess the possibilities are endless?

DB Yes, and another area that I think particularly benefits from the Internet of Things is health care: you can now get smart devices that measure your heart rate, your blood pressure … and for people who have diabetes there is even a smart insulin pump. The pump, which is attached to your body, monitors the insulin levels in your blood and automatically injects insulin when you need it. And because it is internet-connected this information can be sent to your doctor, who can monitor your health remotely.

P Sounds great.

8.3)))
P So we've talked about the benefits … What about the risks? I mean, the problem with technology is that it breaks down sometimes.

DB Yes, that's right. If you're too dependent on internet-connected things and your Wi-fi connection fails or you have a power cut, then you're in trouble.

P Absolutely. And what worries me too is privacy. Who will have access to our personal data, and what will it be used for? That will be a great concern for a lot of people, I'm sure.

DB Yes, it will. Privacy is a big issue, and security too, because every connected device can be hacked.

P Yes. Having your computer hacked, or your fridge, is bad, but imagine if your car or your insulin pump was hacked – now that's a scary thought!

DB It is! But I think there will be ways for people to protect their privacy and security. I think what's more of a real worry is how much space all this data will take up on the internet. It could really slow down people's broadband.

P True. Ah well, we shall see. Duncan, many thanks for coming in.

8.4)))
Cars which are internet-connected can book themselves in for a service.
My car, which is internet-connected, can book itself in for a service.

8.5)))
1   The man who lives in the flat above mine plays loud music.
2   John, who lives next door to me, has a smart fridge.
3   My friend Sarah, who works in IT, often helps me when I have computer problems.
4   The woman whose desk is next to mine is on holiday.
5   The tablet that you gave me for my birthday is really useful.

8.6)))
aubergines   avocados   beef   chillies
citrus fruit   coffee   courgettes   dairy products
onions   papayas   peanuts   pineapples
potatoes   rice   sweetcorn   tomatoes
turkey   vanilla   wheat

8.8)))
Chillies are grown all over the world. They're from the same family as tomatoes, potatoes and aubergines. Although they make your mouth burn, they are also thought to have a number of health benefits. For example, they can help with stomach problems, breathing problems and can reduce the feeling of pain.

8.9)))
Vanilla is the most popular spice in the world. Its sweet, slightly smoky taste is often used in ice cream and other sweet dishes. It is the second most expensive spice on the market because it requires a lot of hard labour to produce. For this reason it is sometimes referred to as 'green gold'.

8.10)))
It's hard to imagine Italian food without tomatoes, Greek food without aubergines, or Thai or Indonesian food without peanut sauce. But before the sixteenth century, these foods were not known outside of South America.

These foods, and many more, were first introduced to the rest of the world during a process known as the 'Columbian Exchange' in the early 16th century. The Columbian Exchange, named after Christopher Columbus, was the exchange of food and other things between the New and Old Worlds.

Fruit and vegetables brought over from South and Central America to Europe included potatoes, tomatoes, sweetcorn, courgettes, aubergines, peanuts, pineapples, papayas, chillies and vanilla. Peanuts and chillies were then introduced to Asia by the Europeans.

It is estimated that 60% of all the crops grown in the world today originated in the Americas. However, nobody could have predicted this at the time, as, initially, the Europeans weren't very enthusiastic about the new foods. For example, it took three centuries before tomatoes and potatoes were accepted. People were suspicious of them, thinking they were dangerous to eat. Of course, both became very important crops in Europe by the nineteenth century. Ireland had become so dependent on potatoes that when the potato crops failed to grow in the 1840s, a million people died of hunger.

The Americas gained many new foods from Europe in return, including apples, citrus fruit, lettuce, cucumber, onions, coffee, tea, wheat and rice. The Europeans also introduced cows to the New World. After that, people living in the Americas could enjoy steak and dairy products for the first time. It's strange to think that before the Columbian Exchange, Argentina – now so strongly associated with beef – had no cows, Mexican cuisine had no cheese and Brazil had no coffee!

Although the first major exchange of foods happened several centuries ago, new foods continue to be introduced between the Old and New Worlds. Quinoa, for example, a grain grown in the Andes mountains, and which was important to the diet of pre-Columbian civilizations, has only in the last few years become hugely popular in the USA, Canada, Europe, Australia, China and Japan. In these parts of the world, quinoa is now considered a 'superfood', as it is extremely rich in protein. It seems that Christopher Columbus, with his food exchange, started a very long-lasting trend!

8.11))

1 These foods, and many more, were first introduced to the rest of the world during a process known as the 'Columbian Exchange' in the early 16th century.
2 However, nobody could have predicted this at the time, as, initially, the Europeans weren't very enthusiastic about the new foods.
3 People were suspicious of them, thinking they were dangerous to eat.
4 Ireland had become so dependent on potatoes that when the potato crops failed to grow in the 1840s, a million people died of hunger.
5 It's strange to think that before the Columbian Exchange, Argentina – now so strongly associated with beef – had no cows, Mexican cuisine had no cheese and Brazil had no coffee!
6 In these parts of the world, quinoa is now considered a 'super food', as it is extremely rich in protein.

8.12))

A So what do you think of the illuminations? Are you glad we came?
Z Oh, definitely. It was well worth coming here. I think it's amazing. What I particularly like is the contrast of old and new; you know, all this modern light and sound technology against the backdrop of the beautiful old buildings.
A Yeah, me too. And the colours are just stunning, aren't they? That projection of the flowers against the town hall was magical, wasn't it?

Z Yes, totally. And I really like the way the buildings seemed to come alive with the moving images … I think the highlight for me was that building with the giant face projected onto it. When the face started moving in time with the music, and making those funny expressions, that was quite something!
A Oh yes, that was pretty dramatic, wasn't it? I found it a bit disturbing, though.
Z Really? I thought it was brilliant!
A Yeah, no, don't get me wrong, I did too – I thought it was very cleverly done – just a bit … scary. It was so huge … and noisy.
Z The only thing I'm not so keen on is the crowds. It's a bit too packed for my liking, especially in the main square. It made me feel a bit claustrophobic.
A Yeah, I know what you mean. Tomorrow, I think we should come back a bit later, when there are fewer people. There's plenty more to see tomorrow, isn't there?
Z Yes, plenty.
A And I'd like to see some of the artworks again. Like the fish in a phone box, for example.
Z Really? I wasn't so keen on that one, to be honest. I didn't really see the point of it.
A The point of it is that it's unusual to see fish in a phone box.
Z Yeah, I know, but it said in the reviews that it was one of the highlights of the event and … I dunno, I just wasn't that impressed. It didn't really live up to my expectations … I think I was expecting something a bit more colourful, maybe … Anyway, I'm getting really chilly. Are you? Shall we go and get a hot drink somewhere?
A Yeah. Good plan!

8.13))

1 What I particularly like is the contrast of old and new.
2 … the colours are just stunning.
3 I really like the way the buildings seem to come alive.
4 … the highlight for me was that building with the giant face …
5 I found it a bit disturbing, though.
6 It's a bit too packed for my liking.
7 I didn't really see the point of it.
8 … I just wasn't that impressed.
9 It didn't really live up to my expectations.

8.14))

1 Fuel efficiency in a car is not a question of speed, but of the number of 'revs' – or 'revolutions' or turns - of the engine, per minute. For most cars, this is around 2,000 revs per minute. That's actually just 56–74 kilometres per hour for the majority of cars. So, 89 kilometres per hour is false.
2 Metal detectors that you walk through at airports use powerful magnets that can damage laptops and some security cameras. So this is true, but it doesn't cause a problem because you aren't allowed to carry electronic devices through these metal detectors anyway. You put them on a separate X-ray machine.
3 A study found that, of the 243 petrol station fires that took place around the world between 1994 and 2005, none were caused by mobile phones. So this is false.

4 There is no evidence that phones and tablets interfere with an aeroplane's navigation or communication. In fact, pilots themselves use information on tablets to help them take off and land a plane. So there is no truth in this.
5 This is false. If you leave a game running, for example, then it will drain the battery, but if you switch to another app, you don't need to close it. The operating system automatically stops it from running.
6 Studies have shown that fibre optic technology works much faster than ordinary ADSL broadband. So this is true.

Unit 9 Nightlife

9.1, 9.2))

Norwegian people are always asking me: 'How do you like the dark?' In Tromsø, where I live, we have something called a 'polar night', when the sun basically doesn't appear for twenty-four hours. And this goes on for sixty days. Imagine that – two months with no daylight. It sounds really depressing, and people automatically assume that I must find it really difficult. But, actually, I love it.

It's certainly very different from my homeland. I originally come from Pakistan where, not only is it considerably warmer than Norway, but the sun sets and rises at pretty much the same time every day. We do have seasons – dry and cool in the winter, hot and wet in the summer – but it's much more dramatic here in Norway.

We actually have two winters here. The first winter is when it's dark all the time; the second winter is when the light gradually starts to come back, but it's still cold and snowy. I love them both, even though I do really feel the cold, but the first winter is really a magical time of year. You might think that everyone would stay indoors, nice and cosy, but they don't. Instead they wrap up warm and get out in the fresh air, skiing and playing in the snow, even if it's under artificial light. November to February is full of light because it's a time of celebrations. There are lights and candles everywhere, as people decorate their houses and gardens.

And then, of course, we may have sixty days of dark, but in the summer we have sixty days when the sun never really sets at all. It only gets slightly darker for about an hour in the middle of the night. They're called 'White Nights', and everyone really makes the most of them. The nights are as lively as the days, with people going to the beach and to outdoor concerts to celebrate the midnight sun. The only downside is that it's a bit difficult to sleep … but, then again, who wants to?

Maybe because it is so different from what I grew up with, I love both the dark days and the white nights. But, if I had to choose … probably the dark days of winter. I still get really excited about snow, even though we get tons of it every year, and it looks so beautiful under the glow of the streetlamps.

9.3))

comfortable   different   family   favourite   interesting   miserable   separate

9.4))

It's not something that I usually do because I really do need my sleep. However, I do find it difficult to sleep on aeroplanes. It was a thirteen-hour flight, and I really tried to get some sleep – I put in the earplugs and I put on the eye mask. But I just can't sleep sitting upright. I closed my eyes, but I didn't sleep at all. Not one bit. I was exhausted when we arrived.

9.5 🔊

A Well, actually there isn't much scientific basis to any of those beliefs …

B Really? So why do so many people believe that the moon landings were faked?

A When the American team first landed on the moon, they planted a flag. In doing so, they accidentally started the myth that the moon landings were faked because the flag appeared to flutter in a slight wind – and clearly there is no wind there. But there's no evidence of a fake.

B What about supermoons? Do they cause tsunamis?

A The moon does have an effect on the tides, but it only makes a small difference, not enough to cause a tsunami. Sometimes there are tsunamis at the same time as a supermoon, but such occurrences are just coincidence. Nor is it true that the other side of the moon is always dark. This is just a myth; its far side is lit by the sun just as often as the side we can see.

B What about the effect of the full moon on human behaviour?

A Again, although a lot of people believe this, there's no real evidence, and there have been several scientific studies which failed to prove it was true.

B But I do think the last one is right though, isn't it?

A Well, if the moon disappeared, the Earth would sometimes lie on its side. This would cause extreme temperatures and different lengths of daylight. On Mars, the axis tilts so much that the ice at its poles has sometimes moved all the way down to the equator. If the same happened here, large areas of Africa would be occasionally covered in ice, making it impossible to live there. At other times, the Earth might revolve on a straighter axis; and, if it did so, there would be no seasons at all. But the Earth would survive.

9.6 🔊

C So, as I said earlier, the proposed new food quarter will be in Regent Court. I'm very pleased to say that we have had quite a few expressions of interest from big restaurant chains.

E If I could just interrupt a second, is it only chains of restaurants, or are we also interested in getting some local restaurant owners to move into the area? I have to say I'm not very happy about the proposal because of the noise and litter it's likely to cause, which wouldn't exactly be good for the environment. However, if it encouraged local business, I might be prepared to support it …

R Sorry, Councillor, can I just say that I'm a local restaurant owner, and I'd definitely be interested in renting one of the units for my restaurant …

C Just a second. Before we open the meeting up to everyone, I'd just like to explain my reasons for proposing this new food quarter.

As you are probably aware, quite a few of the shop units are currently empty, so I firmly believe that renting them out to restaurants would be a great way of bringing life back to the town …

9.7 🔊

1 **A** If I could just interrupt a second, I think that …
   B If I could just interrupt a second, I think that …
2 **A** Excuse me for interrupting, but I think that …
   B Excuse me for interrupting, but I think that …
3 **A** I'd like to say something, if I may. I think …
   B I'd like to say something, if I may. I think …
4 **A** Can I just say, I think …
   B Can I just say, I think …
5 **A** Just a second, I think …
   B Just a second, I think …

9.8 🔊

If I could just interrupt a second, …
Excuse me for interrupting, but …
I'd like to say something, if I may.
Can I just say, …
Just a second, …

9.9 🔊

1 What things do you automatically do in the mornings?
2 How do you feel about working in rooms with only artificial light?
3 Do you find winter depressing? Why/Why not?

9.10 🔊

vegetable every camera restaurant mystery

9.11 🔊

A So, in our last meeting we agreed that we would …
B Excuse me for interrupting, but can I just ask when the last meeting was?
A Yes, it was last month. Anyway, we agreed that we would try and raise as much money as possible for charity.
B I'd like to comment on that. I think we should vote on which charity we raise the money for.
A Yes, I think that's a good idea. So, as I was saying, …
C If I could just interrupt a second, shouldn't we agree on the charity first?
A If I could just finish what I was saying, …

Unit 10 Senses

10.1 🔊

There are two people sitting on what looks like a small yellow and orange rubber boat, holding a real paddle. It appears that the boat is being swept along a wild river and that it's about to crash down a waterfall, right into the mouth of an enormous grey crocodile waiting for them at the bottom. The crocodile is half-submerged in the water, but its eyes are bright orange and very threatening. The people in the boat are screaming, and the woman is waving her hands in the air.

There's a man crouching on the ground with his back against a low concrete wall. It looks as if he's on a tiny ledge at the top of a tall burning building. Lots of people are looking up from

the street below, including two police officers, who seem to be shouting up to him. Batman and Robin are climbing up a rope to rescue him. Batman is wearing his usual long black leather boots and a cape and mask, and Robin is in a red and green costume with a shiny yellow cape and black mask.

10.2 🔊

Two hunters are out in the wood when one of them collapses. He doesn't seem to be breathing. The other guy takes out his phone and calls the emergency services. He gasps, 'My friend is dead! What should I do?' The operator says, 'Calm down. I can help. First, let's make sure he's dead.' There is a silence, then a shot is heard. When he gets back on the phone, the guy says, 'OK, now what?'

10.3 🔊

P What makes us laugh? And do we all find the same things funny? It's often said that different nationalities have different senses of humour, but is there any evidence for that?

E Well, there was some research done a few years back into the world's funniest joke by a group of researchers who called themselves LaughLab. They received over 40,000 jokes from quite a number of different countries and they did seem to identify some differences. According to the study, people from Ireland, the UK, Australia and New Zealand showed a strong preference for jokes with some kind of wordplay or pun, you know, where a word has two meanings. Americans and Canadians seemed to prefer jokes where someone looked stupid or was made to look stupid by another person. And many European countries, such as France, Denmark and Belgium, liked to make a joke out of topics that usually make us feel anxious, like illness and death. If you joke about it, it doesn't make you as anxious, I suppose.

10.4 🔊

P … Yes, maybe … But you do have to be careful about humour, don't you? I'm very careful about telling jokes to people I don't know, in case I offend them.

E Yes, there are quite a lot of jokes I don't tell unless I know the people pretty well! What one person thinks is hilarious, another might find really distasteful, or just annoying.

P Do jokes have anything in common, though? What actually makes us laugh?

E Well, there's usually something unexpected in there. We talk about a punchline at the end of a joke – the final line that hits us and makes us laugh. For example, there's a famous Groucho Marx joke in the film *Animal Crackers*. He says: 'One morning, I shot an elephant in my pyjamas … How he got into my pyjamas, I'll never know!' We usually laugh as soon as we realize that we've been mentally going in the wrong direction. That's why there's a strong link between a sense of humour and being intelligent, because your brain has got to react pretty quickly to get the joke. It's also one of the ways in which you can still tell the difference between a computer and a human.

P What? When you tell a computer a joke, it won't laugh?

E Ha, ha, no, obviously it won't laugh, but it won't even get the joke. Understanding a joke requires a lot of world knowledge, linguistic knowledge and that ability to suddenly shift quickly from what you were expecting to hear. Even young children struggle with this until they get to about five. You hear them telling jokes that just don't make any sense at all.

P Sometimes that's funnier than a proper joke, though …

10.5))))

E And many European countries, such as France, Denmark and Belgium, liked to make a joke out of topics that usually make us feel anxious, like illness and death. If you joke about it, it doesn't make you as anxious, I suppose.

P … Yes, maybe … But you do have to be careful about humour, don't you? I'm very careful about telling jokes to people I don't know, in case I offend them.

E Yes, there are quite a lot of jokes I don't tell unless I know the people pretty well! What one person thinks is hilarious, another might find really distasteful, or just annoying.

P Do jokes have anything in common though? What actually makes us laugh?

E Well, there's usually something unexpected in there. We talk about a punchline at the end of a joke – the final line that hits us and makes us laugh. For example, there's a famous Groucho Marx joke in the film *Animal Crackers*. He says: 'One morning, I shot an elephant in my pyjamas … How he got into my pyjamas, I'll never know!' We usually laugh as soon as we realize that we've been mentally going in the wrong direction. That's why there's a strong link between a sense of humour and being intelligent, because your brain has got to react pretty quickly to get the joke. It's also one of the ways in which you can still tell the difference between a computer and a human.

P What, when you tell a computer a joke, it won't laugh?

E Ha, ha, no, obviously it won't laugh, but it won't even get the joke. Understanding a joke requires a lot of world knowledge, linguistic knowledge and that ability to suddenly shift quickly from what you were expecting to hear. Even young children struggle with this until they get to about five. You hear them telling jokes that just don't make any sense at all.

P Sometimes that's funnier than a proper joke, though …

10.6))))
annoying   childish   comical   distasteful
hilarious   irritating   pointless   predictable
ridiculous   tedious   thought-provoking   witty

10.7))))
For thousands of years, ever since the great Greek philosopher Plato identified them, people have divided the taste of food into four different types: sweet, sour, bitter and salty. However, in 1908, a Japanese chemist, Kikunae Ikeda, sensed that his seaweed soup had a flavour which was not one of the classic four tastes. He knew that the flavour was also found in tomatoes, cheese, such as hard Parmesan cheese, and meat, though not so much in very lean meat, or raw meat. Eventually

he identified it as glutamic acid, but he named it umami, which means 'delicious' in Japanese. Umami is best described as a kind of savoury taste, which makes something taste really good. It's very noticeable in many Asian foods, such as soya, asparagus, shrimp and green tea, but it is also strong in foods which combine meat, cheese and tomato, such as Italian meatballs or a cheeseburger with tomato ketchup.

10.9))))
1 put back   5 had come
2 old man   6 nice shirt
3 brown paper   7 cheese shop
4 short cut

10.10))))
Umami encourages people to eat, which may be why it is now added to many foods in the form of monosodium glutamate. It may also affect your choice of drinks while on board an aeroplane. According to Charles Spence, professor of experimental psychology at Oxford University, tomato juice should taste better than other drinks. In fact, many people on aeroplanes do seem to choose it. This could be because the umami flavour is one of the only tastes strong enough to be perceived over the sound of the engines. In fact, Professor Spence claims to have found that the sense of sound actually has quite an impact on how we taste things.

Through his research, Professor Spence discovered that diners believed food tasted bitter when listening to low-pitched notes played by brass instruments, while listening to high-pitched notes played by the piano made it taste sweeter. So, sweet-sounding music could be used to make diners think that what they are eating is up to 10% sweeter than it actually is, allowing the chef to reduce sugar without affecting the taste. Other kinds of music could make food taste less salty or less sour.

Ever wondered why crisps come in noisy packets? They don't make the crisps last any longer, but they do add to the sensation of crunchiness. The actual sound of the food must also be considered because we associate the sound of crunchiness with food being fresher. Another piece of Professor Spence's research recorded people biting into potato crisps and then played back the crunching sound. When they played the crunches at a louder volume, people rated the crisps as being fresher and tastier.

Professor Spence also found that a dessert placed on a white plate tasted 10% sweeter than one served on a black plate, indicating that the sense of sight also affects how food tastes. Restaurants are starting to take some of these ideas on board, playing music to match the food and not only thinking about whether the food looks nice, but also how the presentation might affect the taste.

10.11))))
Two extracts of music:
'Trois Gymnopédies' by Erik Satie
'Davidsbündlertänze' by Robert Schumann

10.12))))
A OK, well my photo is of a market. There's a man in the foreground cooking something.
B Sorry, did you say 'cooking'?
A Yes.

B That's a difference, then. My photo shows a market, too, but I can't see anyone cooking anything. And I don't think I can see any men either. They all seem to be women. They're wearing headscarves, or straw hats and brightly coloured dresses.
A Mine's a mixture of men and women. I don't think anyone is wearing a hat or a headscarf. Er, what else? What are they selling? My photo shows some different fruit and vegetables. I can see a lot of bananas.
B Ah, mine are selling fruit and vegetables, too, and lots of bananas … but I bet your sellers aren't on the water.
A I'm not quite sure what you mean by 'on the water' …
B I mean they're in boats.
A In boats?
B You look a bit confused … you know … it's a floating market. All the sellers are in boats on the river.
A Oh, I see. No, I think my sellers are definitely on land. So, they're the same in that it's a market, they're selling fruit and vegetables; and different in that I've got men and women selling and you've got only women, and your sellers are in boats.

10.13))))
1 Sorry, did you say cooking?
2 I'm not quite sure what you mean by on the water …
3 You look a bit confused … you know … it's a *floating* market.

10.14))))
1 The scientist [beep] the animals over a three-month period.
2 As he [beep] into her dark brown eyes, he realized he was falling in love.
3 You need to check your homework again – I've [beep] quite a few mistakes.
4 He [beep] at me every time I say anything – it's really making me nervous.
5 Everyone [beep] at her bright red and purple fur coat.
6 I didn't have time to read the paper today; I just [beep] at the headlines.

10.15))))
1 very silly or unreasonable
2 not interesting and taking too long
3 not worth doing or watching
4 clever and amusing
5 stupid or silly
6 unpleasant or offensive

10.16))))
1 American children, and adults, do watch a lot of TV, but not as much as that. The average for a child in the USA is four hours a day.
2 Amazingly, the second statement is true. Babies can distinguish between different languages before they are born.
3 The third statement is also true. It seems that boys are generally less interested in reading than girls, and using a touch-screen device can help to get them more involved.
4 Babies cannot see very well when they are born, but they can definitely see a face that is quite close to them.
5 People used to think that listening to Mozart made children more intelligent, but, in fact, the research was done using adults, not

children, and the effect only lasted about fifteen minutes.

6   This percentage was true in 2010 – it's probably a lot more than 45% now. So be careful what you put online!

10.17)))

1   So, are you saying that …?
2   I'm sorry, I didn't quite catch that.
3   Do you see what I mean?
4   You look a bit confused.
5   Am I right in thinking that …
6   I'm not entirely sure what you mean by

Unit 11 Media

11.1)))

Story 1

In France, a supermarket chain has been selling 'ugly' fruit and vegetables to customers at a discounted rate to raise awareness of the problem of food waste and provide customers with a cheaper shopping alternative. The aim of the campaign is to highlight the fact that millions of tonnes of food are wasted every year because many supermarket buyers refuse to buy odd-shaped fruit and vegetables from farmers.

Customers were invited to blind-taste both the ugly and standard fruit and they admitted that they tasted exactly the same. The supermarket claims that the campaign was a success. All the ugly fruit and vegetables were sold out within three days and the number of customers rose by 24% during that period. The supermarket has announced that it is now looking at rolling out the campaign across all of its stores in France.

Story 2

A new species of monkey has been discovered in the forests of Myanmar, formerly known as Burma. A team of wildlife conservationists, based in Cambridge in the UK, made the discovery after hunters reported seeing a monkey which was unlike anything else in the area. The monkeys have a wide, turned-up nose, which fills with water when it rains. The local people assured the conservationists that the monkeys would be easy to locate because whenever it was raining, water would get up their noses and they could be heard sneezing. Consequently, the monkeys spend rainy days sitting with their heads between their knees to avoid this. Although the discovery of a new species is exciting, conservationists have warned that these monkeys were already on the endangered species list.

Story 3

In Norway, two teenagers found cash worth $81,500 in a bag on a train and handed it in to the police. The money belonged to an elderly man who had left the bag on the seat. The bag also contained a passport belonging to the man. The teenagers immediately called the police to inform them that they had found the money. Police have praised the teenagers for being honest, but the teens denied acting heroically, pointing out that the cash wasn't actually theirs and it hadn't occurred to them to keep it. The police were unable to confirm whether the teenagers had received a reward for their honesty.

11.2)))

1   The supermarket has announced it will continue the campaign.
2   The supermarket claims that the campaign was a success.
3   The teenagers pointed out that the cash wasn't actually theirs.
4   Hunters reported seeing an unusual monkey in the area.

11.3)))

admit   announce   assure   confirm   deny   inform   invite   persuade   refuse   remind   report

11.4)))

1   Don't forget to email him.
2   I did not copy her essay.
3   I'm not eating that.
4   Yes, I'm sorry – I drove very carelessly.
5   Don't worry, I won't be late.
6   Would you like to come to the concert with me?

11.5)))

I   Excuse me, could you spare a few minutes to answer some questions for a survey about the role of online news in people's lives?
L/R Sure./OK.
I   Great. So if I could just ask you your names …
L   Luke.
R   Rosie.
I   Right, so first of all, can you tell me how often you look at online news sites?
L   It's the first thing I do when I wake up in the morning and the last thing I do before going to sleep. I also check them several times a day – I don't know, ten times, fifteen? Maybe more …
R   More, I'd say …
L   I suppose I do find it quite addictive. Not because I need to know everything that's happening in the news but just because I need something to fill the time when I've got nothing to do, like when I'm on the train or when the adverts come on TV.
I   Rosie? How often do you use online news sites?
R   Not often, to be honest. I don't have a smartphone, so I don't read the news on my phone. Also, I have a computer-based job and I'd rather not spend my life staring at a computer screen, so I tend to watch the news on TV in the morning before I go to work.
I   So you never read the news online?
R   Obviously I do occasionally, on my laptop, but there's so much information it's hard to know sometimes where to start. I also don't trust a lot of what's online – apart from a very small number of sites, I don't feel the news is very objective. It's often not based on facts.
I   And do either of you ever read a printed newspaper?
L   What, you mean an actual paper newspaper? No, never. Too expensive, and the size – especially the big ones, the broadsheets – they're unmanageable, so difficult to hold when you're on the train or whatever.
R   I read printed newspapers. I like the physical feel of them. I sometimes read the free ones you get at the underground stations. But I'd never actually pay for one.
I   So tell me what kind of news sites you like.

L   Well, I like to read a combination of serious news sites. You know, the online, app versions of serious newspapers, which give reliable news – news that you can believe. But I also like more informal sites, like BuzzFeed, which, as well as being entertaining, are often quite informative. You can learn a lot from them; but the main reason I like to read those is that they are specifically aimed at my generation – so, people in their twenties.
R   I'm not so keen on that kind of site.
I   What do you like?
R   I'm particularly interested in local and regional news and stuff that's relevant to my life and work. The other thing I like – and Luke doesn't approve of this at all – is looking at celebrity photos and gossip. But you know, I have a very stressful job and sometimes I need to read something light-hearted, something that doesn't require too much mental effort.
I   Absolutely! Well, thank you both very much for taking the time to answer my questions. It's been very helpful.
L   You're welcome.

11.6)))

Conversation 1

M   Did you see that story about the Mexican woman who's just turned 127?
F   127? Seriously?
M   Yes, she's the oldest person who has ever lived, apparently. According to the article, she claims she was born in 1887 – imagine that!
F   Blimey … so she must have lived through a few interesting historical events, then …
M   I know … And it says in the article I read that she's got something like seventy-three great-grandchildren and fifty-five great-great-grandchildren. The sad thing is that several members of her family have already died before her.
F   Well, yes sad, but it's hardly surprising, really.
M   Apparently, although her physical health is not that great, she's really mentally aware and still tells some incredible stories of the Mexican Revolution.
F   So is she in the *Guinness Book of Records*, then?
M   Well, apparently not, because she hasn't got any proof of her age. She claims she lost her birth certificate while moving house forty years ago.
F   Oh … gosh.

Conversation 2

F   Did you read about that guy who's just run a marathon wearing a diving suit?
M   A diving suit?
F   Yes, but not a modern, tight-fitting diving suit, but one of those old-fashioned ones from the 1940s.
M   Weren't they really heavy in those days?
F   Yes, this suit was incredibly heavy, around fifty-nine kilos or something.
M   You're kidding! That must have slowed him down a bit!
F   Er yes, just a bit. It took him six days, supposedly.
M   Wow! That's amazing. So who is this guy?
F   Oh, his name's Lloyd something or other. I can't remember his last name, but he's English and from what it said in the article,

171

he's quite well known for doing these charity marathons dressed up in costumes. What's amazing about him is that he was diagnosed with leukaemia several years ago. He survived that and has since raised something in the region of £5 million for charity.

M That is impressive.

F Yeah. The article had some really funny pictures of him doing the run. Here ... look ... I'll show you on my phone ...

11.7))

1 This is a situation in which people, groups or countries are involved in a serious disagreement or argument. It also describes a violent situation or period of fighting between countries.

2 This verb means to be badly affected by a disease, pain, sadness or the lack of something.

3 This means carrying a weapon, for example a gun.

4 This describes something that makes you feel anxious, upset or shocked.

5 This describes something that gives you hope.

6 This describes an important development that may lead to an agreement or achievement.

Unit 12 Life stages

12.1, 12.2, 12.3))

Speaker 1
Many parents have a second child for the sake of their first – to stop them being lonely and spoilt. But that's just a stereotype, and I believe one child is ideal. Having one child has enabled me to devote plenty of time, money and energy to her. In my view, the more kids you have, the less time and energy you are able to give to each one. I also know that if I'd had more children, I'd have been less happy as I'd have had to give up too much in my life. And, to have a happy child, you need to be a happy parent.

Speaker 2
I have four children. I didn't plan four, but that's how many I've got and, in retrospect, I now believe that's the perfect number. The idea of having fewer or more is as unthinkable as having fewer or more arms or legs. Of course, the physical strain of bringing up four is enormous, but the joy each one brings is immeasurable. Although our home sometimes feels like a zoo and we are like a travelling circus whenever we go abroad, there is great comfort in being part of a six-member team. Having an even number means each child has an automatic playmate. If two are playing together, the other ones have each other and don't feel left out.

Speaker 3
I believe we have a responsibility to be mindful of the world's growing population. Each baby we bring into the world puts extra pressure on the world's resources – energy, food, forests, water and so forth. And people from rich countries use more than their fair share of these resources. For that reason, I feel no couple should have more than two children – one to replace each parent. I read the other day that if every couple in a rich country had one less child, they would save 9,441 tonnes of carbon dioxide over their lifetime. Makes you think, doesn't it?

Speaker 4
I'd like to make the case for not having children. Society puts a lot of pressure on us to have children, but it's not right for everyone. There are countless reasons why I chose to be childfree. If I'd had children, I wouldn't have so much time now to devote to my husband and my career. I'd have very little privacy; my beautiful house would be full of plastic toys; my travels would be limited to school vacations and child-friendly destinations; and I could list dozens more reasons.

Speaker 5
I'm in favour of having as many children as you can manage. I'd say at least six is the ideal number. When you raise a large family – in my case, seven – you create a little community that supports itself through the ups and downs of life. Friends often quote school fees as being a reason not to have a large family. But if you're lucky enough to live in a country with great state schools, then that isn't an issue. There are those that say that having lots of children is ecologically irresponsible. But my family are productive, tax-paying, environmentally aware and all contribute positively to society.

Speaker 6
I didn't mean to have three children. The second of my pregnancies produced twins. And, as a result, I ended up with what I believe is the ideal number. Three children means three sibling relationships. So if two of the siblings fall out or are on bad terms, at least they've got another sibling to turn to. The other thing, and I know this sounds selfish, but let's be honest about it, the more children you have, the greater the chances that at least one of them will be successful enough to support me financially and care for me in my old age.

12.4))

1 I would have done things differently.
2 I might have given it a try.
3 I couldn't have managed on my own.
4 I wouldn't have enjoyed it.

12.5))

P 'Regrets – I've had a few' or so said the great Frank Sinatra in his famous song 'My Way', and today we want to hear all about your regrets, those silly mistakes you've made in life, the things you said or did that you really wish you hadn't or those missed opportunities that left you thinking 'Oh, if only I could turn back time ... I'd do things very differently ...'. Well, now's your chance to call in and get it all off your chest! OK, well on the line we have Greg from Glasgow. Greg, tell us your regret.

G My biggest regret is ignoring my dad's advice to buy a flat while properties weren't too expensive. He even offered to give me some money for the deposit. This was about six years ago when a small flat was just about affordable. But I didn't because ... well, I dunno ... I just couldn't be bothered to save up, and I didn't think there was any hurry, I suppose. Now, even the tiniest flat costs an absolute fortune and I can't even think about buying one. If only I'd listened to my dad. I could kick myself now.

P I bet you could. Sorry to hear that, Greg ... and I'm sure there are lots of people in your position.

Next, we hear from Jade in Bristol. Jade, what happened to you?

J Something I really regret is the time when a very good friend told me she was splitting up with her boyfriend. I'd never really liked him and I said: 'Well, I think that's a good decision ... and to be honest, I never really understood what you saw in him anyway.' She was quite offended by that and then the inevitable happened – they got back together again. Now things are really awkward between us. So now of course I'm thinking 'If only I hadn't opened my big mouth!'. I wish I could be a bit less honest sometimes ...

P Oh my goodness – well, you won't be making that mistake again, will you?
And next – Bill, from London.

B I regret getting rid of all my LPs. But it was my wife that kind of insisted. She kept going on at me, you know, saying: 'I wish you'd sell those records. They take up so much space and you never play them ...' I thought 'maybe she has a point'. So I did, but I knew it was a mistake instantly. Recently, I've got into listening to records again, at a friend's house – I love the sound of records, the covers ... so much more enjoyable than digital music. So I've decided to start again with my record collection.

P It's true – there is something unique about the sound of records. Good luck with rebuilding your collection, Bill!
And we've got time for just one more story – here's Michelle, from Manchester.

M One of my biggest regrets is not standing up to a colleague who used to bully me in my last job. She'd criticize my work, make me look stupid in front of other people and generally do everything she could to knock my confidence. And I just let her do it because I was new to the job, and I didn't dare answer back or challenge her behaviour. I wouldn't tolerate it now – I just wish I'd had the courage to challenge her at the time.

P Bullies, eh? Who needs them! Glad to hear you wouldn't tolerate them now.
Well, it's great to hear your stories – keep them coming in, but first, the news ...

12.6))

1 If only I'd listened to my dad.
2 Oh, if only I hadn't opened my big mouth!
3 I wish I could be a bit less honest sometimes ...
4 I wish you'd sell those records.
5 I just wish I'd had the courage to challenge her at the time.

12.7))

P Every era has a social group that rebels against society in some way. In the 60s, it was hippies; in the 70s, punks; in the 80s it was goths. Now, the latest subculture to hit the international scene is the hipster. But what precisely is a hipster? Here to tell us more about this distinctive group is Carla Nielsen, a future trendspotter, who works for a marketing agency. Carla, describe for us the principal characteristics of a hipster.

CN Well, hipsters are young people – in their 20s and 30s, usually – who reject mainstream culture. You know, so they're kind of anti anything that's popular. That includes art, music, clothes and so on. Instead, they prefer alternative music and fashion. They tend to be well-educated people. Some are students, others are professionals, and many of them work in creative fields like media or publishing ... that sort of thing.

12.8))
1 ... they're kind of anti anything that's popular.
2 That includes art, music, clothes and so on.
3 Many of them work in creative fields like media or publishing ... that sort of thing.

12.10))
1 His beard is a sort of orange colour.
2 Her look is kind of hard to describe.
3 The bike basket's useful for carrying laptops, shopping bags or whatever.
4 He writes a blog about hipster fashion, music and stuff like that.
5 He wears formal clothes like ties, waistcoats and so on.

12.11))
1 Hipsters reject mainstream culture: music, clothes, books and stuff like that.
2 Some hipsters are vegan so they don't eat eggs or milk or whatever.
3 It's a shop that sells old books and posters and so on.
4 He's into 1930s music, like jazz, blues and that kind of thing.
5 She likes the sort of clothes you'd buy from a vintage clothes shop.
6 The area is full of hipster barber shops, cafés and places like that.

12.12))
P   And how would I recognize a hipster if I bumped into one in the street?
CN Well, your stereotypical hipster wears tight-fitting jeans, and large thick-rimmed glasses – whether they need them or not. They wear old-fashioned, retro-style shirts ... you know, with checked or flowery patterns, often bought from vintage or second-hand clothes shops. Another typical hipster feature is the long beard or turned-up moustache. You rarely see a clean-shaven male hipster.
P   And the female hipsters?
CN Well, they're less easy to identify, but, like the men, they wear old-fashioned clothing. Floral-patterned dresses, or cardigans – the sort of things their grandmothers might have worn.
P   So for hipsters, old-fashioned is cool?
CN Yes, and that applies to the things they own. So they love low-tech objects like record players, old-style cameras, typewriters ... that kind of thing ... But what I should explain about hipsters is that they don't actually want to be labelled as hipsters. They don't want to be part of a group, they want to be seen as individuals.
P   Oh right, I see. And that, I suppose, makes them different from punks, or goths or whatever ... who are happy to identify with these labels.
CN Exactly.
P   So where do hipsters hang out?
CN Well, there are hipster neighbourhoods in many major cities around the world, which are full of trendy hipster cafés, galleries, second-hand shops, and so on. They tend to be districts that are historically poor and run-down but are now fashionable places to live and work.

P   Uh huh, so ... so tell me more about the kind of music hipsters are into.
CN Oh, well, all sorts of bands really, as long as they're obscure and nobody else has heard of them. Hipsters are very critical of mainstream music and of those who like it. The same with film, books and art. That's why hipsters aren't very popular. They think their tastes are superior to others.
P   I see, I'm getting the picture ... So apart from a taste for little-known bands and artists, how else are hipsters different from other people?
CN Well, they're anti-consumerism. That's why they like to buy second-hand things and why they believe in mending things when they break, rather than always buying something new. They're also very green – so they buy eco-friendly products, like shampoo. A lot of them are vegetarians or vegans.
P   So I presume they like to travel everywhere by bike?
CN Absolutely. In fact the ultimate cool hipster accessory is the fixed-wheel bike. Or 'fixie' as they're known. They're sort of like modern versions of retro-style bikes with just one gear. They're the in-thing in urban cultures all over the world. You must have seen them around.
P   Yes, I have ... So tell me, how does a hipster like to spend their spare time?
CN As you may predict, hipsters are keen on old-fashioned pastimes, like knitting, woodwork, growing your own fruit and vegetables, making home-made jam, baking cakes and stuff like that ... but probably the most stereotypical hipster pastime is retro-photography, which involves taking photos on a smartphone using an app which makes the images look as though they were taken with a vintage-style camera.
P   Then posting the images on social media?
CN Oh yes ... because hipsters are very keen on showing off their pictures to everyone they know.
P   Really?... so my final question to you as a future trendspotter ... Do you think 'hipsterism' is here to stay?
CN Well, I think it's already been around long enough to be more than just a passing trend, and it's travelled to many different countries. I think we'll always have this group of young people that value independent thinking and fashion and culture. But like all trends, it will change and evolve.
P   Well, thank you for coming on the programme – it's been fascinating.
CN My pleasure.

12.13))
Speaker 1
I'm so pleased I decided to change degree courses. I started off doing languages, French and German – I'd always got really excellent grades in them at school, but at university level I just couldn't keep up. I was skipping lectures, not turning up to classes, because I found the whole thing so difficult. Anyway, so I changed to psychology. That was such a good move. I couldn't have wished for a better course. I ended up with a good result in my degree. I'm very grateful to the tutors for being understanding and allowing me to switch.

Speaker 2
I'm so glad I decided to go and work as a teacher in Istanbul for two years. I'd been working for an accountancy firm in London prior to that, but I knew it wasn't really for me. I wanted to experience life in another country and Istanbul had always fascinated me. Getting to grips with a new culture and language was quite a challenge at first, but I gained so much from the experience, and it's really helped me to put aspects of my own culture into perspective. So thank goodness I didn't listen to my parents, who tried to dissuade me from giving up my career in accounting. And, of course, if I hadn't gone to Turkey I wouldn't have met my wife.

Speaker 3
A couple of years ago, I decided to go freelance – and what a good decision that was! I really appreciate having the freedom to do as much or as little work as I want. What actually happened was that I was made redundant from my job in advertising. Although it was a terrible shock at the time – a real kick in the teeth – I gradually got over it and started to build up my own advertising consultancy business, which is going very well. In retrospect, losing my job was a blessing in disguise. I don't think I would have had the courage or motivation to set up on my own if I hadn't been forced to by my circumstances.

Speaker 4
Two years ago, I gave up smoking. I'd been smoking for several years before that. I'd tried to give up a couple of times before, but my motivation was stronger this time because my wife was pregnant with our first child. It's such a relief not to be a slave to cigarettes any more. And when I think of all the money I wasted, I could really kick myself. Obviously, with hindsight, I should never have started and I wouldn't have done if I'd known how addictive it would be. But never mind – what's done is done and there's no point in crying over spilt milk, is there?

12.14))
1 I couldn't have wished for a better course.
2 I'm very grateful to the tutors for allowing me to switch.
3 So thank goodness I didn't listen to my parents.
4 In retrospect, losing my job was a blessing in disguise.
5 When I think of all the money I wasted, I could really kick myself.
6 With hindsight I should never have started.
7 What's done is done.
8 ... there's no point in crying over spilt milk ...

12.15))
1	tech	5	made
2	known	6	down
3	fitting	7	shaven
4	friendly		

Irregular verbs

Infinitive	Past simple	Past participle
be	was/were	been
beat	beat	beaten
become	became	become
begin	began	begun
bite	bit	bitten
blow	blew	blown
break	broke	broken
bring	brought	brought
build	built	built
burn	burnt	burnt
buy	bought	bought
can	could	been able to
catch	caught	caught
choose	chose	chosen
come	came	come
cost	cost	cost
cut	cut	cut
deal	dealt	dealt
dig	dug	dug
do	did	done
draw	drew	drawn
dream	dreamt/dreamed	dreamt/dreamed
drink	drank	drunk
drive	drove	driven
eat	ate	eaten
fall	fell	fallen
feed	fed	fed
feel	felt	felt
fight	fought	fought
find	found	found
fly	flew	flown
forget	forgot	forgotten
forgive	forgave	forgiven
freeze	froze	frozen
get	got	got
give	gave	given
go	went	gone/been
grow	grew	grown
have	had	had
hear	heard	heard
hide	hid	hidden
hit	hit	hit
hold	held	held
hurt	hurt	hurt
keep	kept	kept
know	knew	known
lay	laid	laid
lead	led	led
learn	learnt/learned	learnt/learned

Infinitive	Past simple	Past participle
leave	left	left
lend	lent	lent
let	let	let
lie	lay	lain
light	lit	lit
lose	lost	lost
make	made	made
mean	meant	meant
meet	met	met
must	had to	had to
pay	paid	paid
put	put	put
read	read	read
ride	rode	ridden
ring	rang	rung
rise	rose	risen
run	ran	run
say	said	said
see	saw	seen
sell	sold	sold
send	sent	sent
set	set	set
shake	shook	shaken
shine	shone	shone
shoot	shot	shot
show	showed	shown/showed
shut	shut	shut
sing	sang	sung
sit	sat	sat
sleep	slept	slept
speak	spoke	spoken
spend	spent	spent
spoil	spoiled/spoilt	spoiled/spoilt
stand	stood	stood
steal	stole	stolen
stick	stuck	stuck
swim	swam	swum
take	took	taken
teach	taught	taught
tear	tore	torn
tell	told	told
think	thought	thought
throw	threw	thrown
understand	understood	understood
wake	woke	woken
wear	wore	worn
win	won	won
write	wrote	written

Phonemic symbols

Single vowel sounds

/iː/	tree /triː/	/ə/	computer /kəmˈpjuːtə(r)/
/ɪ/	his /hɪz/	/ɜː/	learn /lɜːn/
/i/	happy /ˈhæpi/	/ɔː/	four /fɔː(r)/
/ʊ/	good /ɡʊd/	/æ/	hat /hæt/
/u/	usual /ˈjuːʒuəl/	/ʌ/	sunny /ˈsʌni/
/uː/	school /skuːl/	/ɑː/	car /kɑː(r)/
/e/	ten /ten/	/ɒ/	clock /klɒk/

Diphthongs (double vowel sounds)

/ɪə/	near /nɪə(r)/	/ɔɪ/	boy /bɔɪ/
/ʊə/	tour /tʊə(r)/	/aɪ/	try /traɪ/
/eə/	wear /weə(r)/	/əʊ/	so /səʊ/
/eɪ/	train /treɪn/	/aʊ/	out /aʊt/

Consonant sounds

/p/	pen /pen/	/s/	see /siː/
/b/	big /bɪg/	/z/	lazy /ˈleɪzi/
/t/	tea /tiː/	/ʃ/	shower /ˈʃaʊə(r)/
/d/	do /duː/	/ʒ/	television /ˈtelɪvɪʒn/
/tʃ/	children /ˈtʃɪldrən/	/m/	man /mæn/
/dʒ/	journey /ˈdʒɜːni/	/n/	never /ˈnevə(r)/
/k/	cat /kæt/	/ŋ/	sing /sɪŋ/
/g/	go /gəʊ/	/h/	hot /hɒt/
/f/	fly /flaɪ/	/l/	like /laɪk/
/v/	very /ˈveri/	/r/	river /ˈrɪvə(r)/
/θ/	thing /θɪŋ/	/w/	water /ˈwɔːtə(r)/
/ð/	this /ðɪs/	/j/	yes /jes/

OXFORD
UNIVERSITY PRESS

Great Clarendon Street, Oxford, OX2 6DP, United Kingdom

Oxford University Press is a department of the University of Oxford.
It furthers the University's objective of excellence in research, scholarship,
and education by publishing worldwide. Oxford is a registered trade
mark of Oxford University Press in the UK and in certain other countries

© Oxford University Press 2015

ISBN: 978 0 19 456583 7

Printed in China

This book is printed on paper from certified and well-managed sources

ACKNOWLEDGEMENTS

*The authors and publisher are grateful to those who have given permission to reproduce
the following extracts and adaptations of copyright material*: p.18 Adapted extract
from 'Henry Box Brown – The Slave Who Mailed Himself To Freedom' by
Ronald E. Franklin, http://hubpages.com, 19 June 2013. Reproduced by
permission of Ronald E. Franklin. p.62–3 Graphs from Office of National
Statistics licensed under the Open Government Licence v.3.0.

Sources: p.43 'When creativity and facts are a good match' by William Stewart,
www.tes.co.uk, 9 May 2014. p.48–9 'Types of boredom: An experience
sampling approach' by Thomas Goetz, Anne C. Frenzel, Nathan C. Hall,
Ulrike E. Nett, Reinhard Pekrun and Anastasiya A. Lipnevich, *Motivation
and Emotion*, Volume 38, Issue 3, 16 November 2013. p.72 'Madrid's smart
parking meters to charge more for most polluting cars' by Ashifa Kassam,
www.theguardian.com, 30 April 2014. p.72 'Proposed new federal traffic
laws target distracted drivers across the UAE' by Roberta Pennington,
www.thenational.ae, 14 April 2014. p.96 'The science of optical illusions',
www.bbc.co.uk, 18 October 2010. p.98 http://laughlab.co.uk p.106–7 TiVo
Spring 2014 Binge-Viewing Survey. p.118 'Woulda, Shoulda, Coulda:
What Do You Regret?' by Melissa Johnson, www.everydayhealth.com,
28 March 2011. p.140 *Thoughts on the Business of Life*, Forbes, 1948. p.140
Thinking Outside the Church: 110 Ways to Connect with Your Spiritual Nature by
Jennifer Leigh Selig and Kelly Gilbert (Andrews McMeel Publishing, 2004).
p.150 https://varonis-assets.s3.amazonaws.com p.150 *Time*, 3 January
1983 p.150 'Top ten social media survival tips' by Simon Mainwaring,
www.wefirstbranding.com, 2011. p.150 Jef Raskin interview with Berkeley
Groks, 3 March 2004. p.150 www.quotegarden.com/internet.html p.157 'Pearls
of Wisdom' by Rush Limbaugh, www.rushlimbaugh.com, 11 November 2013.
p.157 'Morrissey Returns!' by Jim Nelson, www.gq.com, 15 October 2012.
p.157 Column 1 by David p. Sentner, *Clearfield Progress*, 12 December 1930.

*The publisher would like to thank the following for their permission to reproduce
photographs*: Alamy pp.11 (man whistling/Tony French), 17 (Mary Kingsley/
Pictorial Press Ltd), 21 (falconry/Ian Middleton, zero gravity/NASA Archive),
22 (camper van/Alvey & Towers Picture Library), 23 (Radharc Images), 34 (Cipd
Offices, London/VIEW Pictures Ltd), 38 (office with windows/Ian Shipley ARC),
39 (man in sleep pod/National Geographic Image Collection), 40 (bicycle/
George Leroy, trees/Alvaro German Vilela), 46 (boy in car/Imagestate Media
Partners Limited – Impact Photos, three children/Justin Kase), 49 (Aurora
Photos), 55 (Stocksnapper), 56 (Sao Paulo/Andre M. Chang/ARDUOPRESS),
58 (community/Alistair Heap), 68 (woman in bed/Sergiy Serdyuk, woman
in car/Image Source Salsa), 72 (logo/Novarc Images), 73 (Jenny Matthews),
83 (Anna Stowe), 88 (children/Keren Su/China Span), 89 (Bill Gozansky),
92 (dancing/Hero Images Inc.), 102 (Majestic Café/Alex Segre, queue in café/
Hemis), 103 (Gavin Hellier), 104 (Indian woman with waterlily/Tim Gainey),
105 (PhotoAlto), 108 (bag/Rob Wilkinson), 110 (zebra/Gallo Images, woman/

Mint Images Limited), 116 (beach family/YAY Media AS), 124 (Blenheim
Palace lake and bridge/Andrew Michael), 124 (Blenheim Palace/Stanislav
Halcin), 127 (Marianne North/The Art Archive), 130 (pavement art/Oleksandr
Rupeta), 131 (market/Herianus Herianus, park/Chad Ehlers), 132 (Old
Paper Studios), 134 (Viking festival/Terrance Klassen, market/Hemis, park/
DuohuaEr), 135 (Richard III/GL Archive); Bournemouth News and Picture
Service p.41 (Tom Wren); Corbis pp.16 (hippo/Kenneth Lilly), 30 (bangles/
Steve Raymer), 66 (coins/Erik S. Lesser), 82 (top/Robert Pratta), 87 (Kazuyoshi
Nomachi), 112 (elderly woman/Ulises Ruiz Basurto), 128 (Simon Lim),
129 (Little Havana festival/Nik Wheeler); Getty pp.18 (Henry Box Brown/
Stock Montage, cotton pickers/Universal ImagesGroup), 20 (Philippe
Desmazes), 21 (gladiators/Andreas Solaro), 30 (woman), 34 (man using digital
tablet/Jordan Siemens), 38 (meeting with beanbags/Hufton Crow), 39 (desk/
National Geographic Image Collection), 40 (bridge/Paul Marotta), 52 (vandal/
WIN-Initiative), 54 (shoe factory, 1952/Keystone-France), 56 (girls/News Free/
CON), 62 (teens walking/Yellow Dog Productions), 63 (Seiya Kawamoto),
64 (house boats in Mission Bay/Thomas Winz), 66 (paintings/Andreas
Solaro, Faberge egg/Peter Macdiarmid), 68 (man with phone/Yiu Yu Hoi),
72 (exhausts/Bloomberg), 82 (middle/Fred Dufour), 86, 88 (medieval women/
DEA/M. Seemuller), 91 (Michael Nichols), 92 (audience), 95, 116 (kitchen
family/Shannon Fagan), 120 (Mike Harrington), 121 (record shop, man on
steps), 122 (lecture, office/Shannon Taggart, wedding), 123 (Mark Kauffman),
125 (Petri Artturi Asikainen), 135 (robot/Johannes Eisele); iStock p.52 (broken
window); Oxford University Press pp.9 (pile of letters), 14 video stills,
22 (plane), 24 video stills , 44 video stills , 54 video stills, 62 (friends on bus),
64 (map), 74 video stills, 84 video stills, 92 (meal), 94 video stills, 100 (lemons),
110 (tablet) 114 video stills, 124 (bed); Rex Features pp.37 (Houspian/REX
Shutterstock), 39 (man on slide/Solent News/REX Shutterstock), 45 (James
Roberts/Rex Shutterstock), 46 (rollercoaster/PYMCA/REX Shutterstock),
57 (Sam Pikesley/REX Shutterstock), 60 (book-crossing/Action Press/REX
Shutterstock), 82 (bottom/Sipa Press/REX Shutterstock), 98 (Startraks Photo/
REX Shutterstock), 106 (*Game of Thrones*/HBO/Everett/REX Shutterstock, *Modern
Family*/ABC Inc/Everett/REX Shutterstock), 107 (*Sherlock*/Hartswood Films/REX
Shutterstock), 112 (London Marathon/REX Shutterstock), 115 (*Downton Abbey*/
Joan Wakeham/REX Shutterstock), 135 (pavement art/Tony Kyriacou/REX
Shutterstock); Shutterstock pp.10, 12, 13, 15, 22 (coach), 24 (Porthminster
beach in St Ives, 24 (harbour village/Adrian Hughes), 34 (busy office/Monkey
Business Images), 44 (Eiffel Tower/kook03), 48, 53, 58 (girl), 60 (convention,
students), 64 (San Francisco/prochasson frederic), 65 (boy, woman on screen,
boy on screen), 80 (all), 85, 88 (train, garden), 90, 94 (Vemork hydroelectric
plant, Norway/Scandphoto), 100 (all except lemons), 101, 104 (red warning flag
on beach/Tamara Kushch), 104 (young Chinese woman/lzf), 108 (strawberries),
110 (landscape), 117, 121 (girls, jam), 131 (phone), 133 (yawning).

Cover Image by Getty Images/teekid

With special thanks to: Julian Beever p.97 (both); Canongate Books p.9 (*Letters
of Note* book cover, Elvis Presley handwritten letter), The Dyson Foundation
pp.36, 127, 133, 135; Thomas Geissmann p.108 (snub-nosed monkey
illustration/Thomas Geissmann/Fauna & Flora International); Beau Lotto
pp.96, 120 (10.1 exercise 1); Penguin Random House p.25 (*Kira Salak: The
Cruellest Journey*/artwork © Remi Benali/Paul Thomas Gooney)

Illustrations by: Tatiana Arocha/Bernstein & Andriulli pp.29, 42, 50, 76, 118; Paul
Boston/Meiklejohn pp.70, 71, 98, 130; Mark Duffin p.129, 134; Dylan Gibson
pp.47; Kerry Hyndman p.59; Joanna Kerr pp.53, 78; Andy Parker pp.26, 32;
Gavin Reece pp.6, 7.

With thanks to Jon Hird for the Grammar reference pages.